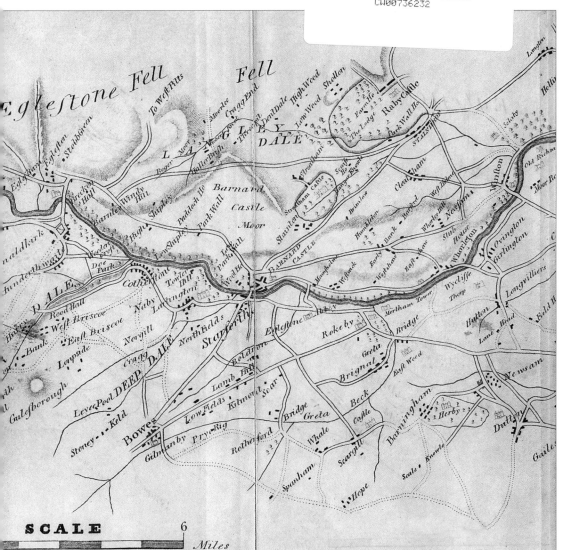

*Teesdale. This map, with slight amendments, appeared in all editions of* A Tour in Teesdale *from 1803.*

*The Discovery of*

# TEESDALE

*High Force of the Tees, engraved by S. Lacey from a drawing by Thomas Allom, 1835.*

*The Discovery of*

# TEESDALE

Michael D. C. Rudd

Phillimore

2007


Published by
PHILLIMORE & CO. LTD
Chichester, West Sussex, England
www.phillimore.co.uk

ISBN 978-1-86077-453-9


Printed and bound in Great Britain

# Contents

# List of Illustrations

*Frontispiece*: High Force of the Tees, Durham. Engraving by S. Lacey after T. Allom, 1835

# Colour Plates

between pages 50 and 51

# Acknowledgements

I should like to thank the following for their help:

The Rt Hon. Sir Andrew Morritt, who since 1986 has shared his knowledge of Rokeby Park, answered numerous questions and allowed me access to his estate in pursuit of artists' viewpoints.

The staff of The Bowes Museum, Barnard Castle, for their generous help, especially with illustrations: Adrian Jenkins, Director; Emma House, Assistant Keeper of Art and Research Assistant to the Director; Dr Howard Coutts, Keeper of Ceramics; Syd Neville, Photographer.

Parkin Raine of Barnard Castle for his help with the photographs of Elijah Yeoman.

Chris Woodley-Stewart, North Pennines AONB Officer, for guidance on the Geopark.

Darlington Library (Centre for Local Studies).

Durham County Record Office.

Durham University Library (Palace Green).

Laing Art Gallery, Tyne and Wear Museums, Newcastle upon Tyne.

The Literary and Philosophical Library, Newcastle upon Tyne.

Newcastle upon Tyne City Library (Local Studies).

North Yorkshire County Council Record Office, Northallerton.

Sunderland Museum: Shauna Gregg, Assistant Keeper of Decorative & Fine Art; Dr Leslie Jessop, Keeper of Biology.

Visitor numbers were kindly supplied by Barnard Castle Tourist Information Office, the Countryside Group at Durham County Council, English Nature (Natural England), and the North Pennines AONB Partnership.

I owe the greatest debt to my wife, Anna, without whose encouragement, advice and forbearance this book would never have been written.

The author and publisher are most grateful to the following owners and trustees of copyright for their permission to publish these images:

The Bowes Museum, 2, 7, 8, 10, 14-17, 19-22, 28, 30-1, 35-42, 46-48, 50, 52-3, 61, 65-71, 74, 78, 83, 86-7, 89-92, 97, 99-100, 102-5, 108, 111, 114-15, II-IV, VIII-X.

George Cuit, The Elder (1743-1818) Winch Bridge on the River Tees, © Christie's Images Ltd.1989, V.

County Durham and Darlington Acute Hospitals NHS Trust, VIII.

Darlington Borough Council, 33-4, 43, 45.

Durham County Record Office, 23-4 (NCB/1/P 102-103); 26-7.

Laing Art Gallery, Tyne and Wear Museums, 29, 44.

Plate VI, Hell Cauldron (pen & ink and watercolour on paper) by Cotman, John Sell (1782-1842) © Leeds Museums and Galleries (City Art Gallery)/The Bridgeman Art Library.

Plate I, The Fall of the Tees, Durham, George Lambert. Private collection: photograph courtesy of Lowell Libson Ltd

The Rt Hon Sir Andrew Morritt © Rokeby Park, 12, 13.

National Railway Museum/Science & Society Picture Library, XI.

North Yorkshire County Council Record Office, 54-5.

Stockton Museum Service, 108.

Quotations (p.151) from *Durham Company* by Una Pope-Hennessy, published by Chatto & Windus, are by kind permission of The Random House Group Ltd.

Plates 112 and 113, and quotations (p.155) from *The Pennine Way Companion* by A. Wainwright, published by Frances Lincoln Ltd, © The Estate of A. Wainwright 1968, 2004, are reproduced by permission of Frances Lincoln Ltd.

Quotations from the *Cholmeley Archive* (Chapter 13) are by permission from the North Yorkshire County Record Office, where the originals are held.

Quotations (pp.xi, xiii and 158) from the North Pennines AONB website are by kind permission of the AONB Partnership.

# *Introduction*

## *'the tumbling river Tees'*

'Teesdale' is the name usually given to the valley of the Tees above the market town of Barnard Castle; it thus includes many tributary valleys, notably those of the Greta, Balder and Lune. Until 1974 the river Tees formed the boundary between County Durham and the North Riding of Yorkshire, and in the higher reaches, between Cumberland and Westmorland. Now County Durham extends further south to include the Greta valley and part of Stainmore; but the headwaters of the Tees near Cross Fell lie firmly in Cumbria.

Before I first visited Teesdale I had heard of High Force and the Meeting of the Waters, and as a student learned of the Great Whin Sill. I later came across the wonderful watercolours of J.M.W. Turner and John Sell Cotman, and the poem *Rokeby* by Sir Walter Scott. In many visits to the valley of the Tees I increasingly wished to know how others – writers, poets, artists, geologists, and tourists – had interpreted the landscape, a landscape of 'tumbling waterfalls, sweeping moorland views, dramatic dales, stone-built villages, snaking stone walls.'[1]

Underlying the story of the discovery of Teesdale is its landscape, and in turn this landscape is the result of its geology. Lead miners were the first to study and name the rocks in which they found the mineral veins; the mining and smelting of lead also changed the scenery of Teesdale and proved a subject for investigation by curious visitors. Throughout the 19th century geologists, professional and amateur, visited Teesdale; what they discovered led to a revised understanding of geological processes, such as the formation of what became known as the Great Whin Sill and the associated 'sugar limestone', and the legacy of the ice age. From the late 17th century botanists came to collect and study the rare flowering plants which survived in Teesdale, due largely to the underlying rocks and the climate.

The first visitors to Teesdale were the Romans. Where their strategically important road over the Pennines crossed the river Greta they built a fort. In 1729 nearby Rokeby Park was re-modelled. This re-building was influenced by the Roman remains at Greta Bridge, and by the current interest in Roman architecture and all things classical stemming from the Grand Tour. Rokeby thus became one of the earliest Palladian villas in England, and its owners would exert a powerful influence on our story.

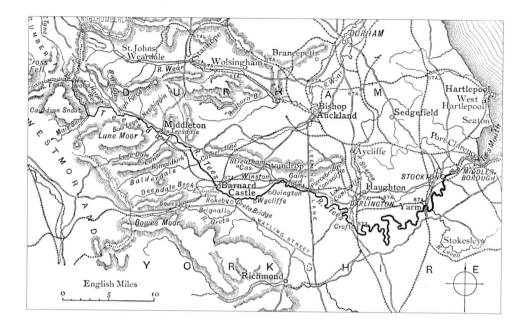

*Above:* **1**  *Map to accompany* Rivers of Great Britain, *1902. 'Teesdale' is that part of the valley above Greta Bridge. The county boundaries changed in 1974.*

*Left:* **2**  *Rokeby. A Rock & Co. engraving for* Views & Scenery of Barnard Castle, *1857.*

From the 16th century the first explorers of Teesdale recorded Rokeby and the Roman remains, although roads, such as they were, did not appear on maps until the 17th century. The earliest drawings of the area were topographical representations of the castles at Barnard Castle and Raby, and the abbey at Egglestone. The first descriptions of the spectacular waterfalls of Cauldron Snout and High Force, where the river Tees flows over the Whin Sill, were published in 1756 – in a novel which exaggerated the wild nature of upper Teesdale. However High Force was being visited before this; a picture dated 1746 shows tourists and their guide at the waterfall. Paintings of Teesdale sights in oils and watercolours appeared in exhibitions from 1762; and engraved copies meant that these scenes reached a wider audience, some of whom were intrepid enough to make their own journey to Teesdale. Engravings were used to illustrate the increasing number of 'Tours' that were published as the roads improved. The earliest tours, written by an agriculturist, a local solicitor and a naturalist, covered an area wider than Teesdale alone. In 1778 the picturesque scenery of Teesdale was endorsed by its own poem *Teisa*, and in 1803 by its own *Tour in Teesdale*, the work of a local solicitor.

Staying at Rokeby Park, the artist John Sell Cotman spent more than a month in the summer of 1805 sketching along the river Greta, producing ground-breaking watercolour studies. Britain's greatest landscape artist, J.M.W. Turner, made four sketching tours to Teesdale, resulting in some of his most inspired and expressive watercolours. Many of Turner's Teesdale scenes were engraved, helping to make the scenery of the dale more widely known.

But it was to be Walter Scott's poem *Rokeby* that after 1813 was to put the area around Greta Bridge firmly on the tourist map. The

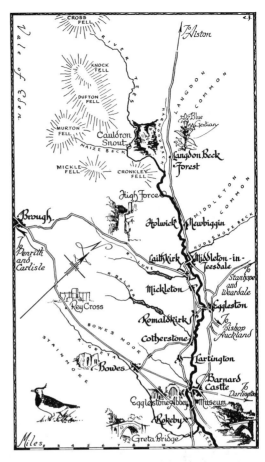

3　*Upper Teesdale. Map by E. Jeffrey after Douglas Ramsden for* Upper Teesdale, *1961.*

expansion of the railways into Teesdale in the 1850s and '60s was reflected in a plethora of guidebooks. These faithfully followed in the footsteps of Scott, as well as those of William Wordsworth and Charles Dickens who had also written about the area, and guided the growing numbers of walkers, cyclists and botanists to the Whin Sill crags and waterfalls. In 1892 a tourist attraction of quite a different kind opened in Barnard Castle – The Bowes Museum.

From the second half of the 20th century the growth in the numbers of tourists visiting Teesdale has been paralleled with an acknowledgement of the need for the conservation of the area's special landscape. The Moor House National Nature Reserve was designated in 1952, that of Upper Teesdale in 1963; these became accessible via the Pennine Way long distance footpath, which was opened in 1965 and has each year brought thousands of walkers past Cauldron Snout and High Force. The upper valley of 'the tumbling river Tees'[2] forms a major part of the North Pennines, which was designated an Area of Outstanding Natural Beauty in 1988. In 2003 the tourist potential of the AONB's geological heritage was recognised when it became the first area in Britain to be awarded the status of European Geopark.

# 1

## Geological Foundations

*'the upper part of Teesdale has a character all of its own,*
*which is derived from the Great Whin Sill'*

The story of tourism in Teesdale has its foundations in its unique landscape; this landscape, physical and human, is largely based on the rocks beneath – the geology. As many geologists, professional and amateur, beat a path to upper Teesdale to try and unravel the story of the rocks, they too became part of the story of the exploration of the dale.

Adam Sedgwick (1785-1873) born in Dent in North Yorkshire, became Professor of Geology at Cambridge in 1818. Three years later Sedgwick made a two days' excursion on horseback from Stockton-on-Tees, visiting an old friend Dr Wallace living near Barnard Castle; the geologist rode up 'the higher part of Teesdale. It is perhaps more beautiful than any valley in the North of England'. Before being driven from this interesting area by incessant rain, Adam Sedgwick describes High Force where 'the whole river is precipitated over a fine mass of columnar basalt'. For some miles above the waterfall he finds this basalt 'arranged in magnificent clusters of pillars'.

Sedgwick returned to upper Teesdale in 1822; while investigating the rocks at High Force, he briefly met by chance John Phillips (1800-74).[1] Phillips had been brought up by his uncle, William Smith (1769-1839) who Sedgwick would later call 'the Father of English Geology' as he devised the idea of sequencing rocks through their fossils, and produced the first geological map of England. John Phillips would become Keeper of the York Museum from 1824, later becoming Professor of Geology at London, Dublin and Oxford; he wrote two books on Yorkshire geology, *Illustrations of the Geology of Yorkshire* (1836), and *The Rivers, Mountains and Sea-coast of Yorkshire* (1852). Adam Sedgwick would make another visit to Teesdale, reading a paper on his findings to the Cambridge Philosophical Society in 1823 and 1824, before publishing an article in the Society's *Transactions* in 1827.

On his Teesdale visits Sedgwick was accompanied by Mark Watson and J. Dent, two 'intelligent practical men', probably lead miners or agents. As he made his way towards Cronkley Scar and beyond to Cross Fell, Sedgwick encountered the three main types of rock, igneous, sedimentary and metamorphic. The geologist was testing the current ideas about the dark 'basaltic greenstone' rocks, then considered to be

4   *The High Force in Teesdale. Lithograph by W. Bevan from a sketch by J. Phillips, c.1852. Phillips noted the 'prismatic greenstone' above an 'indurated and prismatized shale' and jointed limestone.*

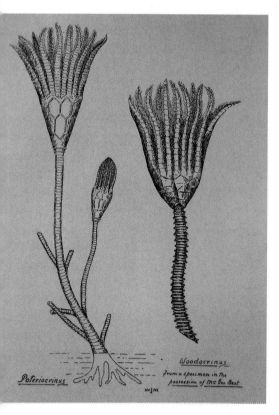

5   *Fossil sea lilies or crinoids. Engraving after W.J. Mountford for* Zig-Zag Ramblings of a Naturalist, *1898. Only the stems are usually found, in Carboniferous limestones.*

similar to the build up of sheets of volcanic lavas which produced what were called the 'trap' or stepped landscapes. This igneous rock, by now called the Great Whin Sill, was found between layers of sedimentary rocks. Sedgwick went from High Force on to Cronkley Scar, to see where the limestone had been changed or metamorphosed into 'sugar limestone'. Investigating the relationships between these three types of rock in upper Teesdale led to a revised understanding of geological processes throughout the country.

Walking up Teesdale from High Force, Sedgwick was aware of the repeated sequence of sedimentary rocks – a hard layer of limestone, perhaps showing fossils telling of its origin on the floor of the sea, followed by a softer shale or mudstone and a hard layer of sandstone, formed in shallow river deltas; sometimes a thin coal seam would represent the vegetation which developed on the delta flats. The order of deposition of these layers or strata had been investigated by mining engineer Westgarth Forster (1772-1835) in *A Treatise on a Section of the Strata, from Newcastle-upon-Tyne, to the mountain of Cross Fell, in Cumberland,* and first published in 1809, with a much expanded edition in 1821. In what he called the 'Lead Measures' Forster had identified 19 such sedimentary sequences

– of limestone, shale and sandstone – named after the limestone in each. Many of the names came from local lead miners and described the thickness of a particular bed (the Five Yard Limestone), one with good fossils (Cockleshell Limestone), or a location where it was easily seen (the Tynebottom and Melmerby Scar Limestones).[2] As well as providing two tables of the strata obtained from Mr Walton, a mine agent at Middleton-in-Teesdale, Adam Sedgwick in his article quotes an extract from Forster's *Section*.

The Great Whin Sill also featured in Forster's coloured section of the strata; he reports how the rock is similar to that at the celebrated Giant's Causeway in Ireland, and gives the thickness of this sill as nearly 30 fathoms (180ft) at Cauldron Snout. This recently published information perhaps spurred both Adam Sedgwick and John Phillips, working separately, to investigate this igneous 'basaltic greenstone'. At the time other geologists, working elsewhere in the Pennines, were debating the origin of this formation, questioning whether it could simply be a series of lava flows or 'regularly interbedded Trap'[3] on the sea floor, which had baked the still soft sedimentary rocks beneath, before in turn having more sediments deposited above its cooled surface. This 'basalt' or 'whin', a quarryman's term for any hard black rock, had created waterfalls at High Force and Cauldron Snout.

Sedgwick in his article gives many examples of where the Whin Sill occurs above quite different sedimentary beds, proving that it 'has not been regularly deposited with the other stratified rocks'. He also reports that the sill has baked the rocks above as well as below it. John Phillips too would later write of the metamorphosed limestone found above the whin, 'converted to a crystallized white rock of very large grain, which easily disintegrates into loose crystalline sand … sometimes called Sugar limestone.' Phillips too pointed out that the sill was also found on different geological levels or horizons – between layers of the Melmerby Scar Limestone at Cronkley, and above the much younger Tynebottom Limestone at High Force; therefore the whin could not have been a build up of lava flows on top of a particular sedimentary layer.

Adam Sedgewick's article of 1827, *On the Association of Trap Rocks with the Mountain Limestone Formation in High Teesdale, &c.*, complete with a map and 11 sections, argued that the Whin Sill was not a lava flow deposited on top of the other sedimentary layers, but was an intrusion or 'lateral injection' forced between and into these rock layers, its heat altering the rocks above and below it. Six years later Thomas Sopwith (1803-79), a land and mine surveyor from Alston to the north of Teesdale, declared that 'the insertion of basaltic rocks among the regular strata at Teesdale is a fact open to the observation of every eye at the waterfall of High Force.' The term 'sill' was adopted for such a roughly horizontal sheet of intrusive igneous rock; so the 'Great Whin Sill' of upper Teesdale became the original sill of the science of geology. Some geologists continued to believe that this whin was built up from a series of surface lava flows from a volcano; it was not until 1877 that its intrusive nature was established beyond doubt and the Great Whin Sill became the accepted type example of a sill.[4] Naturally, the Whin Sill provided a distinctive rocky plant habitat, and the metamorphism of the nearby rocks produced different soils

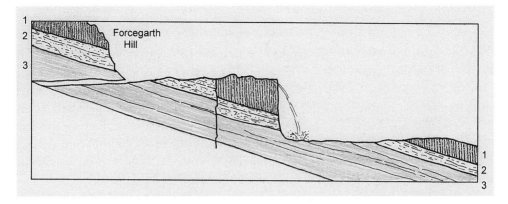

**6**  *Section between Forcegarth Hill and bed of River below High Foss. Redrawn in 1898 for* Zig-Zag
Ramblings of a Naturalist, *after Sedgwick, 1827. Sedgwick labels the Whin Sill at 1 and a dark crinoid
limestone at 3.*

which in turn had an effect on the plants that would grow; we will investigate these
plants and the botanists that came to study them in a later chapter.

As well as investigating the Great Whin Sill, Adam Sedgwick noted a major
structural feature crossing Teesdale between Cauldron Snout and High Force.
Westgarth Forster had described this great Burtreeford 'dyke' or fault, with the rocks
to the east being thrown down nearly eighty fathoms. On the map accompanying
his article, Sedgwick marks this fault, along with the Teesdale Fault and the outcrop
of the 'Trap' or Whin Sill. The mining engineer Forster as well as the mine surveyor
Thomas Sopwith were naturally interested in the veins of lead in smaller cracks in
the sedimentary rocks of Teesdale.

The origin of these mineral veins, their association with the Whin Sill, and the
whole structural history of the area were not thoroughly investigated until the 20th
century. The minerals were probably deposited by fluids coming from the same
hot magma which formed the Whin Sill, now identified as a quartz-dolerite. From
painstaking work on the zoning of minerals in the veins, Kingsley Dunham (1910-
2001; knighted 1972) in 1934 suggested the existence of a solidified mass of granite
beneath the north Pennine area; a gravity survey in 1957 added further evidence
for this, and it was proved by the drilling of the Rookhope borehole in 1961.
The heat from this Weardale Granite was probably responsible for circulating the
mineralising fluids which produced the veins of lead, though the exact mechanism
is still debated.

A more recent episode in the geological history of the area drew interested
geologists to Teesdale. John Phillips in 1852 described large isolated blocks of rock
or 'erratics' which were quite different from the local rocks on which they were
found. On the summit of Stainmore from one such block,

> we may look back across the Vale of Eden, over many other such scattered erratics,
> almost to the very point of the [Shap] Fell from which they were torn, and speculate
> on the power employed, and the ancient condition of land and sea which could render

possible this almost miraculous transport of heavy rocks across deep valleys and over lofty hills.

This 'strangest phenomena of physical geography' took place along the valley of the Greta; on the eastern side of Stainmore the erratics of Shap granite radiate out towards Romaldkirk, Cotherstone, Barnard Castle, and Brignall, and even reach the vale of York. Phillips had either not heard of the work of Swiss geologist Louis Agassiz (1807-1873), or did not accept his ideas. Agassiz had studied the glaciers in Switzerland, and seen how they could transport huge blocks of rock and smaller material, depositing them as erratics and moraine; in 1840 he had published his theory of the 'Ice Age', though it was not widely accepted for some time.

John Phillips in 1852 suggested that the recently improved inn near High Force would be found very convenient for exploring Upper Teesdale. By July 1865 another scientist would be following this advice and be investigating the work of ice in Teesdale. Joseph Dalton Hooker (1817-1911; knighted 1877) was the Assistant Director of the Royal Botanic Gardens at Kew, shortly to take over as Director from his father Sir W.J. Hooker (1785-1865). After long expeditions to the Antarctic and Himalayas, J.D. Hooker had brought his wife to the *High Force Inn* in Teesdale for health reasons. Though his choice of area may perhaps have been influenced by the knowledge of the rare Teesdale plants through his father (Chapter 10), he seems to have spent some of the time studying the glaciation of the dale. In a letter to his friend Charles Darwin (1809-82) Hooker wrote: 'I am studying the moraines all day long'. It was not long before Darwin was congratulating Hooker on his article *Moraines of the Tees Valley* in *The Reader* of 15 July 1865.

Hooker obviously knew of and accepted Louis Agassiz's theories; he describes the moraines between High Force and Cauldron Snout as being as well developed and as clearly marked as any to be found in the Alps or Himalayas. The moraines, both lateral at the valley sides, and medial (or middle) for example where the Lunedale glacier joined the main Tees valley glacier, are of loose material, loaded with angular blocks and covered with boulders. Besides these glacial depositional features, there are signs of the erosive force of a great glacier which filled the valley of the Tees – the 'moutonnéed surfaces of hills' where the ice had frozen onto and plucked out blocks of rock, and an abundance of 'scored surfaces and polished rocks' where the ice, loaded with rocks frozen into its base had acted like a giant file. Hooker believes that the Tees has altered its course little since the great glacier disappeared, and he distinguishes between the small effect of the river itself on wearing down the Whin Sill, and the erosive action of the pebbles and boulders carried by the river, especially in flood.

Professional and amateur geologists found much to collect and investigate in Teesdale, their writings in turn attracting more visitors. G.A. Lebour, Professor of Geology at Newcastle upon Tyne brought out *Outlines of the Geology of Northumberland and Durham* in 1886. Lebour sets out the controversy over the origin of the Great Whin Sill, concluding 'that the Whin Sill has been injected between the strata after their deposition and consolidation is now sufficiently evident'. Lebour dates the intrusion of the Whin Sill to the late Carboniferous period with its 'extraordinary repeated

7 *Cauldron Snout.*
*Photograph by Elijah Yeoman of*
*Barnard Castle. Two ladies are*
*viewing the Tees tumbling over*
*the columnar Whin Sill.*

alternations of open sea, land-locked sea, lake, land, estuary, and shore to which we owe the thousands of feet of grits, shales, under-clays, coals and limestones.'

Robert Calvert's book, *Notes on the Geology & Natural History of the County of Durham*, published in Bishop Auckland in 1884, was perhaps aimed at a more general audience. Calvert describes the 'Spar' minerals found in the veins, and hints at their widespread collection – 'the finer and smaller pieces being highly prized for cabinet specimens or general ornament, and the larger for garden rockeries'. In their spare time, lead miners would assemble the minerals, together with small mirrors, in spar-boxes; there were spar-box exhibitions and competitions in the 1880s and 1890s in neighbouring Weardale, where better mineral specimens were found; one spar-box from Teesdale has survived.[5] As well as describing fluorspar, quartz and barytes, Calvert gives hints on how to tell them apart, testing their hardness with a knife, or testing with acids. When describing the valley of the Tees, Calvert notes how the vegetation gives clues as to the underlying rock; the hill tops are covered with ling or heather, a sure sign of millstone grit, and short grass indicates an outcrop of limestone. Robert Calvert gives details of how to get to Cauldron Snout, which should be visited after a thunderstorm or heavy rain rather than during what he calls 'pic-nic weather'; he also lists the rare alpine plants nearby, the result of the geology and the elevation of the site. As well as describing the splendour of High Force, borrowing heavily from the writings of previous visitors, Calvert explains how the waterfall has receded. From the plunge pool below the falls, the river

> flows through the deep gorge worn by the rushing waters during the long periods that the fall has been gradually receding westward to its present position. [The softer rocks underlying the Whin Sill are] more easily worn and carried away by the fall and eddy of the water thus undermining the cliff, so that through the continued action of the stream, frost, and other agencies, large masses of rock are dislodged.

Calvert should have added another 'agency' to his list of factors affecting the recession of High Force; but the effect of melting ice would be recognised by another local naturalist.

The Darlington Naturalist's Field Club was founded in 1891, with some links to earlier societies of 1793 and 1860; in 1896 the club changed its name to the Darlington and Teesdale Naturalists' Field Club, and took the first edition of Richard T. Manson's book *Zig-Zag Ramblings of a Naturalist* as the basis of its work. The second edition of this book in 1898 included illustrations of fossils and geological sections; with reference to specific localities, it set out to explain the geology of the area in fairly simple terms. Manson describes how the Tees once covered a much greater area than at present, during and at the end of the Ice Age. 'When the ice and snow melted from the hills – ice and snow, remember, that far exceeded in quantity any that are deposited now

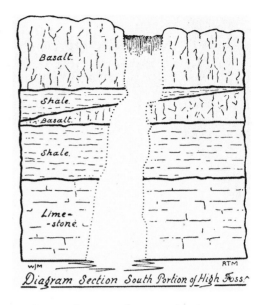

**8** *Diagram Section South Portion of High Foss. Drawn by W.J. Mountford after R.T. Manson for* Zig-Zag Ramblings of a Naturalist, *1898. This is not to scale.*

– ... torrents of water [were] poured in immense volumes from the elevated lands, tearing, crashing and scooping all before them.'

Manson thinks that there should be a tablet or plaque at the *High Force Hotel* to commemorate the chance meeting near there in 1822 of the two great early geologists John Phillips and Adam Sedgwick. Discussing the origins of the Whin Sill, Manson reproduces Sedgwick's section of the strata above and below High Force, showing how a fault leads to the repetition of the basalt or Whin Sill. A more detailed section through the rocks at High Force seems to be based on local observations; Manson credits Henry Redfearn of Forest-in-Teesdale with investigating the wedge of shale in the almost inaccessible upper part of this section.

Geologists came to Teesdale to investigate the rocks, their structure and the history of their formation. Writers and artists would depict the wonders of the waterfalls over the Whin Sill; botanists came to study the rare flowering plants surviving on the sugar limestone; tourists were drawn to the natural scenery and the trappings of lead mining. It is clear that geology underlies not only the fabric of Teesdale, but also the story of its discovery.

## 2

## *Classical Foundations*

*'a pretty addition to the marbles at Rokeby'*

In the 18th century landscape painting in Britain developed from the Classical through the Picturesque to the Romantic. Teesdale not only witnessed this development but also played an important part in it. A special role was taken by Rokeby Park near the junction of the rivers Greta and Tees (see plate 2). J.B.S. Morritt, Rokeby's owner, wrote in 1811, 'The scenery of our rivers deserves to become classic ground.' Before this, during the 18th century, Rokeby itself had indeed become classic ground.

The Reverend T.D. Whitaker, in his antiquarian work *An History of Richmondshire* of 1823, wrote of Greta Bridge lying on a branch of the great Roman road, which led to Bowes (plate 1), and thence north-westward to Carlisle. Within the Rokeby estate were several significant antiquities including the rectangular Roman station Maglovæ guarding the crossing of the river Greta (plates 54 & 55), and the Premonstratensian Egglestone Abbey. Mortham Tower still displayed the Rokeby arms of three rooks (see plate 59). Whitaker traced the foundations of an early Rokeby church near the junction of the Tees and Greta, where he found a small nave and a few headstones. The parish register contained the names of Rookbys and Rokebys.

> On the whole, the several features of Rokeby and Mortham combining the union of the Teese and Greta, with their rocks and native woods; the venerable but almost disappearing fragments of the old parish church, with the gravestones just peeping above the green swarth; the memory of the brave, the pious, the spirited family, whose residence so long animated the scene; the Roman station, partly within the park, and the near prospect of Egglestone Abbey, with which in life and death the Rokebys were so nearly connected, must be allowed to constitute in the eye of taste, or in the exercise of recollection, one of the most enchanting residences in the north of England.

A vicar of Rokeby in the 17th century recorded how a London merchant, William Robinson, purchased the manor of Rokeby from Sir Thomas Rokeby, who was still living in Mortham Tower in 1610 (see plate VIII). Robinson built a new house where the present Rokeby Hall stands. Soon after inheriting Rokeby, Sir Thomas Robinson (*c.*1702-77), an amateur architect, began to consider replacing this old house. Having turned down plans by others for not having 'so many Palladian strokes

**9** *Rokeby Hall. Engraving by F. Mansell after Nathaniel Whittock, 1830, for* A History of the County of York.

**10** *Roman Antiquities. Engraving for* An History of Richmondshire, *1823.*

**11** *Arms of Rokeby at Mortham Tower. Illustration by G.P. Rhodes for* A Picturesque History of Yorkshire, *1901.*

about them', Robinson proceeded to design his new house himself in the fashionable style associated with Lord Burlington (1695-1753) and Yorkshireman William Kent (1685-1748). In Italy, Lord Burlington studied the architecture of Andrea Palladio (1508-80), returning home with 'Palladian' plans and William Kent who had lived in Italy for ten years. Burlington sponsored a number of books on classical architecture, including Kent's *Designs of Inigo Jones* in 1727 and Robert Castell's *The Villas of the Ancients Illustrated* in 1728. Like many of the neo-Palladians, Burlington studied Roman remains in Britain as well as in Italy, financing a survey of some Roman sites in Yorkshire.

Lord William Howard of Naworth, Cumberland (1563-1640) was one of the first collectors of Roman remains along nearby Hadrian's Wall; his great grandson Charles Howard became the 1st Earl of Carlisle. Sir Thomas Robinson married Elizabeth Howard, the eldest daughter of the 3rd Earl in 1728; at least some of Lord William Howard's Roman antiquities were sent to Rokeby, adding to those collected by Robinson at Greta Bridge. Barnard Castle solicitor William Hutchinson, returning from *An Excursion to the Lakes* in 1773 (Chapter 7), found Rokeby 'a repository of curiosities', reflecting Robinson's 'fine taste': 'In the Tuscan hall and musæum there is a large collection of antiquities, in sculpture, statues, monuments, altars, vessels and inscriptions ... gathered from ... Egypt, India, Italy and many other foreign parts, as well as those found in this country.' In his book, Hutchinson includes two plates of Roman vessels, altars and inscriptions, either found near Rokeby or brought from Naworth (plates 14 &15).

Aware of the Roman connections of his estate, Sir Thomas Robinson was also much influenced by Lord Burlington's taste in Roman architecture. Building began in 1729 to Sir Thomas Robinson's design, although he and Lady Robinson were themselves away on the Grand Tour from August 1729 to January 1731. Rokeby became one of the earliest Palladian villas in England. According to Hutchinson, a tablet of marble at the gate to Rokeby commemorated the completion of the house in 1730.

An 18th-century painting of the *North Front of Rookby House, Offices and part of the Park*, still on display in the house, shows Robinson rigorously following Palladio's classic villa layout and using some of Burlington's and Kent's designs. The house was approached through a courtyard with wings containing stables and offices; there was a central hall with apartments on either side; the repeated use of a pyramidal roof and a terracotta-coloured stucco completed what has been described as one of the purest examples of the neo-Palladian villa in Britain. In designing twin towers instead of the usual four, Robinson seems to have gone back to Pliny the Younger (62-114) and the description of his villa at Laurentinum. By 1753 Sir Thomas Robinson was altering his original design, replacing the external staircase with a more fashionable front door and entrance hall on the ground floor; the intended Palladian-inspired *bagnio* or bath and billiard room were replaced by a print room. Another oil painting still at Rokeby, *South Front of Rookby House, Offices and Gateways towards the Park*, must date from after 1753 as it depicts Sir Thomas Robinson showing off this

**12** *The north front of Rookby. An 18th-century oil painting of this neo-Palladian villa.*

altered design of his house, probably to his father-in-law the Earl of Carlisle; various antiquities are shown prominently in the foreground.

The layout of the park at Rokeby, especially as shown in Robinson's plan of 1741, also has its basis in Pliny's descriptions, this time of his villa at Tuscum, reconstructed in Castell's engraving in *Villas of the Ancients*. This book gave encouragement and authority to the new style of irregular gardening in 18th-century England. As Sir Thomas Robinson wrote to his father-in-law Lord Carlisle in 1734:

> There is a new taste in gardening just arisen ... that a general alteration of some of the most notable gardens in the Kingdom is begun, after Mr Kent's notion of gardening, viz. to lay them out, and work without level or line ... The celebrated gardens of Claremont, Chiswick, and Stowe are now full of labourers, to modernise the expensive works finished in them, even since every one's memory.

This 'new taste' in gardening owed something to poetry. The poet James Thomson (1700-48) joined the Burlington set soon after arriving in London in 1726; his *Seasons* were published between 1726 and 1730, and William Kent illustrated the collected volumes. According to the literary historian Joseph Warton (1728-90), the *Seasons* 'have been very instrumental in diffusing a general taste for the beauties of nature and landscape'. Poet and garden designer Alexander Pope (1688-1744) commented in 1734 that 'all gardening is landscape painting ... just like a landscape hung up'. *The Newcastle General Magazine* in January 1748 included a description of Pope's garden at Twickenham, and in April 1755 praised again 'the modern art of laying out ground ... regularity banished, prospects opened, the country called in, nature rescued and improved, and art decently concealing herself under her own perfections'.

At Rokeby various features of this landscaping were apparent. From the main entrance at Greta Bridge the visitor had a prospect of Mortham Tower and there

**13** *The south front of Rookby. Sir Thomas Robinson shows off his new design. Eighteenth-century oil painting.*

was a perimeter drive; the Palladian villa was placed in a 'hippodrome', a 'fine level lawn, surrounded with plantations' leading to the surrounding country, which included cultivated hills and the steep rocky banks of the river. A feature which would later be praised by visiting writers was a prospect house next to Dairy Bridge overlooking the river Greta, which in turn was contained by a great stone wall. A rather unexpected source provides another insight into Sir Thomas Robinson's partly executed landscaping plans. In 1812 the poet Robert Southey described another 18th-century painting (of the east aspect) which he saw hanging at Rokeby; the river Greta was 'metamorphosed by four dams into a piece of water as smooth and as still as a canal, and [made] to appear at the end of a smooth shaven green'.

Here, on the walk beside the Greta at Rokeby, Hutchinson sums up the 18th-century 'new taste', and refers to the influence of Rome:

> Nothing can excel the nobleness and solemnity of this walk; it is calculated for contemplation and religious rhapsody; every mind must feel the influence of the scene, and, forgetting the giddy engagements of lighter pleasures, yield to sublimer sentiments; … Near Rookby was a Roman station … In these walks, and under these shades, the Deæ Nymphæ were invoked, and the rites of Silvanus and Ceres were once performed.

Robinson also designed Thorpe Grange, to the east of Rokeby, and Rokeby church. However, by June 1765 his London interests prompted him to sell Rokeby. The estate was advertised in the *London Evening Post* as including 'a modern built Mansion House, Offices and Museum, and with or without the Furniture, Library, Pictures, Statues, Busts, Sculptures, Bronzes and other Curiosities'.

Four years later John Sawrey Morritt bought Rokeby. After the great flood of 1771 he paid for the rebuilding of two bridges, Greta Bridge and Abbey Bridge. J.S. Morritt's eldest son, John Bacon Sawrey Morritt (1771-1843), inherited Rokeby in 1791. For some reason Robinson had left his architectural drawings of Rokeby, two of them engraved

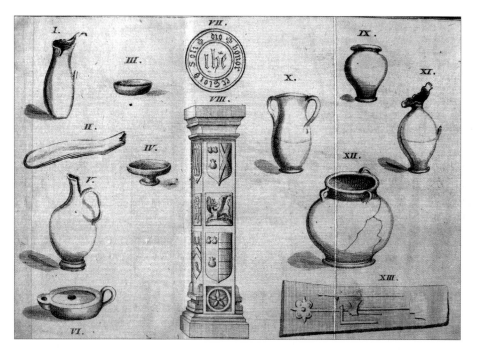

**14**   *Roman Vases and other Antiquities at Rookby, Engraving for* An Excursion to the Lakes, *1776. VIII (a pillar from a font) and XIII (a tombstone) came from Egglestone Abbey.*

by architect Isaac Ware (*c.*1704-66), but none of his books; amongst his pictures in the sale were those of Rokeby, three views of his house in Whitehall, and a portrait signed by William Kent.[1] J.B.S. Morritt added to the many pictures and 'curiosities', some collected on his own two-year Grand Tour from 1794, when he toured extensively in Greece and Turkey especially to investigate sites associated with Homer's *Iliad* and *Odyssey*. In a letter from Athens to his sister Morritt wrote that 'you are in a perfect gallery of marbles in these lands'. He later wrote to his aunt, 'We found a little statue, half-buried in the ground, which we dug up … If I can get it well restored in Italy, it will figure in the Rokeby collection; and its greatest charm perhaps will be that I found it myself.' J.B.S. Morritt supported Lord Elgin over the Parthenon marbles controversy, and himself made 'a pretty addition to the marbles at Rokeby'. Later, in 1813, he bought the painting *Venus at her Mirror* by the Spanish painter Diego Velázquez (1599-1660) which would later be known as the *Rokeby Venus*.[2] J.B.S. Morritt was a founder member of the Travellers' Club in 1819, but before then he and his Rokeby estate had helped an artist (John Sell Cotman, Chapter 12) and a writer (Walter Scott, Chapter 13) produce works which would bring many travellers to Teesdale.

J.B.S. Morritt may also have given hospitality to the clergyman and poet William Mason (1724-97). Mason designed a number of flower gardens, and wrote *The English Garden: A Poem in four books*; these were published between 1772 and 1781, a combined edition being printed in York in 1783. In *The English Garden* Mason, in setting out practical ideas for landscaping and gardening, acknowledges

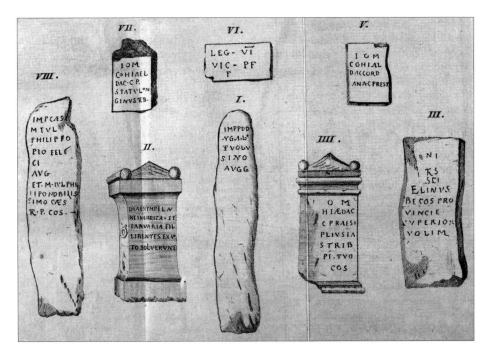

**15** *Roman Inscriptions at Rookby. Engraving for* An Excursion to the Lakes, *1776. I to III were found near Rokeby; IIII to VII came from Naworth.*

poets such as Spenser and Milton as the inspiration for landscape sensibility, and Pope as a landscape gardener. He advises that landscaping should be performed with 'Poet's feeling and Painter's eye'. A number of tour writers suggest that Mason visited Rokeby, a suggestion perhaps borne out by parts of the poem itself.

The author of the first (1803) edition of *A Tour in Teesdale* (Chapter 11), also published in York, suggested that Mason had given Morritt gardening advice:

> It should not be forgotten, that the late Mr Mason was a frequent inmate at Rokeby; and probably, by his correct and chaste judgement, it has been saved from tawdry and fantastic embellishments. It is in his Practical English Garden, where
>
> Art is called<br>Only to second Nature, and supply<br>All that the Nymph forgot, or left forlorn.

These lines are from Book 1 of Mason's *The English Garden* and refer to Edmund Spenser's *Fairie Queene* (1590-6). A footnote in *A Tour in Teesdale* suggests that an earlier passage in Mason's poem 'contains so many striking circumstances belonging to Rokeby, that one should be tempted to suppose, that the poet had it in his eye when he wrote'.

In the second edition of *A Tour in Teesdale* the author decides to quote this earlier passage from *The English Garden* in full, italicising the lines supposedly referring to Rokeby:

And yet, my Albion! in that fair domain
Which Ocean made thy dowry, when his love
Tempestuous tore thee from reluctant Gaul,
And bad thee be his Queen, there still remains
Full many a lovely unfrequented wild,
Where change like this is needless; where no lines
Of hedge-row, avenue, or of platform square
Demand destruction.[3] In thy fair domain,
Yes, my lov'd Albion! many a glade is found
The haunt of wood-gods only: where if art
E'er dar'd to tread; 'twas with unsandal'd feet,
Printless, as if the place were holy ground.
And there are scenes, where, tho' she whilom trod,
Led by the worst of guides, fell Tyranny,
And ruthless Superstition, we now trace
Her footsteps with delight; and pleas'd revere
What once we should have hated. But to Time,
Not her, the praise is due: his gradual touch
Has moulder'd into beauty many a tow'r,
Which, when it frown'd with all its battlements,
Was only terrible: and many a fane
Monastic, which, when deck'd with all its spires,
Serv'd but to feed some pamper'd Abbot's pride,
And awe th'unletter'd vulgar. Generous youth,
Whoe'er thou art, that listens to my lay,
And feel'st thy soul assent to what I sing,
Happy art thou if thou can'st call thine own
Such scenes as these; *where Nature and where Time*
*Have work'd congenial; where a scatter'd host*
*Of antique oaks darken thy sidelong hills;*
*While, rushing[4] thro' their branches, rifted cliffs*
*Dart their white heads, and glitter thro' the gloom.*
*More happy still, if one superior rock*
*Bear on its brow the shiver'd fragment huge*
*Of some old Norman fortress; happier far,*
*Ah! then most happy, if thy vale below*
*Wash, with the crystal coolness of its rills,*
*Some mouldering abbey's ivy-vested wall."*

Mason is here reflecting the 'new taste in gardening' that Sir Thomas Robinson described, sweeping away the formality of previous designs. It is easy to see the estate of Rokeby in the italicised section describing a classic landscape in no need of embellishment; here are the cliffs along the Greta river with Mortham Tower above, and nearby Egglestone Abbey.

When Robert Southey visited Rokeby in 1812 he wrote to his wife how J.B.S. Morritt had escorted him around the grounds; his account confirms the idea of Mason visiting the house. The inside of the summer-house overlooking the river 'was ornamented by Mason the poet: one day he set the whole family to work in

**16**  *A tomb brought from Egglestone Abbey and placed in Rokeby Park. Engraving for* An History of
Richmondshire, *1823.*

cutting out ornaments in coloured paper from antique designs, directing the whole
himself. It is still in good preservation.'

Later guide books to Teesdale (discussed in Chapter 18) quote from Book 3 of
*The English Garden*:

> then let down thy torrent: then
> Rejoice; as if the thund'ring Tees* himself
> Reign'd there amid his cataracts sublime.

Mason's footnote refers to High Force, or the Fall of the Tees 'esteemed one of the
greatest in England'. *Rambles in Teesdale* (1877) states that Mason 'loved to linger
in the "shadowy glades" of Rokeby'; and a *History & Directory of North Yorkshire*
in 1890 repeats the assertion that 'Rokeby was the frequent resort of Mason, the
poet.'

Before Mason drew on Teesdale for his poem other visitors had explored the area,
describing and mapping the Tees and the Roman remains; it is to these 'explorers'
that we now turn.

# 3

## The Early 'Explorers'

### 'The Castelle of Barnard stondith stately apon Tese'

The first travellers to visit Teesdale had no maps to guide them. In 1535 John Leland, then aged about 32, received a commission from Henry VIII to survey the monastic libraries for antiquities. In 1536 the dissolution of the monasteries began, their libraries being ransacked. Leland collected as well as catalogued the monastic manuscripts, so that they might 'be brought out of deadly darkenesse to lyvely light'. At the end of 1545 Leland wrote his *New Year's Gift*, a report to Henry VIII on his work and his plans for it. Leland's manuscript notes, or copies of them, were eventually published as an *Itinerary* in 1712.

Leland hopes that his description of the country will allow an accurate map to be made. He estimates the mileage between towns, and notes the source and tributaries of each river he comes across:

> Yad More hath the Hedde of Tese, then it takith a Course emong Rokkes, and reseyving divers other smaul Hopes or Bekkes, and cummith much by wild ground for a 8. or x. Miles to Ægleston Bridge wel archid: then to Barnard Castel Bridge, very fair of 3. Arches.

While not mentioning the waterfalls between the source of the Tees and Eggleston, Leland does note the rocky terrain and comments on the bridges. Stainmore allows communication from Yorkshire by way of Bowes, but what we now know as a Roman marching camp at Rey Cross is of equal interest:

> There is a place an viii Mile plaine West from Bowis, a Thorough-fare in Richemontshire cawlid Maiden Castel, where is a greate rounde Hepe a 60. Foote in Cumpace of rude Stones, sum smaul, sum bygge, and be set in *formam pyramidis*; and yn the Toppe of them al ys set one Stone *in conum*, beying a Yard and a half in length. So that the hole may be counted an xviii. Foote hy, and ys set on a hill in the very Egge of Stanemore.[1]

Leland here seems to be describing the Rey Cross stone, then on top of a cairn or heap of stones; 'Maiden Castle' today refers to a fortlet a few miles to the west.

From Durham, Leland visits Bishop Auckland before staying at Raby, the largest inhabited castle in the North, and a strong building; two of the three parks belonging to Raby are stocked with deer. Barnard Castle is quite a pretty town, fairly well built

**17** *Part of Christopher Saxton's map of County Durham, c.1607; details of Teesdale lying in Yorkshire are included. Roads are not shown, only bridges.*

and with a good market; the well-moated castle stands proudly above the Tees; in the church there are two tombs, perhaps of the Balliols. At Egglestone Abbey Leland notices the (packhorse) bridge over Thorsgill, still to be seen today, and two very fine tombs of grey marble to Sir Ralph Bowes and one of the Rokebys. Here, on each side of the river Tees, Leland remarks on the 'very fair marble' worked at Barnard Castle and Egglestone Abbey. There are two miles of pasture, corn and wood to Greta Bridge, which has two or three arches; the village of 'Gretey' is on Watling Street. At 'Mr Rokesby's Place' the river Greta flows into the Tees.

John Rudd may have been the first to attempt an accurate topographical map showing the river Tees. Rudd was vicar of Dewsbury and a prebend at Durham Cathedral. In 1561 he was granted a dispensation from residence at Durham for two years to allow him to travel and map more of the country. Queen Elizabeth I was facing rebellion with the Rising of the North and Lord Burghley, her chief minister, particularly appreciated the importance of maps. It is likely that the famous early mapmaker Christopher Saxton (*c*.1543-1610) accompanied John Rudd as his apprentice. Some time after 1570 Saxton began a survey of England and Wales, the first maps being dated 1574. A complete atlas came out in 1579; though much of it was based on Rudd's surveys and manuscript estate maps, the atlas comprised the first set of county maps and would influence map production for some time.

In 1612-13 Michael Drayton (1563-1631), a poet who was part of a circle that may have included Shakespeare, published a book of poems with the title *Poly-Olbion* or *Chorographical Description of all the Tracts, Rivers, Mountains, Forests and other parts of the Renowned Isle of Great Britain*, containing 18 illustrative county maps; a second part with 12 extra maps appeared in 1622. The maps, possibly engraved by William Hole, are not geographical but allegorical in nature; nymphs adorn the rivers, and figures crowned with castles and spires indicate towns. The poem, too, concentrates on the rivers; the Tees divides the counties of Durham and Yorkshire, and receives tributaries from both:

> Tees as a bordering flood (who thought herself divine)
> Confining in her course that county Palatine,
> And York, the greatest shire, doth instantly begin
> To rouse herself: quoth she, doth every rillet win
> Applause for their small worths, and I, that am a queen
> With those poor brooks compar'd, shall I alone be seen
> Thus silently to pass, and not be heard to sing?
>
> .    .    .    .    .    .
>
> But as in all these tracts, there's scarce a flood of fame
> But she some valley hath, which her brave name doth bear!
> My Teesdale nam'd of me, so likewise have I here,
> At my first setting forth, through which I nimbly slide!
> Then Yorkshire, which doth lie upon my setting side,
> Me Lune and Bauder lends, as in the song before
> Th' industrious muse hath show'd: my Dunelmenian shore
> Sends Huyd to help my course, with some few other becks,
> Which time (as it should seem) so utterly neglects
> That they are nameless yet; then do I bid adieu
> To Bernard's battled towers, and seriously pursue
> My course to Neptune's court.

William Camden (1551-1623) failed to furnish the first (1586) edition of his *Britannia* with maps, but maps were engraved for the sixth Latin edition of 1607, and re-appeared in the first English edition of 1610 and in the new translation of the work by Holland in 1637, *Britain, or a chorographical description of the most flourishing Kingdomes of England, Scotland, and Ireland ... Beautified with Mappes of the several Shires of England: Written first in Latine by William Camden ... translated newly into English by Philémon Holland ... Revised, amended and enlarged*. The maps were mostly engraved by William Kip and William Hole, and were largely based on those by Christopher Saxton. Stainmore lay in the part of Yorkshire called Richmondshire; in the 1610 edition Camden mentions the inn at Spital, Rey Cross and Maiden Castle.

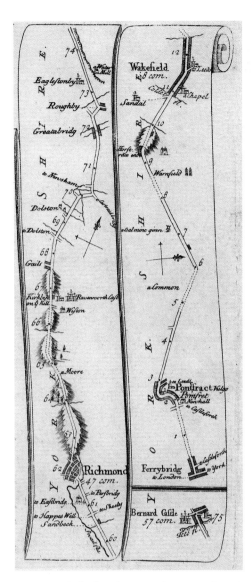

**18** *Part of John Senex's strip road map, number 95; the road from Ferrybridge to Barnard Castle, and a branch road from Ferrybridge to Wakefield. Published 1719.*

Heere beginneth to rise that high hilly and solitary Country exposed to wind and raine, which, because it is stony, is called in our native language Stanemore. All heere round about is nothing but a wild desert, unlesse it bee an homely Hostelry, or Inne, in the very middest thereof, called The Spitle on Stanmore, for to entertaine waifaring persons, and neere to it is a fragment of a crosse, which wee call Rerecrosse, the Scots Reicrosse, as one would say *The Kings Crosse* ... And a litle lower, upon the Romanes high street, there stood a little Fort of the Romans built four square, which at this day they call Maiden-Castle. From whence, as the borderers reported, the said High way went with many windings in and out, as farre as to *Caer Vorran* in Northumberland.

Camden goes on to describe the bishopric of Durham with the river Tees on its way to Barnard Castle, where the hard limestone or 'marble' at Egglestone Abbey is quarried:

The river that boundeth the South part of this country is called by Latin writers *Teisis* and *Teesa*, commonly Tees ... Tees springeth out of that stony country called Stanemore, and, carrying with him away in his chanell along, many brooks and beckes on each side, and running through rockes (out of which at Egleston, where there is a marble Quarroy, and where Conan Earle of Britaine and Richmond founded a small Abbay), first beateth upon Bernard Castle, built and so named by Bernard Balliol the great grandfathers father of John Balliol King of the Scots.

Camden gives an account of Staindrop and the Nevill family of Raby castle (see map, plate 19). The village of Staindrop was given to the monks of Durham Cathedral by King Cnut in 1031. Behind the church a small monastery or 'college' was founded in 1408 by Ralph Nevill, Earl of Westmorland. The Lords of Raby, buried in splendid tombs in the church, lost Raby castle following their support for the Rising of the North in 1569.[2]

The only indication of roads on the earlier maps was the inclusion of bridges over the rivers. In 1675 John Ogilby (1600-76) published the first really accurate set of road maps. He had the main roads measured with a 'Wheel Dimensurator' or 'waywiser' and

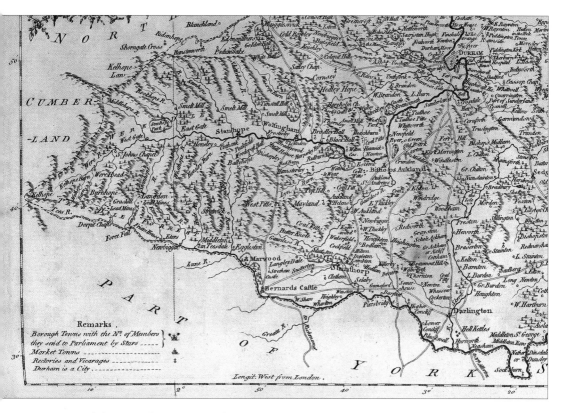

**19**   *Part of Thomas Kitchin's New Map of Durham, Drawn from the best Authorities, 1764; showing lead mines and High Force as the 'Force Fall'.*

recorded places, junctions with side roads, rivers and hills; there were descriptive notes on the country on either side of the road, such as 'Common' or 'Arable', and the material used in the construction of the bridges was noted. Ogilby used the standard mile of 1,760 yards which had been introduced by statute in 1593 but had never replaced the old 'long', 'middle' and 'short' miles which had long confused travellers. A scale of one inch to one mile is used, with the number of miles between towns marked beside the road. Ogilby's maps were published in an atlas named *Britannia – a Geographical and Historical Description of the Principal Roads thereof*; each map had the road drawn as if on a strip of rolled paper, with compass roses showing the orientation of each strip. Pages with accompanying notes were interleaved with the 100 pages of strip maps. Four issues of *Britannia* were published between 1675 and 1676, with a reprint in 1698.

Ogilby's atlas was too large to use on the road, and in 1719 John Senex published a smaller, quarto, copy:

An Actual SURVEY Of all the PRINCIPAL ROADS of ENGLAND and WALES; Described by One Hundred MAPS from Copper Plates. On which are delineated All the CITIES, TOWNS, VILLAGES, CHURCHES, HOUSES, and Places of Note throughout each Road. As ALSO Directions to the Curious Traveller what is worth observing throughout his Journey.

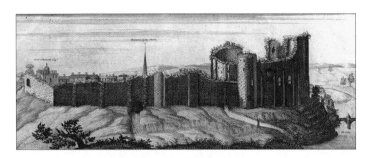

**20** *West View of Barnard Castle. Nathaniel and Samuel Buck, 1728.*

With a scale of less than half an inch to one mile, Senex's more portable maps omit some of Ogilby's detail; bridges are no longer of stone or wood, but the spelling of place-names is copied. Map number 95 is *The Road from Ferrybridge to Boroughbridge, continued to Bernards Castle*. Barnard Castle is 75 miles from Ferrybridge and correctly placed in the Bishoprick of Durham rather than in Yorkshire; however, 'Greatabridg' is no longer shown as being built of stone and the 'Water Mill' at 'Eaglestonby' is placed on the wrong side of the River Tees. Senex's quarto copies of Ogilby's maps were soon followed in 1720 by Emanuel Bowen's octavo version named *Britannia Depicta* or *Ogilby Improved*.

Thomas Kitchin (1718-84) was a prolific map engraver and publisher, contributing county maps to many publications. His *New Map of Durham, Drawn from the best Authorities* shows roads, but none in Teesdale above Barnard Castle; two sets of lead mines are shown. High Force is labelled as 'Force Fall'; on his map of the North Riding of Yorkshire (plate 35) Kitchin labels this as 'Fall 60 Feet'. John Cary (1754-1835) set up in London as an engraver, map and print seller, and surveyor about 1783. Cary's *New and Correct English Atlas* was first published in 12 parts between 1787 and 1789. Although the text page accompanying his map of the County of Durham includes 'The Force of Teesdale' as one of 'The most extensive Views in this County', High Force is not named on the map; lead mines are shown, however. From 1790 small county maps by John Cary were published in the *Traveller's Companion*, which showed the results of a new survey of the turnpike roads. This *Companion* became increasingly popular and had a good deal of influence on the early work of the Ordnance Survey Office which was established in 1791.

Francis Place (1647-1728) was born to an affluent family in Dinsdale near Darlington; after a short time at Gray's Inn in London he made it clear to his father that he preferred the fine arts to law. He met Wenceslaus Hollar (1607-77) of Prague, who had come to London in 1636 and was an accomplished etcher. Place probably adopted Hollar's pen and ink style, which was concerned with the accurate or 'topographical' portrayal of a place, and learnt the technique of etching in Hollar's London studio. Place had a wide circle of acquaintances, including nobility, merchants and professional people; some of these, with Place and the artist George Lambert, formed the York Virtuosi, which gathered to discuss artistic and scientific questions of the day. About 1700 Place began to concentrate on landscape drawing, being the first English artist to do so; he travelled, often with Lambert, around England, Wales and into Ireland, drawing and etching 'prospects' of towns, though most of his drawings seem to have been made for his own

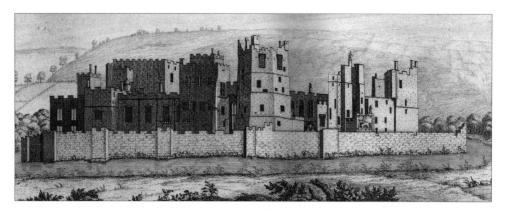

**21**  *South-east View of Raby Castle in the Bishoprick of Durham. Nathaniel and Samuel Buck, 1728.*

satisfaction rather than produced for etching. As well as many drawings of York, and one of Richmond, drawings of Barnard Castle survive, but in private hands.

Antiquarian John Warburton (1661-1759) was a collector of excise, and from 1720 a College of Arms Herald. While on government business his travels took him to the houses of the gentry and past many churches and castles. Planning an illustrated history of Yorkshire, Warburton employed Samuel Buck (1696-1779) from about 1719 to draw buildings of interest. Although the history of Yorkshire never materialised, Buck's Yorkshire sketchbook has survived. As well as a view of Barnard Castle from Startforth, there are sketches of Egglestone Abbey, Wycliffe, Lartington Hall, Mortham Tower and Rokeby. This last is of interest as it shows the house before Sir Thomas Robinson started to rebuild it in 1729.

After five years working for John Warburton, Samuel Buck, with his brother Nathaniel, began the task of creating a visual record of the ancient monuments in England and Wales; these images were termed 'views' and were still firmly in the topographic tradition. Eventually 428 views of abbeys and castles, four views of seats and 83 large general views of cities and towns were printed, and sold separately or collected into volumes. *The South-East View of Raby Castle, in the Bishoprick of Durham* was dedicated to 'To the Right Honourable Thomas, Earl of Strafford … Baron of Raby' with an appended history of the castle. *The West View of Bernard Castle in the Bishoprick of Durham* was dedicated 'To the Rt. Honble. Gilbert Ld. Bernard'. This view, also dated 1728, has labels indicating the river Tees and the church.

Another artist employed to make topographical drawings was Samuel Hieronymus Grimm (1733-94). Grimm came to England from Switzerland in 1768 and worked for a number of patrons, including Sir Richard Kaye, for whom he toured the country to depict 'everything curious' of antiquarian interest. At Raby Castle in 1773 Grimm made a sketch of the interior of the hall, and a more finished drawing in Indian ink and wash of the castle set in its park.

The author of *Robinson Crusoe*, Daniel Defoe (*c.*1661-1731) wrote his *Tour Through England and Wales* (1724-6) as a popular guidebook. He travelled through the north of England five times, using a different route on each occasion, 'that I

**22** *Barnard Castle. A Rock & Co. engraving for* Views & Scenery of Barnard Castle, *1857, before Thorngate footbridge was constructed in 1871.*

might see every thing that was to be seen'. His main interest was economic; he hurries over the country to record manufacturing, perhaps pausing to note some picturesque sight. So, Defoe finds Barnard Castle 'an antient town, and pretty well built, but not large'; he notes that yarn stockings and leather goods for horses are made there. Defoe finds the Tees 'a most terrible river, so rapid', explaining that it very quickly rises in time of flood. Defoe finds all hills 'terrible' and 'frightful'; those of Lancashire and Yorkshire are high and formidable, with 'a kind of inhospitable terror in them'. There are no rich valleys, no mineral wealth, 'but all barren and wild, of no use or advantage either to man or beast'; the Pennines are like a wall of brass. Defoe does not seem to have ventured from Barnard Castle further up Teesdale, where he would have seen some evidence of mineral wealth.

Some twenty years later George Smith (*c*.1700-73)[3] of Brampton in Cumberland was drawn to make the ascent of Cross Fell near the headwaters of the Tees. In his account of his journey, published in the *Gentleman's Magazine* in 1747, Smith explains the attraction of such a venture:

> A mountain that is generally ten months bury'd in snow, and eleven in clouds, cannot fail of exciting the attraction and curiosity of a traveller … Cross-fell, tho' distinguished in none of our county maps, is most singularly eminent … emitting considerable streams to both seas. This insensible ascent … being in a manner encompassed with other desolate and barren mountains, … retains the snow much longer than any other we can see in Britain.

On 13 August 1747 Smith and a companion hire a guide at Alston and are soon joined by two other explorers 'out of the same curiosity'. Smith gives enough detail to enable their route to be followed on a map, along Black Burn, past Greencastle Tarn and numerous swallow holes, to the disused lead mines near Bullman Cleugh. They then ride through 'very broken morassy wastes' and across scree slopes which force them to dismount. From the 'inconceivably barren' summit plain of Cross Fell, Skiddaw, Ingleborough and the Cheviots are all visible.

The publication of 'A Journey up to Cross-fell Mountain', along with articles in the *Gentleman's Magazine* on George Smith's ascents of other Cumbrian mountains, soon led to articles by others in the rival *Universal Magazine* and *London Magazine*. The mountains of Britain, though perhaps still seen as barren and wild, were finding their place on the explorer's itinerary. Travellers were also keen to see the trappings of lead mining, the topic to which we now turn.

# 4

## Lead Mining

*'Come me little washer lad comes lets away*
*We're bound down for slavery for fourpence a day'*

Although it is likely that the Romans mined for lead in Teesdale, records relating to lead mining are found only from the 17th century. Lead sulphide or galena, along with other minerals such as zinc, fluorspar and barites, occurs in fissure veins, deposited by mineralising fluids emanating from the same hot magma which formed the Whin Sill in the Carboniferous rocks of Teesdale.

Thomas Sopwith (1803-79), a land and mine surveyor, published a volume of three *Geological sections of … Lead Mines in Alston Moor and Teesdale* in 1828, and *An Account of the Mining Districts of Alston Moor, Weardale and Teesdale* in 1833, having kept a private diary over four years while working as an assistant and then partner, in a firm in Alston. The surveyor thought that the machinery and curious processes used in preparing the ore for smelting, and the beautiful specimens displayed in the shops of mineral dealers, 'all tend to combine the most rational enjoyment with the most agreeable exercise, and to fill up a succession of those intellectual treats which it is the object of the tourists to obtain'. Sopwith's description of a visit to a lead mine demonstrates that this was a common occurrence. The visitors, suitably dressed in clothes usually provided by the inn landlord, are each given a candle and ride in horse-drawn wagons into the mine adit or 'level'. A level is usually six feet high and three feet wide at the bottom, gradually widening to four feet in the middle, and then arched at the top. The level is usually driven in a soft 'freestone' or a 'hazle', a mining term for a hard sandstone. Access to where the lead vein above is being worked was by a primitive staircase of 'stemples' or boards up a 'rise' or shaft, the process of throwing the worked stone down the shaft having been halted while the visitors were in the mine: 'to a stranger the idea of climbing fifty or a hundred feet on so perilous a footing is seldom unattended with some sense of fearful apprehension.' Having arrived at the 'drift' the visitor can watch the miners working the ore, often witnessing a demonstration of blasting with gunpowder.

In his *Plan of the Silver-Band Lead Mine* on Cronkley Fell, Sopwith includes a section through the rocks showing the levels, as well as explanatory notes. The levels are driven along the course of three veins, the Silver Band, Old Band and West Veins, in 'hazle', which is to Westgarth Forster's Tyne Bottom Plate, some way above the

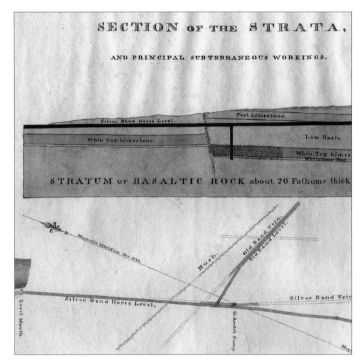

**23**  *The Silver-Band Lead Mine at Cronkley: Section & Plan (part). Engraving by Thomas Sopwith, 1828.*

Great Whin Sill which is here about twenty fathoms thick. Thomas Sopwith's plan of the associated washing floor (plate 24) may be compared with his description of the visitors to a mine being 'much entertained with the ingenious and cunning devices' used to extract the lead ore from the mined rock. They watch the waggons from each partnership of miners dump the 'bouse' or mixed stone and ore into the partitioned bouse teams. The bouse is broken into small pieces, by hand on 'knocking stones' or in a crushing mill powered by a water wheel. Then the crushed bouse undergoes various processes of washing 'to obtain every particle of ore'; after using 'grates', 'tubs' and 'buddles', even the ore from the sediment collected in the slime pits is separated out. The resulting shining ore is collected in the 'bingsteads' and then conveyed to the smelt-mills, where the lead, and perhaps silver, are extracted.

A number of writers suggest or record visits to the lead mines. In the fifth edition of his *Tour in Teesdale* in 1834, Richard Garland (see Chapter 11) suggests that a visit to the lead mines and works north west of Middleton (probably Coldberry, added to Garland's map in the second edition of 1813) 'will amply repay the trouble of visiting'. In July 1840 Samuel King, returning from a botanical excursion in Teesdale, visited the lead mines at Middleton-in-Teesdale. In a manuscript for a talk to a Mechanics Institute, Francis Cockshott in 1847 described the Eggleston smelt mill: the rough ore is loaded in at the top level and descends through the various processes, including the furnace where the impurities rise as slag and are skimmed off, and the pure lead is run out into 'pigs' at the lowest level. The mill could be seen by any 'respectable person' applying for a note of admission at Middleton-in-Teesdale.

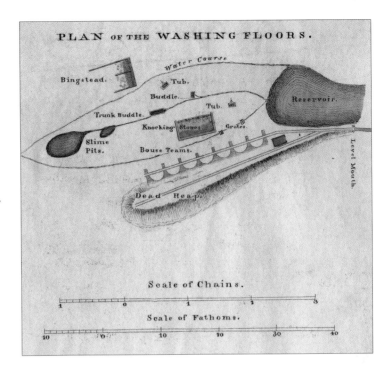

**24** *Plan of the Washing Floors at the Silver-Band Lead Mine at Cronkley.*

At that time Cockshott thought there were over forty lead mines belonging to the London Lead Company. At Middleton the lead mines were the chief attraction in 1857, *The Hand-Book to Teesdale* stating that the mine managers permitted visitors. Twenty years later the authors of *Rambles in Teesdale* noted that the Skears Gill lead mines and the Eggleston smelt mill were open to visitors; as well as seeing the smelting and refining processes the tourist could watch the silver content of the lead being tested in the assay house.

James Backhouse in 1896 mentions the smelt mill at Blackton near Eggleston; the crushing and washing mills at Coldberry were by then in ruins. Backhouse describes the Lady Rake Lead Mine near Harwood as one of the London Lead Company's most important and most productive mines, where the washing and dressing floors are extensive and complete. The modern system of ore-washing, whereby every available particle of lead is sifted out by means of its greater weight, may be seen to great advantage. An interesting feature is the hydraulic balance adopted for drawing 'work', as the output is called in mining language, from the shaft.

At some point, perhaps from the 1860s, tourists would hear the song *Fourpence a day* attributed to Teesdale lead miner Thomas Raine: it was about the boys who worked on the 'washing rakes' where the waste was washed from the crushed ore-bearing rock.

> The ore is waiting in the tubs, the snow is on the fell;
> Canny folks are sleeping yet the lead is reet to sell;
> Come my little washer lad, come, let's away,
> We're bound down to slavery for fourpence a day.

**25**   *Cross Fell. Illustration for* Rivers of Great Britain, *1902.*

It's early in the morning we rise at five o'clock
And the little slaves come to the door to knock, knock, knock.
Come, my little washer lad, come, let's away,
It's very hard to work for fourpence a day.

My father was a miner and lived down in the town;
'Twas hard work and poverty that always kept him down.
He aimed for me to go to school but brass he couldn't pay
So I had to go to the washing rake for fourpence a day.

My mother rises out of bed with tears on her cheeks,
Puts my wallet on my shoulders which has to serve a week.
It often fills her great big heart when she unto me does say,
'I never thought thou would have worked for fourpence a day'.

Fourpence a day, my lad, and very hard to work
And never a pleasant look from a gruffy looking Turk.
His conscience it may fail and his heart it may give way,
Then he'll raise us our wages to ninepence a day.

Another aspect of the lead-mining scene which attracted tourists was the accommodation for the miners. Mine lodging 'shops' were built near the more remote mines from 1818. Francis Cockshott describes a typical lodging shop he visited in the summer of 1847. This remote shop, not far from the head of the

Tees on the slopes of Cross Fell, and over 2,000 feet above sea level, was nearing completion:

> They stay here about five months in the year, dig out the lead ore; break it up with hammers into small pieces, then wash it and then carry it for a short way in bags to where there is a track for donkeys or ponies to travel on. There are three or four men and about the same number of boys, but no females. Poor fellows they never see but each other except an occasional tourist or the man who comes with the ponies for the lead, bringing with him provisions.

At that time the 'occasional tourist' must have been very determined to have reached this spot; today the Pennine Way follows the track which Cockshott describes. A little further down Teesdale, above the Weel, Cockshott visits another 'groover's hovel'. This shop consists of a single room partitioned into two, with a loft above. The only furniture is a table propped beneath the window and two sloping planks with bundles of heather which act as beds. During the summer the miners come up every Monday, returning home near High Force on the Saturday. These may have been the men who Cockshott describes as making a sort of gin or whisky from the berries of the juniper bushes near High Force.

In 1864 more than two-thirds of the Teesdale lead miners lived in lodging shops during the working week. However, by 1894 *The Teesdale Mercury*, reporting a monthly meeting of the Teesdale Sanitary Board, listed only six mine shops still occupied in Teesdale: High Manors Gill, Low Manors Gill, Wiregill, Little Eggleshope, Lady Rake and Green Hurth. These were inhabited four days a week by about 250 men and boys.

As well as describing the rocks of the area, Westgarth Forster's *A Treatise on a Section of the Strata, from Newcastle-upon-Tyne, to the mountain of Cross Fell, in Cumberland*, provides further information on the lead industry. He lists 38 mines in Teesdale in 1809, mostly belonging to the London Lead Company. This company entered the dale in 1753, when it leased Ravelin Mines near Newbiggin; in about 1820 the Company built Blackton Mill near Eggleston to smelt its Teesdale ores. Other smelt mills were at Langdon, Newbiggin, and the Eggleston High, Middle and Low Mills. In the 18th and 19th centuries the greater part of the population of the upper dales depended upon lead mining for a living. In 1857 the chief agent of the London Lead Company reckoned that nine-tenths of the population of Teesdale were connected with the mines.

One of the most productive mines was Coldberry, producing about 500 tons of lead ore each year. Coldberry Gutter was an impressive hush worked mainly in the 18th century in the late 1850s; today it is still highly visible as a great notch in the skyline north west of Middleton-in-Teesdale. Richard Garland in 1813 (Chapter 11) explained the practice of hushing, where constrained water is suddenly released to wash away soil and rock from on top of a possible vein of lead; it is likely that some dislodging of rock by blasting would also have been used in this process.

There were often over 350 men employed in the Teesdale mines. However, lead prices fell in the 1830s and after about 1850 the London Lead Company was

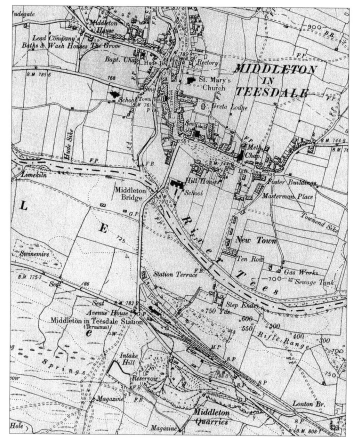

**26** *Ordnance Survey map of Middleton-in-Teesdale, 1898. The London Lead Company's buildings include New Town, Masterman Place and Middleton House, as well as the Baths. The railway station lies to the south of the river Tees.*

dependent on only four mines for most of its production, Coldberry, Little Eggleshope, Flakebridge and Wiregill. With the total collapse of lead prices in about 1880, the lead-mining industry went into decline. James Backhouse in 1896 reports how a large number of men from the district had been induced to emigrate. The London Lead Company withdrew from the dale in 1902.

But, in the heyday of the lead industry, another tourist attraction had been built. In 1833 Thomas Sopwith could suggest that tourists inspect a 'new town': the London Lead Company was constructing Masterman Place on the edge of Middleton-in-Teesdale. The Company had purchased an estate there in 1815 and over a span of fifty years it built more than a hundred 'extremely neat and comfortable' cottages, which ranged from the two-roomed cottages of Ten Row and New Town Terrace, each with its long garden, to the block of superior dwellings for the under managers, surveyor and doctor. Baths, offices, chapels and school were built, and after 1880 Middleton-in-Teesdale became the head office of the Company, at Middleton House built in 1815 for the Company's Superintendent. As well as providing a school in Middleton-in-Teesdale in 1819 (rebuilt in 1861), where boys attended from the age of six to 12, girls to 14, the Company bought books to form libraries and later donated money towards a further supply of books. A Mechanics' Institute was constructed with Company support.

The London Lead Company also adjusted the way in which the lead miners were paid. The usual system of payment was the quarterly 'bargain', in which the Company's agent provided details of the lead veins and places that were to be worked, and the miners offered to work at a certain rate. The miners had to balance their knowledge of the geology against the current price of lead, and make a 'bargain' for the rate of pay for the next quarter: so much per fathom of ground opened up or per bing of ore produced. After some food shortages, the Company made the bargains independent of the price of lead, to enable the miners to have a decent wage; in 1815 corn was issued at cost price, and in 1820 a kind of co-operative was organised. Food conditions worsened in the 1840s and the Company helped with the formation of miners' Corn Associations, the forerunners of Co-operative Societies. To stop the credit traders who advanced goods to the miners at exorbitant prices, the Company bought a Ready Money Shop where the shopkeeper could sell only for cash. These various arrangements, and the schools, were opened up to all residents in the area with Company mines. Other recreational activities were encouraged by the Company, such as cricket clubs and bands, and by 1827 responsibility was taken on for medical help for the miners. Other villages benefited as well: in 1877 the London Lead Company built a Mechanics' Institute reading and lecture room at Eggleston.

The London Lead Company's activities had further benefits, this time for the tourist as well, in the form of improved roads. To improve the transport of ore, lead and provisions along Lunedale, the Company improved the road and built new bridges, as at Grains o' th' Beck and Rennygill near the Lunehead mines; in 1817 the road from Middleton to Brough was rebuilt as a turnpike. However, conditions further north, towards Alston, were much worse; Thomas Sopwith in 1833 wrote that

> the want of good or even of tolerable roads was for a long period the principal cause of the mining districts being so little known. About 50 years ago, scarcely a regularly formed road was to be found in them; goods were chiefly conveyed on horses or galloways, which followed the soundest track over the moors.

Since then many roads which have been constructed have merely followed these tracks 'in the most inconvenient and circuitous directions' and are so steep as to terrify those unaccustomed to mountainous districts. Sopwith recalls that it was in 1824 that Lord Lowther had travelled from Alston to Teesdale by Yadmoss, in the first carriage that had passed over 'that dreary and exposed fell'. It was over Yad Moss that the Scottish army had escaped from Edward III, then in Weardale, by laying boughs to prevent their sinking in the bog. Sopwith goes on to report that the road from Yad Moss into Teesdale was shortly to be improved.

The Earl of Derwentwater's vast estates in the north of England were confiscated in 1716 after the abortive Jacobite Rebellion and in 1735 given to the Greenwich Hospital, which leased the mineral rights to the London Lead Company. In 1822 Edward Locker, the Secretary to the Hospital Board, recommended extensive road improvements centred on Alston. John Loudon McAdam (1756-1836) was engaged to survey the proposed routes and the subsequent Act of Parliament authorising the necessary turnpikes was passed in 1824. Despite the London Lead Company putting over £7,000 into the scheme, and the Greenwich Hospital £5,000, not all the proposals were carried out. *A Map of the Road proposed to make Turnpike from Alston in the County of Cumberland, by Middleton in the County of Durham, to the South End of Abbey Bridge in the North Riding of the County of York: as projected by John Loudon McAdam Esqr.,* and surveyed in 1823, was one of the maps which

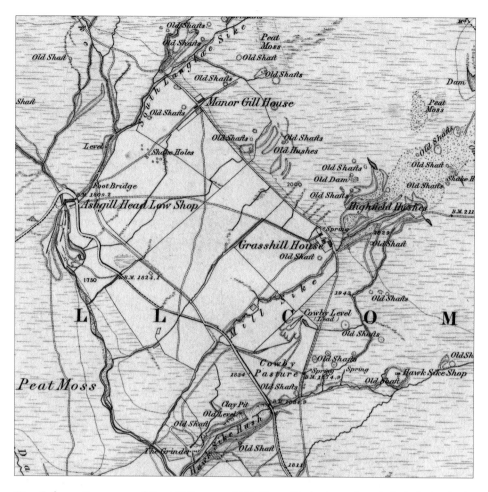

**27** *Ordnance Survey map of Grasshill Common, 1858. Signs of lead mining abound: shafts, hushes, levels and mine 'shops'. The turnpike road contours around Ashgill Head.*

accompanied the Bill. Of the eight sections of suggested improvement shown on this map, only three were carried out; these are followed by the modern road, with the old road they replaced still largely visible as a minor road or track. About four miles of new road between Bowlees and Langdon Beck took a route nearer to the river Tees, incidentally making access to High Force much easier. The major realignment of the road was from Langdon Beck to the summit of Yad Moss, where the new route avoided the Harwood Beck valley by contouring around the fellside of Grasshill Common above, and passing the mine lodging 'shop', Ashgill Head Low Shop.

The improved roads did not help the first real tourist to 'discover' Teesdale, just as the London Lead Company came into the dale; in fact, he exaggerated the difficulties of access to enhance his account.

*5*

## *Thomas Amory's Life of John Buncle, Esq.*

*'that very wild and wonderful land'*

It is usual to cite the wars with France from 1793 as what made travel on the continent difficult and encouraged the Picturesque Tour within Britain itself, but by 1786 Thomas Hurtley could already record how 'men of Sense and real information' were beginning 'to visit, to admire, ... to pourtray ... the majestic scenery of our own Clime'. In 1766 a much-quoted letter from Dr John Brown of Newcastle was published in the *London Chronicle*, stating that the 'beauty, horror and immensity' of the Lake District scenery would need 'the united powers of Claude, Salvator, and Poussin'[1] to describe it. However, the scenery of Teesdale had been publicised a decade before this.

In 1756 readers of Thomas Amory's *The Life of John Buncle* were no doubt exclaiming at the first detailed descriptions of actual wild scenery to appear in a novel. Thomas Amory (*c.*1690-1788) grew up in Ireland, which he left about 1729; by 1755 he was living in Westminster. The second volume of *The Life of John Buncle, Esq: containing various observations and reflections made in several parts of the world and many extraordinary relations* was published in 1766. The fact that Amory's son referred to 'my father (John Buncle), Thomas Amory' indicates the problem of trying to separate true biographical information from this fictionalised account. The highly imaginative story of the matrimonial ventures of the eccentric hero is interspersed with various digressions and descriptions of the 'very wild and wonderful land' of Teesdale he passed through. Although Amory, as John Buncle, dates his excursion to 1725, and mentions further visits to the area in 1739 and 1752, we cannot be sure that any of the dates he gives are true.

Amory, accompanied by his servant O'Fin, rode from Whitehaven and, apparently searching for his university friend Charles Turner, approached upper Teesdale from the west and Stainmore. They stayed at Lamb's inn at Brough, and then, on 8 June, Amory saw Stainmore for the first time; Italian scenes well known from the Grand Tour came to mind:

> I travelled into a vast valley, enclosed by mountains whose tops were above the clouds, and soon came into a country that is wilder than the campagna of Rome, or the uncultivated vales of the Alps and Appenines. Warm with a classical enthusiasm, I journeyed on ...

> For several hours I travelled over mountains tremendous to behold, and through vales the most enchanting in the world.

Five days later Amory further shows an awareness of the more sublime aspects of the Picturesque; the way is difficult, with 'numberless windings round impassable hills' and 'rivers it was impossible to cross', the air is thin, and almost inevitably there is a thunderstorm:

> The mountains, the rocky precipices, the woods and the waters, appeared in various striking situations every mile I travelled on, and formed the most astonishing points of view. Sometimes I was above the clouds, and then crept to enchanting vallies below. Here glens were seen that looked as if the mountains had been rent asunder to form the amazing scenes, and there, forests and falling streams covered the sides of the hills. Rivers in many places, in the most beautiful cascades, were tumbling along; and cataracts from the tops of mountains came roaring down. The whole was grand, wonderful, and fine.

Because Amory's landscape descriptions are exaggerated and an amalgamation of various scenes, it is not possible to follow his journey on a map. However, ostensibly on 14 June 1725, after deliberating on the origin of a lake on the top of a hill (there are three on Dufton Fell), he was apparently making his way towards the north-eastern part of Westmoreland when he gives what may well be the first description of Cauldron Snout:

> I came to a great glen, where a river made a rumbling noise over rocks and inequalities of many kinds, and formed a very wild, wonderful scene. The river was broad and deep, and on an easy descent to it, was an assemblage of stones, that ran in length about a hundred feet, in breadth thirty feet, and somewhat resembling the Giant's Causeway, in the county of Antrim …

Amory goes on to describe what must be the columns of the intrusive Whin Sill; the extrusive basalt lava flows of the Giant's Causeway give rise to similar features:

> The assemblage of stones I am speaking of are columns with several corners, that rise three yards above the ground and are joined as if done by art … These columns have five and six sides, a few of them seven; and a number of them nicely and exactly placed together make one large pillar from one foot to two in diameter.

Amory may have known of the engravings by Francis Vivarès of the Giant's Causeway from Susanna Drury's panoramic paintings of 1740. Having compared the 'great glen' of Cauldron Snout with the Giant's Causeway, Amory thinks of Niagara Falls four days later as he gives what is surely the first description of High Force:

> We rode through a river, that was up to the horses bellies, very rapid, and a bad bottom, and then proceeded along a steep hill side … till we came to a rich low land, that was covered with flowers and aromatic shrubs … surrounded with stony mountains, … and from the top of one of the lowest of them, a cataract descends, like the fall of the river Niagara in Canada.

The Teesdale 'Niagara' is typically exaggerated in Picturesque style: 'Swifter than an arrow from a bow the rapid water comes headlong down in a fall of an hundred and

**28**  *Caldron Snout. Engraving after W. Hutchinson (1781) for* The History and Antiquities of the County Palatine of Durham, *1794.*

forty feet, which is three feet more than the descent of Niagara.' The river here is only half the size of that at Niagara, but

> it is a great and prodigious cadence of water, and tumbles perpendicularly in as surprising a manner, from as horrible a precipice; and in this very nearly resembles the Niagara Fall; that as you stand below, as near the fall as it is safe to go, you see the river come down a sloping mountain for a great way, as if it descended from the clouds. It is a grand and amazing scene.

Perhaps aware that his descriptions of wild scenery break new ground for a novel, Amory gives footnote advice to the reader with 'the curiosity and heart' to 'wander over this wild and romantic part of our world, at the hazard of your neck, and the danger of being starved'. He starts by correcting earlier writers; he finds several hamlets in the Stainmore area of Richmondshire that are not mentioned by Camden or Thomas Cox,[2] and is sure that they 'never so much as saw this country at a distance'. Amory seems unaware of the fact that his own descriptions of Stainmore, 'that vast tract of mountains, glens, and valleys, forest, rock, and water, the most wonderful land in the world', often lack topographic accuracy. Even when giving directions to an inn which is likely to be at North Stainmore, Amory cannot resist a little scaremongering; he recalls being pursued by two highwaymen and escaping only because of the excellence of his horse.

Even when supposedly giving instructions on how to reach 'that very wild and wonderful land' of upper Teesdale or Stainmore, Amory is ambiguous. His vague instructions do include making for the 'headlong torrents' and mountains from Eggleston; this helps to confirm my attribution of his descriptions to Cauldron Snout and High Force. One way to 'the Stanemore Alps' involves hiring a guide at Bowes who 'will bring you as he did me once through a very surprising way of deep bottoms to a public house at Eggleston'; from there another guide brings the traveller 'to mountains upon mountains, rapid rivers and headlong torrents, that form amazing and tremendous scenes'. However, this route is neither comfortable nor very safe; it is better to ride from Greta Bridge to Barnard Castle and on to Eggleston and then 'set out for the mountains'.

After six weeks of wandering around 'the northern fells of Westmoreland, and the bad part of Yorkshire-Stanemore' and searching York and other towns for his friend, Amory decides to head back to his cottage in Westmorland. He makes a detour to see the Roman fort at Greta Bridge, and 'passed the day in looking over all the antiquities and curiosities I could find there'.

*John Buncle* proved popular enough to be reprinted in 1770 and 1825, and to be translated into German in 1782. Amory's descriptions of the scenery of Teesdale were read and used by later travellers. We will see how Arthur Young acknowledged Amory's novel when he made 'a little excursion into Stainmore, of which I had read such wonders in the life of John Buncle'.

*6*

# The Picturesque in Paintings and Engravings

*'a picturesque and picturizing journey to the North'*

The Lakes poet Robert Southey (1774-1843) used the pseudonym Don Manuel Alvarez Espriella to write *Letters From England,* an account of a tour of the country supposedly from a foreigner's perspective. By 1807 Southey could write of the passion for the Picturesque that had sprung up in the previous 30 years; he identified the Picturesque as a new science with its new language, and extolled the 'beautiful landscapes in water-colour, in which the English excel all other nations'. The portable nature of the watercolour and the immediacy of its execution meant that it was better suited to recording the scenes made popular by the taste for 'summer travelling' that Southey had recognised. Two years before Southey's account the Society of Painters in Water-Colours had held its first exhibition, and in 1808 an observer was struck by the overwhelming proportion of landscapes at an exhibition of the Associated Artists in Watercolours:

> In pacing round the rooms the spectator experiences sensations somewhat similar to those of an outside passenger on a mail-coach making a picturesque and picturizing journey to the North. Mountains and cataracts, rivers, lakes and woods, deep romantic glens and sublime sweeps of country, engage his eye in endless and ever-varying succession.

In painting, as well as a change in the medium used, there was a change in content or emphasis. Advice for artists producing 'beautiful landscapes', as opposed to the earlier topographical representations of Francis Place or the Buck brothers for example, was available in the new language of the Picturesque. The Revd William Gilpin (1724-1804) was the headmaster of Cheam school in Surrey in 1755-85, and vicar of Boldre in Hampshire in 1777-1804; he is now best known as the forerunner of the Romantic movement. William Mason[1] and Horace Walpole (1717-97) persuaded Gilpin to publish his accounts of his summer journeys and they were extremely influential in popularising the appreciation of natural landscape. Gilpin first introduced the phrase 'picturesque beauty', and in *Observations, relative chiefly to Picturesque Beauty, Made in the Year 1772, On Several Parts of England; particularly the Mountains, and Lakes of Cumberland, and Westmoreland* (1786), analysed a picturesque view as containing a mountain to fill the 'offskip' or background, a lake the nearer distance, and trees, rocks or cascades for the foreground. Gilpin was at Greta Bridge shortly after the floods of 1771 which destroyed many bridges in northern England, and wrote:

> At Greta we found much devastation from the late high floods. The bridge was beaten down; and large fragments of it carried away, through the violence of the stream. With these, and huge stones torn from the adjoining cliffs, the bed of the river was choaked.

In the Bodleian Library in Oxford there is a watercolour sketch by Gilpin of the ruined Greta Bridge in his manuscript *Tour Through Cumberland & Westmoreland* of 1772.

William Gilpin was particularly concerned with the Lake District, and today it is generally assumed that the first tourists in search of picturesque scenery were to be found here. Interest in the Lakes appeared to start with the Revd Dr John Brown's *Description of the Lake at Keswick*, first published as a letter in the *London Chronicle* in April 1766. The following year this letter was published in Newcastle as a pamphlet, *Description of the Lake and Vale of Keswick*. From this pamphlet the Barnard Castle solicitor William Hutchinson, in his *Excursion to the Lakes, in Westmoreland and Cumberland* (published in 1776), may have been the first to quote what was to become the famous description of Keswick:

> the full perfection of Keswick consists of three circumstances, beauty, horror and immensity united ... But to give you a complete idea of these three perfections, as they are joined in Keswick, would require the united powers of Claude, Salvator, and Poussin. The first should throw his delicate sunshine over the cultivated vales, the scattered cots, the groves, the lake, and wooded islands. The second should dash out the horror of the rugged cliffs, the steeps, the hanging woods, and foaming waterfalls; while the grand pencil of Poussin should crown the whole with the majesty of the impending mountains.

Although some see this *Description*, invoking the European 17th-century paintings of Claude Lorrain, Salvator Rosa and Gaspard Poussin, as heralding the start of tourism in the Lake District, one artist has left us proof of tourists and a guide in Teesdale some 20 years earlier.

The first representation of a picturesque landscape in Teesdale is by George Lambert (1700-65): *The Falls of the Tees, Durham* (1746, in pastels; plate I) pre-dates the widespread use of watercolours. Four years earlier, 'Lambert the Landskip painter has begun to do Landskips in Crayons, which are very pleasant and are takeing ... done with less trouble & Study, than with Oyl Colours.'[2] The chief scenery painter at Covent Garden from 1732, Lambert showed an eye for picturesque arrangements, and was responsible to some extent for introducing the conventions of Claude and Poussin into British landscape painting. He was the first Chairman of the Society of Artists in 1761, and was elected its first President shortly before his death. For his pastel at High Force, Lambert chose a low viewpoint that let the sides of the gorge of recession lead past the guide, to the visitors on the mound of fallen rocks at the edge of the plunge pool, and then to the waterfall. There is only one fall, indicating a fairly low water in the Tees; the columnar whin sill overlying the horizontally bedded limestone is depicted quite realistically. When Lambert exhibited a copy of this picture in oils at the Society of Artists in 1762, the catalogue listed it as *The Great Fall of the Tees. N.B. – This river divides the counties of York and Durham*. To this copy of his earlier work Lambert adds another local guide in the foreground, and two tourists high up on the southern bank. An oil painting by George Lambert suggests that the artist may have visited Teesdale by 1741: a 'capriccio' or invented river scene has a bridge and Italianate castle which appear to be based on Barnard Castle.[3]

One of the pioneers of landscape painting in watercolour was Paul Sandby (1730-1809); he was also the first to use the aquatint process in England, the etching technique which allowed watercolours to be effectively reproduced. The only recorded Teesdale watercolour by Sandby is *Middleton High Force*.

The growing taste for paintings in watercolour is reflected in increasing patronage for the medium. Physician and amateur painter Dr Thomas Monro was one of the collectors of works by artists such as Paul Sandby, Thomas Hearne and Edward Dayes. Monro ran a sort of informal academy, and had young artists such as Thomas Girtin and J.M.W. Turner at his London home, to study and copy these paintings. With Sir George Beaumont of Leicestershire, Thomas Hearne (1744-1817) made two tours which included Durham and Yorkshire in 1777 and 1778. Hearne's watercolour *Barnard Castle* (plate II) from 1788 shows the artist's meticulous detail in the bridge and the houses, one thatched, of Bridge Street. Above are the Round Tower, Mortham Tower, Great Hall and Constable Tower of the castle; in the foreground an angler attends to his line and a woman washes clothes. It seems likely that Thomas Hearne advised both Girtin and Turner on their sketching tours to the north of England.

Another artist who influenced both Girtin and Turner was the topographical watercolourist Edward Dayes (1768-1804). His watercolour of 1791, *The Abbey Bridge* (plate III), shows a fisherman seated on the rocks below the castellated bridge rebuilt after the floods of 1771; it bears the hallmarks of Dayes's style, pastel shades of pinks and greens with grey shadows.

Thomas Girtin's watercolour *Barnard Castle* (plate IV) shows signs of the artist's training. From 1789 Girtin (1775-1802) was apprenticed to Edward Dayes, and from 1794 he copied drawings at Dr Thomas Monro's. Girtin's apprenticeship ended in 1796, and he immediately made his own tour of the north, visiting the churches, abbeys and castles of Yorkshire, Durham and Northumberland that he had previously seen only in paint. Largely through the patronage of Edward Lascelles of Harewood near Leeds, Girtin would return to the north a number of times before he died young in 1802. In *Barnard Castle*, Girtin, using a palette similar to Dayes', only faintly echoes Hearne's view from upstream of the castle; he pushes the bridge further downriver and shows us more of the river bank in front of the castle.

An artist's sketch shows his first response to a landscape and, fortunately, some sketchbooks featuring Teesdale have survived. John Glover (1767-1849) at 19 was appointed as writing master in the Free School in Appleby, where he found time to pursue drawing. In 1805 Glover became a member of the Society of Painters in Water-

**29** *At the Junction of the Tees and Greta. Sketch by John Glover, 1805.*

**30** *The High Force. Engraving after Thomas Smith, 1751. The inscription gives a height of 23 yards for the fall.*

Colours and exhibited 23 works in the opening exhibition. His 'Durham' sketchbook covers the period 20 to 30 September 1805. After many sketches in Durham itself, the artist moved on to sketch Raby Castle, Barnard Castle and Eggleston Abbey. But he seems to have lavished most care on some of his sketches made along the river Greta, applying tonal washes and making colour notes alongside. On the page facing the sketch titled 'At the Junction of the Tees and Greata', Glover adds, 'A singularly rich map of light on the right hand particularly by light reflected in the water and back again on some of the rock – becoming warmer each time.' In a morning sketch made further up the Greta, Glover notes a purple tint in the air on the distant wood, and a 'beautiful mellow warm tone' reflected onto the rocks in the river bed. If John Glover had visited the Greta a few weeks earlier he would have met John Sell Cotman, whose work we consider in a later chapter. The following year, in the second exhibition of the Society of Painters in Water-Colours, Glover showed *On the Greta, Yorkshire.*

**31**  *View of the remarkable Cataract on the River Teese [sic]. Engraving, c.1771.*

Only the rich could afford to buy paintings, but collections of landscape prints were soon being made available to middle-class collectors and tourists. Thomas Smith 'of Derby' (d.1767) was one of the earliest professional painters of country houses and well-known picturesque spots. Few of his original landscape paintings seem to have survived, but we can envisage them today because many of them were engraved. The engraving by J. Mason of Thomas Smith's *The High Force* is dated 1751, ten years before the famous engraving of his painting of Derwentwater was published. The engraving of High Force has this inscription:

> The High Force. This Cataract is on the River Teese, which divides the Counties of York, and Durham; it falls down a Rock of Granate, about 23 yards into a Large Circular Bason; the South side belongs to Ld. Carlisle, and Geo. Bowes Esq. the North to Ld. Barnard, to whom this View is Inscrib'd by their most Obedt. Servt. Tho. Smith.

In the foreground, on the north bank of the river, is a tree which seems to be inspired by those painted by Salvator Rosa; from here we watch an angler with rod and net at the edge of the plunge pool, into which pour two separate falls of water. This engraving was much copied, as in *View of the remarkable CATARACT, on the River Teese, which divides the Counties of York & Durham* in *The Complete English Traveller* by Nathaniel Spencer (a pseudonym for Robert Sanders), published by John Cooke in 1771. This smaller copy retains the foreground figures and the angler, but is a much cruder representation of the rocks, water and vegetation. The same copper plate was used eight years later in *The Modern Universal British Traveller*, as traces of the earlier engraved lettering may be seen beneath the title. We shall see how the height of the waterfall, 23 yards or 69 feet, quoted in the inscription to Mason's engraving, is used by later writers in their descriptions of High Force. Some of this copying came by way of Nathaniel Spencer's text of 1771,

**32** *View of Barnard Castle. Sketched by Thomas Hearne in 1778 and engraved in 1799 by William Byrne.*

which relied not only on Mason's engraving but also Arthur Young's description, published the previous year and discussed in the next chapter. Spencer wrote:

> The water of the river having collected itself together at the top of a frightful precipice falls down with such a prodigious force that it is heard at a great distance; for the perpendicular is twenty-three yards. The force of the water dashing against the rocks fills the mind with horror, but the scattered rays of the sun shining through the misty particles gives the whole the appearance of a most beautiful rainbow.

Following the trend set by Samuel and Nathaniel Buck's *Antiquities*, reissued in 1774, and Francis Grose's *Antiquities of England and Wales* from 1773, Thomas Hearne began *The Antiquities of Great Britain* in collaboration with the engraver and publisher William Byrne. Issued in parts, 52 prints appeared between 1778 and 1786, before a ten-year hiatus and the publication of a further 32 plates. Hearne's *View of Barnard Castle*, sketched in 1778 and engraved by Byrne, was published in 1799 as number 13 of volume two. In the view looking downstream, and in the accompanying text, the defensive position of the castle 'on the brink of a high rock, of above eighty perpendicular feet, above the Tees' is emphasised. The buttressed Great Hall and 15th-century oriel window ('a bow window hung on corbles') in the Great Chamber are clearly depicted, along with the 'circular tower of excellent masonry, in ashler work', 30 feet in diameter. There is a building, perhaps a chapel, in the centre of the bridge, and a family strolls on the path beneath the castle while two women wash clothes on the Yorkshire side.

Hearne's *View of Eggleston Abbey* was published in 1782. As well as the east window and the north transept, the east range, used as a farmhouse from the 16th century, is shown, and a cart load of hay is being brought in. Although Samuel Middiman's engraving after Thomas Girtin's *Eggleston Abbey* shows the same

**33**  *Eggleston Abbey.
Engraved by William
Byrne after Thomas
Hearne, 1782.*

**34**  *Eggleston
Abbey. Engraved by
S. Middiman after
Thomas Girtin,
1805.*

buildings, Girtin chooses a viewpoint on the north bank of the Tees. As with his watercolour of Barnard Castle, this allows him to show the building in its setting and give the river Tees more prominence. With their emphasis on antiquities, both these engravings ignore the Abbey mill.

Engravings or prints had been collected for some time; some collectors chose to hang them on their walls, as with Sir Thomas Robinson's 'print room' at Rokeby, still to be seen today. Landscape prints were also collected to prepare for a tour, or to illustrate a tour journal, the equivalent to the modern tourist consulting a travel guide and bringing back postcards or photographs of the places visited. John Byng collected prints in anticipation of his *Tour to the North* in 1792; these included Thomas Smith's *High Force*, and Samuel Buck's *Bernard Castle* and *Eggleston Abbey*.

# 7

## Published Tours

*'A morning's ride well worth a journey of a thousand miles to travel'*

We know from his letters that the poet Thomas Gray (1716-71) visited Barnard Castle and Rokeby in July 1767 and passed through Teesdale and over Stainmore in 1769 on his way to tour the Lakes, on both occasions travelling from Old Park near Bishop Auckland in County Durham (see Kitchin's map, plate 19), the home of his friend Thomas Wharton. Thomas Gray's *Catalogue of the Antiquities, Houses, Parks, Plantations, Scenes, and Situations in England and Wales, arranged according to the alphabetical order of the several Counties* was published in 1773. The list was originally drawn up on the blank pages of Kitchin's *English Atlas*, and was partly based on Gray's summer tours. The Teesdale entries are found under Durham and the North Riding of Yorkshire. The antiquities include Raby Castle, Egglestone Abbey, Bowes Castle and Barnard Castle, with the walk from the town through the Holmes to Towler Hill; Rokeby is listed under 'Houses, Parks, Plantations', High Force or 'The Force in Teesdale, West of Middleton' comes under 'Scenes and Situations'. This *Catalogue* must have had some influence on tourists to Teesdale, directly and through other writers; the walk at Barnard Castle to Towler Hill is mentioned in a *History* of 1794 and a *Tour* of 1803.

Arthur Young (1741-1820), who became the first Secretary to the Board of Agriculture in 1793, took over the family farm in Hertfordshire during the agricultural revolution. He squandered so much money on agricultural improvements that he took up writing about farming to pay the bills. In June 1768 the 27-year-old Arthur set off in a chaise on his *Six Months Tour through the North of England. Containing, An Account of the present State of Agriculture, Manufactures and Population, … Interspersed with … Views of some picturesque Scenes, which occurred in the Course of the Journey.* As well as advertising for innovative landowners to contact him before his 2,500 mile journey, Young made other contacts at York races, though he had to ply some with drink to gain 'unprejudiced intelligence'.

It was Thomas Amory's description of upper Teesdale, published twelve years earlier, that diverted Young from his survey of agricultural practice to make a diversion into Stainmore, 'of which I had read such wonders in the life of *John Buncle*'. Young finds the turnpike road across Stainmore 'a most excellent one; firm, dry, level,

**35**  *A New Map of the North Riding of Yorkshire. Thomas Kitchin, 1764. High Force is marked 'Fall 60 Feet'; the road over Stainmore is shown.*

and free from loose stones'. In his little garden the turnpike keeper grows excellent potatoes, good beans and admirable turnips. Staying at the 'middling' *George Inn* at Greta Bridge, Young visits Rokeby Park, suggesting that travellers will find it worth viewing. He takes three pages to list the sculptures and paintings, and particularly mentions the copies of pictures in needlework by Anne Morritt (1726-97) which are still in the house. Young describes the prospect house near Dairy Bridge as a tea room, 'very romantically situated on the rocky banks of the Greta, raging like a torrent over the rocks, and tumbling in a romantic manner under the windows'.

Young now makes for 'the greatest natural curiosity in this part of the world', High Force. Teesdale, especially from Barnard Castle to High Force, captivates the tour writer: 'I never yet travelled such a line of country so astonishingly fine, containing so noble a variety.' There are mountains, fertile valleys, woods, precipices, winding streams and raging torrents with beautiful cascades – 'a morning's ride well worth a journey of a thousand miles to travel'. Towards Eggleston the road runs along a steep woody precipice, the traveller looking down in a 'most exquisitely picturesque' way over the tops of tall trees to the meandering Tees. Eggleston is 'romantically situated among rocks, steeps of wood, raging torrents, beautiful cascades, a fine assemblage of the noble touches of nature'. Towards Middleton-in-Teesdale (at 'Fogsforth' on plate 51), Young stops and describes 'the most glorious prospect … that imagination can picture'. The agricultural scene of enclosed fields, scattered trees and villages is improved for Young by the river Tees, which 'breaks into noble sheets of water' below. This viewpoint is used by subsequent tour writers, and today at Whistle Crag an information board and parking space induce tourists to stop and experience a wonderful view first publicised over 230 years ago.

After Middleton-in-Teesdale Young prepares the tourist for the awesome High Force; the countryside from now on is more characteristic of 'the terrible sublime than the pleasing or beautiful'. 'Here you ride through rapid streams, struggle along the sides of rocks, cross bleak mountains, and ride up the channel of torrents as the only sure way over bogs.' Although Young gives his own opinion of the height of the waterfall, and introduces some new imagery, he uses some of Amory's words to note the 'prodigious roar' of the waterfall as he scrambles to the earlier writer's viewpoint. Young writes:

> Making use of our hands as well as feet, and descending almost like a parrot, we crawled from rock to rock, and reached from bough to bough, till we got to the bottom under this noble fall. Noble indeed! for the whole river (no trifling one), divided by one rock into two vast torrents, pours down a perpendicular precipice of near fourscore feet. The deluging force of the water throws up such a foam and misty rain, that the sun never shines without a large and brilliant rain-bow appearing.

In describing the gorge below High Force, Young is torn between using his favourite adjective 'romantic' and the sublimity of the scene; even the woods hang and the

**36** *High Force. Engraving after a drawing by Arthur Young, c.1770. Young shows the Tees in flood.*

cliffs threaten: 'The whole scene is gloriously romantic, for on every side it is walled in with pendant rocks an hundred feet high; here projecting in bold and threatening cliffs, and there covered with hanging woods … The scene is truly sublime.' Young attempts a 'slight sketch' of the waterfall, showing the two falls of water and the foam, but fears that it is far short of the original.

It is here that we learn Young has a guide, at least for High Force, for the writer is so overwhelmed by this waterfall, that he dismisses the guide and promptly loses his way, attempting to penetrate further up Teesdale. He comes upon 'a most enchanting landscape, as if dropt from heaven' and then parades his knowledge of the 17th-century continental artists then in vogue: 'Would to heaven I could unite in one sketch the cheerfulness of Zuccarelli with the gloomy terrors of Poussin, the glowing brilliance of Claude with the romantic wildness of Salvator Rosa.' Unfortunately, although describing the black mountains, thick woods, a cascade, a cottage and haystacks, Young does not tell us the location of the scene.

Eventually he finds his way back to Bowes and the 'middling' turnpike road and remembers that he is reporting on agriculture; on the way to Brough he stops many times on the excellent road to examine the soil and rail against the occupiers for not cultivating the moors. The Earl of Darlington's agricultural practices at Raby Castle come in for high praise. However, it is Young's description of 'picturesque Scenes' that would soon be copied or referred to in subsequent writers' tours.

The Barnard Castle solicitor William Hutchinson (1732-1814) made *An Excursion to the Lakes, in Westmoreland and Cumberland; with a Tour Through Part of the Northern Counties, in the Year 1773 and 1774*, published in 1776. On his way to the Lakes he stops at Bowes and describes the dimensions and building materials of the Norman castle (built around 1136), and the remains of the Roman fort of *Lavatrae* with signs of its bath and aqueduct. In one of the plates Hutchinson depicts Roman coins found on the site; he quotes Camden on seeing an altar to Hadrian in the church at Bowes. At Spital there used to be an old hospital, the Spittel upon Stainmore, and at the turnpike house on Stainmore there is a Roman guide post; Rey Cross marks the boundary between Yorkshire and Westmorland (plates 17 & 35). The turnpike passes through the earth banks of a large entrenchment now identified as a Roman marching camp and Hutchinson includes a plate showing this camp and Maiden Castle fortlet. At Stainmore there are echoes of Thomas Amory, though the language of the picturesque is not quite so over-drawn. Stainmore feels the fury of storms from west and east; it is a dreary view:

> The hills were cloathed in heath, and all around a scene of barrenness and deformity; the lower grounds were rent with torrents, which impetuously poured from the steeps in winter; and chasms harrowed on the sides of hills, yawned with ragged rocks, or black and rotten earth … all was wilderness and horrid waste.

On his way back from the Lakes and on his tour through part of the northern counties, William Hutchinson makes it clear on his journey down Teesdale that he has read Arthur Young's account published four years earlier. (He had obviously met Young and mentions having visited the agriculturist's farm in Hertfordshire.) Although, as we have seen, it was Thomas Amory who first described Cauldron Snout, it is William Hutchinson who first gives us a named description of this 'cataract' surrounded by barren and desolate hills:

> The Caldron Snoot is worth the traveller's observation. After the river has slept in a long and serene canal, it pours its streams down continued precipices, and falls for several hundred yards, where it is tossed from rock to rock, and making a prodigious noise, hurries forward in sheets of foam.

Here we recognise several phrases and descriptors from Young's account of High Force, and naturally at this latter fall Hutchinson borrows further from the earlier writer.

The High Force is 'an august scene', the noblest cascade Hutchinson had ever seen. Although initially he seeks out his own viewpoint on the brink of High Force, and makes his own observation about the two falls of over 80 feet, one 'precipitate' and the other over a flight of shelves, these still make a tremendous noise and a perfect rainbow in the spray. However, the solicitor does give what may well be the first description of a picnic in the area:

> Beneath us on the rocks, a party on pleasure, consisting of several gentlemen and ladies, sat enjoying the beauties of the scene … the rocks were spread with their repast, and the servant attending catched the living spring to mix their wine. Deep in a grot they sat, shadowed with hanging oaks, which grew on the cliffs.

Hutchinson continues, retaining Young's foam and the depth of the gorge but adding further dimensions and description. Some distance below the fall, lofty, bold, perpendicular rocks surround a natural amphitheatre 100 feet high, 'resembling the shaken walls and battlements of a ruined castle', with a 40ft deep plunge pool into which the thundering 'cataract pours forth its precipitate streams in sheets of foam'.

At Wynch Bridge Hutchinson succeeds in evoking the sublime aspects of the scene without any previous description to rely on. The river is forced through a narrow channel and 'precipitates into a deep gulph with vast tumult'. Over this is a narrow wooden bridge suspended from two long chains; leaning on the hand rail increases the swinging motion of the bridge: 'beneath you yawns a black and horrid chasm, sixty feet in depth, where the torrent rushes with a mighty noise amongst broken rocks'. He heightens the anticipation of the potential tourist by recording how a passer-by astonished them by making the bridge swing and then crossing as steadily as a tightrope walker. Wynch (or Winch) Bridge was perhaps the first chain bridge in the country when constructed by subscription in around 1741; it was replaced c.1830 by a bridge of similar construction a few yards upstream. This later bridge, now restored, remains today; the modern tourist can re-create something of the early tourist's sublime experience.

After Middleton, Hutchinson obtains the view of the junction of the River Lune with the Tees 'which Mr Young so highly extols', though the solicitor mistakenly states that it is the confluence with the Balder. In contrast, the view from Eggleston is merely picturesque, with the meandering river, scattered villages and cottages agreeably disposed amongst the green enclosures. Romaldkirk is shrouded with trees and shut in by hills. West of Barnard Castle, 'Toller' or Towler Hill provides another prospect: the mile of river is framed by a hanging oak wood over high rocks on one side and meadows on the other; the ruined castle stands above the stone bridge connecting the counties of Durham and Yorkshire; in the background lies part of the town and an expanse of cultivated land. From the village of Startforth on the Yorkshire bank is a view of the south-west front of the ivy-covered castle with 'an awful and solemn aspect'; the view is extended to the left by the river bordered with woods and meadows and terminated by some bold rocks fringed with oaks; to the right the winding river falls in cascades, with the Hambleton Hills beyond.

Below Barnard Castle, the banks of the Tees afford the most romantic walks. A terrace gives a good view of the elevated Egglestone Abbey; beneath it the Tees falls in cascades over the marble rocks, foaming through the Rokeby new bridge or Abbey Bridge. An engraving by Hutchinson of 'Athelstan Abby' is included to illustrate this

**37** *Athelstan Abby. Engraving after William Hutchinson for his* Excursion to the Lakes, *1776.*

description; amongst the ruins only the east window is perfectly preserved. The steep river banks lead the eye to Rokeby Hall on one side and part of Barnard Castle on the other. The Abbey Bridge, 58 feet above the 'narrow channel of rugged rocks', also provides similar romantic views along the 'august avenues' of oaks besides the river Tees. Some of these viewpoints would appear in the writings of later tourists.

Hutchinson ends his Tour at Rokeby (map, plate 55); the Hall is a beautiful Italian-style building set in a fine lawn surrounded by stately trees. Like Arthur Young, Hutchinson describes Sir Thomas Robinson's collection of antiquities (plates 14 & 15). However, the solicitor also praises the walks along the river Greta; perpendicular rocks 40 feet high are covered with large oak trees, while the river 'falls from rock to rock with hoarse murmurs, where deep chaldrons are worn in the stone by the incessant rolling of flints moved by the stream … Nothing can excel the nobleness and solemnity of this walk.'

On the other side of the Greta is Mortham Tower, a fine square structure with turrets built, according to an inscribed date and coat of arms, in 1166 by the Rokebys. Near Rokeby was a Roman station, the remains being apparent behind the *George* inn. Having earlier (1771) described the effects of the recent floods along the Tees, with damage to the bridge and houses at Barnard Castle, Hutchinson ends his *Excursion* at the elegant new bridge at Greta Bridge rebuilt by J.S. Morritt, who had bought Rokeby in 1765, after the same flood.

In the third volume (1794) of *The History and Antiquities of the County Palatine of Durham* William Hutchinson expands on his earlier descriptions of Teesdale, which 'everywhere abounds with the noblest and most romantic landscapes: from Gainford to the head of the river … there is the greatest variety of picturesque, pastoral, and august scenery, that any vale in the north of England affords'. The solicitor quotes two 17th-century diaries to show how inhospitable the upper dale could be. In 1614 nine people were lost in 'a great snow', six yards deep; the severe winter of 1634 was followed the next year by a 'very great flood' of the Tees; and in 1673 over 400 red deer in Teesdale Forest were destroyed in the snow. Hutchinson includes engravings,

**38** *Tees Force. Engraving by John Bailey after William Hutchinson, 1784.*

some from his own drawings finished from sketches by his brother Robert, who died after their first excursion to the Lakes.

At Cauldron Snout the columnar Whin Sill is noted as the river Tees is 'hurried down from steep to steep … dashed and distracted by opposing rocks … and resounding from the lofty shores, that tremble on their thousand columns'. Though the grandeur of the scene defies description and illustration, the historian supplies an engraving (plate 28) and adds to his earlier account a suitably sublime description of the bridge. This consists of a single piece of timber 40 feet long, laid 'over the deepest and most awful part of the gulph … where only passengers who have a brain befitted to aerial flight, may go without horror'. From here, with echoes of John Leland's 'rokkes' and 'much wild ground', Hutchinson describes the 'rocks, cascades and wild shores' which line the river Tees to its source on the lower slopes of Cross Fell.

The engraving *Tees Force* by local artist John Bailey shows three visitors at the top of the falls and two on fallen blocks at the base, matching Hutchinson's descriptions of these viewpoints in his earlier *Excursion*. For his re-written account of High Force there are signs that the solicitor has re-read Young's account of the waterfall, as the earlier writer's adjective 'prodigious' and his term 'hanging woods' are borrowed: Hutchinson does add his own colour notes as he details the vegetation: 'the slopes are decorated with hanging woods, the fissures and openings of the cliffs, with creeping shrubs; and ancient yew trees, here and there scatter their solemn green over the grey rocks, or suspend their rusty branches from the precipices.' Picnicking groups continue to use the grottoes along the northern bank of the river, complete with a supply of water to mix with their wine: 'a delightful scene for beauty, song, and wine!' At Wynch Bridge Hutchinson re-writes his earlier description, emphasising the sublime nature of the suspension bridge, 'planked in such a manner, that the traveller experiences all the tremulous motion of the chain, and sees himself suspended over a roaring gulph, on an agitated, restless gang-way, to which few strangers dare trust themselves'. Hutchinson also includes an engraving, which would be reproduced in 1823 for *The Gentleman's Magazine*.

**I** *The Fall of the Tees, Durham. Pastels by George Lambert, 1746.*

**II** *Barnard Castle. Watercolour by Thomas Hearne, 1788.*

**III** *Abbey Bridge. Watercolour by Edward Dayes, 1791.*

**IV** *Barnard Castle. Watercolour by Thomas Girtin, 1808.*

V  *Winch Bridge on the River Tees. Oil painting by George Cuit the Elder.*

VI  *Hell Cauldron. Watercolour with pen and ink by John Sell Cotman, 1805.*

**VII**  Bartsia alpina. *Coloured engraving by James Sowerby, 1796.*

**VIII**  *Mortham Tower. Oil painting, 19th-century.*

**IX**  *The Meeting of the Waters. Watercolour by William Callow, 1872.*

**X**  *Cross Fell, source of Tees. Watercolour by Benjamin Heslop, 1891.*

NEAR BARNARD CASTLE

# TEESDALE BY L·N·E·R
## IT'S QUICKER BY RAIL
FULL INFORMATION FROM L·N·E·R OFFICES AND AGENCIES

**XI** *Teesdale by LNER; Near Barnard Castle. Railway poster after E.W. Haslehust, 1930s.*

**XII** *Cauldron Snout on the Tees. Book illustration from a watercolour by Alfred Heaton Cooper, c.1924.*

**XIII**  *High Force, Teesdale. Book illustration, 1907.*

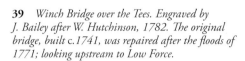

**39** *Winch Bridge over the Tees. Engraved by J. Bailey after W. Hutchinson, 1782. The original bridge, built c.1741, was repaired after the floods of 1771; looking upstream to Low Force.*

Near Eggleston Hutchinson describes a 'highly romantic and picturesque' prospect or view at Foxgyll, encompassing about fifteen miles. As well as Eggleston, there is Romaldkirk and its chapel Laithkirk, Mickleton and Middleton-in-Teesdale; the columnar Whin Sill provides part of the background. Hutchinson then returns to Arthur Young's 'most glorious prospect' from nearby Foggerthwaite, now Whistle Crag. This lower view, from the road high above the river, is narrower but not concealed by high land; Mickleton's townfield is striped with corn, grass and fallow and the Lune winds down a narrow valley to join the Tees. An engraving of Eggleston after C. Gibson matches Hutchinson's account of the house, close to the river and surrounded by sycamores and extensive plantations.

Hutchinson includes an engraving of the church at Barnard Castle. As well as discussing the declining manufacture of woollen goods and the flourishing stocking trade, the history of the town and castle naturally predominates; the Roman road crossed the Tees at a ford, giving Street-ford or Stratford (Startforth) its name; and Hutchinson quotes Leland's description of the town. There are a number of walks from Barnard Castle; that to Towler Hill to the west follows Thomas Gray's listing (p.44) 20 years previously. To the south east a path beside the river leads to Abbey Bridge and views already fully described in Hutchinson's *Excursion*. On the title page an engraved 'View on the River Tees near Barnard Castle' shows the Abbey through this bridge. Some six miles away, Raby Castle is the seat of the Earl of Darlington; it is a 'noble pile of stately towers', giving the most perfect idea of a great feudal baron's palace. Descriptions of Raby from Grose's *Antiquities of England and Wales* and from Thomas Pennant accompany an engraving by John Bailey.

Befitting a history, Hutchinson gives some account of lead mining in Teesdale; the Romans probably mined here, and there is evidence of the industry since the time of Edward VI. In 1781 the smelters in the district received 5,617 'bings' of ore,

**40**   *Eggleston. Engraved by J. Bailey after C. Gibson, 1783.*

a bing being equivalent to about 8 cwt; each 4½ bings produced a 'fother', or 22 cwt of lead and 10 ounces of silver.

In 1773 the Flintshire landowner and naturalist Thomas Pennant (1726-98) was on his mainly antiquarian *Tour from Alston-Moor to Harrowgate, and Brimham Crags* when he decided to vary the route he had taken the previous year and cross the river Tees at Barnard Castle. In this way he was able to see Raby Castle, and the artist Moses Griffiths who travelled with him was able to sketch the castle for an engraving to illustrate the *Tour*. The Earl of Darlington, though at breakfast, received Pennant very politely. The castle was 'an irregular but magnificent pile' with square towers, and partly surrounded by a moat. Lord Darlington rides around his grounds with Pennant, who remarks on the handsome farm house with a castle front, an amazing stock of hay and large plantations. The terraced grounds give a view into Yorkshire; Pennant thinks that the projected serpentine river will be very fine, but will be disgraced near its end by some 'drip-drip-a-drips, miscalled cascades'.

At Staindrop Pennant stops long enough simply to record the tombs in the church; the reports on Streatlam suggest that it is not worth visiting, so the naturalist refers his readers to Grose's account. Barnard Castle was founded about 1170 by Bernard Baliol and stands high above the Tees; its front is almost totally clothed with thick ivy, and the ditch cut out of solid rock. The castle affords a beautiful view up the Tees, with its wooded banks, and to the two-arched bridge. Egglestone Abbey was built in the late Gothic style above the river Tees; here Pennant refers to Leland's description of the two tombs and the quarrying of marble from the river. Below the abbey is Morritt's magnificent single-arch bridge, 'flung from rock to rock' high above the river.

At Rokeby, 'an elegant house in the Italian style', Pennant gives a long account of the collection in the house, together with a brief description of the Greta; these

*Right:* **41** *Title page of* The History and Antiquities of the County Palatine of Durham, *1794. The View on the River Tees near Barnard Castle engraved by J. Lowes.*

*Above:* **42** *Raby Castle, South East Aspect. Drawn and engraved by J. Bailey, 1784 for W. Hutchinson's* The History and Antiquities of the County Palatine of Durham.

closely follow the accounts of Young and Hutchinson. The 'piles of stone of most tremendous and uncommon magnitude', perhaps brought down by the floods of 1771, do seem to come from Pennant's own observation.

Pennant's *Tour* was not published until 1804; in it he records how he first met William Hutchinson at Penrith in 1773 and later at Barnard Castle. Pennant does not seem to have ventured into Teesdale beyond Barnard Castle; when he comes to describe the waterfalls he gives detailed references to the three engravings in Hutchinson's *History* and uses the solicitor's words. Along the Tees, which rises on Cross Fell, 'We are told that Nature has been … wildly prodigal of the awful and picturesque scenery, exhibited in the time-worn rocky-bed.' The first 'wonder' is Wynch Bridge, which is flung over the river, its chains 'stretched from rock to rock' over a 60 ft chasm. Re-written from Hutchinson's account, the bridge at Cauldron Snout is 'attended with ten thousand more horrors' than that at Wynch Bridge; a single beam 40 feet in length crosses the deepest part of the river, 'foaming and roaring' through a 200 yard long chasm of columnar rocks. The third cataract has no such crossing, it is 'a magnificent exertion of nature. Here, at High Force, we read again of parties of picnickers in the grottoes admiring the 'dreadful noise and vast spray' as the double fall of water descends 82 feet into a deep basin.

By 1782 the Hon. John Byng, whose own manuscript *Tour to the North* we shall shortly consider, could write that 'Tour writing is the very rage of the times'. Teesdale had its fair share of such *Tours*, written both by visitors from outside the region and by locals. We next discuss how local artists and poets perceived Teesdale and influenced travellers coming to the dale.

## 8

## *Local Artists and Poets*

*'For vast thy height, and rapid is thy course;*
*From rock sublime, O justly call'd, High Force!'*

As well as providing drawings or watercolours for engravings in local histories, artists from Teesdale and the surrounding region were busy supplying the demand for paintings to hang on the walls of the local gentry.

Still hanging at Rokeby are three 18th-century oil paintings of the site; two are of the house from the north and from the west, and one is of Greta Bridge with the south lodge. At one time these were tentatively attributed to George Cuit, but there is little evidence for this. George Cuit the Elder (1743-1818)[1] was born in Moulton near Richmond in Yorkshire, about 14 miles south-east of Barnard Castle. His talent for drawing attracted the interest of Sir Lawrence Dundas, who had bought the Aske estate nearby in 1763, and in 1769 he was sent to study art in Rome for six years. On his return he sought to establish himself as an artist in London, but ill health forced him to return to Richmond. 'There he quietly passed the remainder of his life, painting with equal exactness the polished features of park scenery and the mansions of the opulent as the moss-grown cliffs and roaring torrents which are so profusely scattered about in Richmond and its vicinity.'[2] In 1792 the travel writer John Byng[3] was recommended 'to seek a Mr Cuit, a painter of merit, who took sketches of this country'. Cuit certainly painted Egglestone Abbey and Wycliffe, and the oils *High Force on the River Tees* and *Winch Bridge* (1782, plate V), which until 1989 were in a private collection in Barnard Castle. At Wynch Bridge (the modern spelling) Cuit shows an angler, with companion and dog, dwarfed by the scale of the columns of whin sill across which the suspension bridge, complete with stabilising chains, is slung; unlike Hutchinson, Cuit turns his back on Low Force and chooses to show a sunlit Staple Crag behind the bridge.

John Bailey (1750-1819) was born near Bowes; showing an early artistic bent, he was placed as a pupil to the engraver Godfrey, who engraved the plates for Francis rose's, *The Antiquities of England and Wales*. Later Bailey became a tutor to his uncle George Dixon's children at Cockfield, near Raby Castle, drawing and engraving in his spare time; he later taught mathematics at Witton-le-Wear, and worked as a land surveyor. Of his Teesdale watercolours which can be traced, there is one of Egglestone Abbey; vegetation is growing in the east window, and the viewer looks over Abbey

**43**   *High Force. Oil painting by Joseph Miller, c.1830.*

Bridge in the middle ground towards Rokeby in the distance. John Bailey made a number of engravings for William Hutchinson's *The History and Antiquities of the County Palatine of Durham* including, as we have seen, those of High Force, Wynch Bridge, Eggleston and Raby Castle (plates 38-42).

Another Teesdale artist was Joseph Miller, who practised at Staindrop near Raby Castle; his paintings are not dated, but the fourth edition of *A Tour in Teesdale* in 1828 was 'embellished with eight views from designs by Joseph Miller', and he exhibited at the Northern Academy in Newcastle in 1829 and 1831. Miller painted both Raby Castle and High Force a number of times, perhaps for the local art market. In one almost theatrical version of High Force the artist has chosen dramatic diagonal lighting and a low viewpoint from the edge of the plunge pool. It is interesting that the viewpoint was that selected by Thomas Amory and Arthur Young; it would be chosen by many other visitors. The composition of the painting, along with the inclusion of the thread of water from the southern or Yorkshire side and the two anglers, echoes J.M.W. Turner's *High Force or Fall of Tees* engraved for a *History of Richmondshire*. Though obviously taken from his own study, as shown by the foam and spray from the falling water, and the shape of the foreground boulders of whin sill, Miller does seem to have been influenced by the famous artist.

George Balmer (*c.*1806-46) lived at Ravensworth, five miles south-east of Greta Bridge. He became best known for his coastal views, but one local work that can be

**44**   *The Rokeby Picnic. Watercolour sketch by William Bewick, 1825.*

traced is his *Glen of the Greta* which was engraved for *Illustrations ... to the Poetical Works of Sir Walter Scott*, published in 1834 by Charles Tilt (plate 61).

For a painting of Cauldron Snout we have to turn to an artist from lower down the Tees valley. William Bewick (1795-1866) left his home in Darlington at the age of 20 to be taught in London by Benjamin Haydon for three years. At Haydon's studio he met William Wordsworth and Sir Walter Scott. While in Scotland in 1823 he painted many portraits, including those of the poet James Thomson and the botanist Sir William Hooker; the following year he stayed with Scott at Abbotsford. Back in Darlington Bewick spent a couple of years obtaining commissions to finance his proposed visit to Italy. In *Cauldron Snout*, painted in 1825, Bewick has had to integrate views from several points down the staircase of falls. He has combined the straightened falls with the long pool of the Weel beyond and vegetation clinging to the columns of whin sill in the foreground; two people are about to cross the railed bridge, perhaps tourists determined to reach the sublime 'station' above what William Hutchinson had described as 'the deepest and most awful part of the gulph'. A 'Sketch by the late William Bewick in the year 1825 at Rokeby' was signed 'E. Pease'; this would be Edward Pease (1767-1858) of Darlington, importantly connected with the famous Stockton and Darlington Railway which opened in the same year. Now known as *The Rokeby Picnic*, the sketch shows a group of people from Darlington who from their dress are obviously Quakers; with hampers and bottles, they are presumably on a visit to Rokeby.

When Anne Wilson had her 1600-line poem *Teisa: a descriptive poem of the River Teese, its towns and antiquities* printed she turned to an unknown engraver for the title page, which shows a bird in front of Barnard Castle. It is tempting to look for connections with the famous wood engraver Thomas Bewick (1753-1828). Bewick is thought of as the father of modern English book illustration, being especially known for his two-volume *History of British Birds* (1797, 1804). He trained as an engraver with Ralph Beilby in Newcastle upon Tyne, in a district of printers and booksellers and in 1777 joined Beilby in a partnership. The following year Anne Wilson had her poem *Teisa* printed in Newcastle.

Anne Wilson labels herself an obscure 'northern female bard'; from sparse references in the poem she appears to be a widow. The poem is influenced by Drayton's Poly-Olbion, and contains direct allusions to Milton's river imagery in *Lycidas* and in *Paradise Lost*. Wilson interjects musings on national and regional history as she traces the course of the Tees from its source.

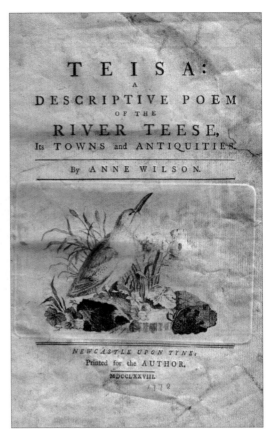

**45** *Title page of* Teisa, *1778.*

From 'a calm transparent Lake' or the Weel, the Tees

> As from the steepy height her waves she throws,
> Impetuous; and white as falling snows!
> But soon from rock to rock they flow along,
> Soft murm'ring as the poets vernal song

at what is Cauldron Snout, where fearless miners have laid a basic bridge over this amazing cataract. Next, another beautiful cataract is seen

> For vast thy height, and rapid is thy course;
> From rock sublime, O justly call'd, High Force!
> …
> From this stupend'ous height, the streams that flow,
> Are swiftly chang'd to flakes of falling snow;

At Wynch Bridge 'artful peasants' have made a bridge of two strong iron chains

> On these rebounding links some boards depend,
> And make a dancing bridge, where peasants go,
> Regardless of th'amazing depth below!

**46**  *Barnard Castle, Durham. Engraving after W. Westall for* Great Britain Illustrated, *1830.*

At Barnard Castle Anne Wilson praises the prospect from Towler Hill of the bridge, castle and town and beyond to distant woods and hills. Startforth also provides pleasing views of the castle and town. Morritt's bridge at Egglestone Abbey might vie with that over the Tiber, and at Rokeby 'lost Eden sure is now revived'. Along the Greta are 'cooling grottos' and craggy rocks arrayed with 'pendant woodbines' and 'clasping ivy'; we will encounter similar imagery to describe this spot from another poet, some 35 years later, writing from one such grotto.

George Layton, a schoolmaster at Bowes, wrote a good deal of poetry about the Tees, and 'a somewhat ambitious poem on Barnard Castle'[4], *Castle–Barnard, a poem,* published in 1823 with wood engravings of the town. Layton seems to be unaware of Anne Wilson's poem and believes his is the first to address Barnard Castle:

> HAIL, Baliol's ward, neglected and unsung!
> No native harp for thee has yet been strung.

The poem describes the castle in detail, with its moat, great round tower and Brackenbury Tower, along with nearby Flatts wood; however, notes to the poem describe the course of the Tees through the Weel and over Cauldron Snout and High Force.

Richard Watson (1833-91) was the son of a lead miner. From the age of six he went to the London Lead Company's school in Middleton-in-Teesdale, and was allowed to leave school two years early at the age of 10 when his father became seriously ill; he started work as a washer boy, separating the lead ore from the waste rock. As a young man he wrote songs and poems for special occasions and for concerts; some of his poems were published by the *Teesdale Mercury*, and he soon became known as 'The Teesdale Poet'. Watson paid for the printing of the first book of his poems, *The Poetical Works of Richard Watson*, in 1862; a larger edition, *Poems and Songs of Teesdale*, came out in 1884, and Watson's grand-daughter brought out a new edition in 1930. Although his poems were very popular in Teesdale, Watson made very little money from them. The poet was more interested in reading and writing than in his job working in the lead mines or on the washing floors; instead of tending a vegetable plot like most miners, and having a spare-time job, he spent many evenings writing, or reciting at functions for no reward; inevitably his family suffered.

Watson's poem *The Teesdale Hills* must have been written after he and his family had spent 10 years away from Teesdale, unsuccessfully seeking a better life in Cumberland and Scotland:

> I've wandered many a weary mile,
> And in strange countries been;
> I've dwelt in towns and on wild moors,
> And curious sights I've seen;
> But still my heart clings to the dale
> Where Tees rolls to the sea,
> Compared with what I've seen I'll say
> The Teesdale hills for me.

One of his most popular poems, with both miners and other readers, was *My Journey to Work*. With his 'week's wallet' of provisions over his shoulder Watson sets out on a Monday morning from Holwick, over Wynch Bridge to Newbiggin and then on to Hardberry Hill with its extensive views. From here can be seen Middleton-in-Teesdale, supported by lead mining, and

> A vapour dense ascends on yonder hill
> From the large smelting works of Blackton mill.

The poet continues down into the valley of Hudeshope Beck, past 'the din of mills and jiggers' from the washing floors of Coldberry Mine, and by Lodge Sike Mine, where his father had mined at what was once the richest mine in Teesdale:

> it has had its run,
> 'Tis now wrought out, its mineral wealth is done,
> Large rubbish heaps along the hillside show
> The vast extent of hollow ground below.

Watson passes Wiregill Mine, where he had worked before leaving Teesdale, and his walk of about eight miles ends at the lodging 'shop' at Little Eggleshope, where he will spend four or five nights before returning home to his family for the weekend.

In the song *Lovely Sweet Vale of the Tees* Watson recalls Walter Scott's poetry[5] which was inspired by the landscape, and praises the beauties of the dale – Cauldron Snout, High Force, the 'rocks, dells, and shady green bowers', and the 'rare ferns and flowers'. It is to these rare plants of Teesdale that we now turn.

# 9

## Botanists

*Gentiana verna, Potentilla fruticosa, Bartsia alpina, Minuartia stricta*

Upper Teesdale has long been visited by botanists who have discovered rare plants there, apparently growing outside their normal habitat. The spring gentian is abundant near the permanent snowline in the Alps; the hoary rock-rose is found in southern Europe; the mountain avens and alpine bartsia grow in the Arctic and the Alps; and the sea-thrift is a plant of the coasts of northern Europe. It is now accepted that these rare plants (the Teesdale 'assemblage') are a relict flora from the end of the Ice Age, assisted by the climatic and geological conditions of the area. The Whin Sill, as well as providing distinctive plant habitats on rocky ground, produced the sugar-limestone when it was injected which resulted in shallow rendzina soils on which many of the rare plants survive. The pronounced upland climate and the remoteness of much of upper Teesdale has limited human interference and allowed the continuance of restricted plant habitats.

By 1805 the authors of *The Botanist's Guide through the Counties of Northumberland and Durham* could list most of the rare plants 'worthy of notice on the romantic banks of the Tees', as communicated by various botanical friends, particularly the Revd John Harriman of Eggleston. However, the recent research of Dr F. Horsman has shown that it was well over 100 years earlier that the Revd Ralph Johnson (a Brignall vicar) and William Oliver (a Middleton-in-Teesdale apothecary) had played a large part in the early discovery of these plants. In 1671 'the father of English botany', John Ray (1627-1705) was in Teesdale while on his third collecting expedition to northern England. By now Ray had produced a *Catalogus Angliae* or *Catalogue of British Plants*, had been elected to the Royal Society and had been accepted as one of the foremost naturalists in Europe. In July 1671 John Ray and his helper Thomas Willisel (who died c.1675), the first professional collector of plants, animals and minerals for the Royal Society, stayed with Ralph Johnson (1629-95) at his Brignall vicarage. Ray, who described Johnson as a great friend, particularly wanted to see *Potentilla fruticosa* or shrubby cinquefoil, which Johnson had discovered locally and which Willisel may have recorded in 1641. In the 1677 edition of his *Catalogue* John Ray records that Ralph Johnson was the first person to find *Potentilla fruticosa* and, as well as showing it to Ray, had supplied a description.

Ralph Johnson's notebook records the discovery of 20 plants in upper Teesdale. *Minuartia verna*, the spring sandwort or 'leadwort', was discovered on Widdybank Fell (see map, plate 51); other finds included alpine saxifrage, alpine bartsia, Scottish asphodel and dwarf birch. Only the discovery of *Potentilla fruticosa*, found at 'Mickle' or High Force, was published at the time, as the others had appeared in Ray's earlier *Catalogue*; at that time the main thrust of botanical study was on description and identification, and no consideration was given to plant distribution. So knowledge of these plants in upper Teesdale was lost for almost a century.

By the time that the apothecary and surgeon William Oliver (1761-1816) arrived in Middleton-in-Teesdale, the Linnaean system of plant classification, using genus and species names and still used today, had started to overtake Ray's more complicated system. Oliver had studied at Edinburgh University and arrived in 1783 with a copy of a Scottish *Flora* and an interest in field botany, originally gained from gathering plant 'simples' for making drugs. William Oliver discovered many of the Teesdale rarities; however these might have remained overlooked if another botanist had not arrived on the scene.

In 1796 John Harriman (1760-1831) moved from Barnard Castle to take up the curacy of Eggleston; he soon made a botanical excursion into upper Teesdale in the company of Oliver. Harriman knew a Darlington botanist of national standing, Edward Robson (1763-1813), who was in touch with the authors of the outstanding *English Botany*, a 36-volume work issued in parts between 1790 and 1814. The beautiful illustrations for this work were by James Sowerby, and James Edward Smith, who had founded the Linnean Society of London in 1788, wrote the accompanying descriptions and named the botanists who had contributed the specimens. *Bartsia alpina* (plate VII) has this annotation:

> The wild recent specimens of this very rare plant, from which our drawing was taken, were gathered July 27, 1796, near Middleton in Teesdale, Durham, by the Rev. Mr Harriman, and Mr Oliver surgeon, of Middleton, and sent us by our liberal correspondent Mr E Robson.

The Darlington Natural History Society was founded in 1793; its first treasurer, Edward Robson, prepared *Plantae Dunelmenses*, a list of the rarer plants of County Durham, for the Society in the following year; included was *Potentilla fruticosa*, to be found growing plentifully at High Force. This was followed by the printing of a list of rare wild plants around Darlington which Robson could offer to other collectors, and a *Plantae Desideratae* or list of specimens which he required for his herbarium of pressed plants. It is apparent from this herbarium that between 1796 and 1810 Oliver sent Robson at least 11 species of plant from upper Teesdale. Harriman would have informed Robson of the plants which Oliver had discovered; Robson would ask Harriman to obtain those not already in *English Botany* – to send to Sowerby for inclusion in *English Botany*.

It is at this point that John Binks (*c.*1766-1817), who at one time was credited with discovering many of the Teesdale rarities, appears. Binks was a lead miner who

Oliver employed to collect duplicates of plants he had collected himself and pressed for his herbarium. While Binks was collecting for Oliver, he himself discovered some of the Teesdale rarities, including perhaps the most famous plant of upper Teesdale, the spring gentian (*Gentiana verna*). Although this plant was well known to the local people, who called it Spring Violet, the authors of *English Botany* credited Binks with collecting the specimen in April 1797, and John Harriman with its identification and with sending it to them. William Oliver had also sent dried specimens, which 'have been carefully compared with the Linnæan Herbarium, and prove this the real *Gentiana verna*'. It seems from his herbarium that Robson collected the spring gentian in 1798 on a collecting trip with William Oliver and John Binks. William Oliver also sent a specimen of *Minuartia verna* to Robson; this is of significance because, as its common name of leadwort indicates, it is a lead tolerant or metallophyte plant. Early lead prospectors are thought to have used such plants to indicate where surface lead veins were producing a lead rich soil; as a lead miner, John Binks may well have been aware of this. Although the specimen (then called *Arenaria verna*) illustrated in *English Botany* had been collected from lead spoil heaps in Derbyshire, Edward Robson had also sent in specimens from Teesdale.

By 1798 over 150 rare plants had been found in Teesdale; of these, 36 were Teesdale rarities found largely by William Oliver. In an 1813 Appendix to the second edition of his *Tour in Teesdale*, Richard Garland (Chapter 11) lists 28 'rare Alpine Plants to be found in and near Teesdale … obligingly communicated by Mr Oliver, Surgeon, at Middleton'.

The pages of the magazine *The Phytologist: a Popular Botanical Miscellany*, produced in monthly numbers from June 1841, were soon filled with accounts of excursions to Teesdale by botanists no doubt drawn by the finds listed and illustrated in *The Botanist's Guide through the Counties of Northumberland and Durham* and *English Botany*. In one such account Samuel Simpson of Lancaster told of how he explored Widdybank Fell in August 1838 to collect alpine bartsia and spring gentian amongst others, and searched Baldersdale for yellow marsh saxifrage. He advised fellow botanists to hire a guide, 'a requisite in search of a plant which is confined in its growth to a very limited area'. Despite getting thoroughly soaked through his Mackintosh cape, Simpson managed to find and collect the fern *Woodsia ilvensis*. Samuel King described how in July 1840 he travelled from Halifax to find the rare saxifrage in Baldersdale. On Cotherstone Moor a local guide showed him the plant; being only able to collect two specimens in flower, King left his address with the guide for the forwarding of further specimens the following year. The landlords of the *Talbot Inn* in Middleton-in-Teesdale and the *High Force Inn* guided King on the next two days. After much searching near Cauldron Snout he saw two small specimens of the Woodsia fern, 'which were instantly secured'; he searched for more, but 'was obliged to leave the spot with an impression that one day or other it would be extinct there'. It is not surprising that this fern, originally extremely rare and found only on dolerite rock scree, is listed as extinct since 1895, wholesale destruction being caused by collectors in the 19th century. John Bell, a mine inspector of

Middleton-in-Teesdale, discovered a new locality for yellow marsh saxifrage between Cross Fell and Cauldron Snout in 1843; nearby he also found Jacob's ladder, now no longer known in upper Teesdale. An article written in March 1843 in *The Phytologist* warned of the 'threatened extermination of rare plants by the rapacity of collectors … since the establishment of railroads and learned Societies'.

The Backhouse family has long been associated with plant finds in Teesdale. The family were Quaker bankers, many with an interest in botany, related to Edward Robson, and running a plant nursery in York from 1815. James Backhouse (1825-90) accompanied his father James Backhouse (1794-1869) on a visit to Teesdale in the summer of 1843. Writing in *The Phytologist*, he described their long walks, finding many of the rare plants they had seen on the previous year's excursion; these included the spring gentian 'in great profusion' on Cronkley Fell and three small plants of the Woodsia fern on Falcon Clints. The next summer the two Backhouses and three Quaker friends spent a week in Teesdale as part of a longer excursion. They took the train from York to Darlington, then to Bishop Auckland and Crook; after a walk of 27 miles they stayed at the *High Force Inn*. The next morning they set out for Widdybank Fell, Cauldron Snout and Falcon Clints, 'which comprehend a district probably the richest in Teesdale for a botanist'. Unable to identify the particular species of a plant which 'occurred very sparingly', Backhouse records how they sent a specimen to Sir William J. Hooker (1785-1865, the first official director of the Royal Botanic Gardens at Kew). Whilst working in Norwich James Backhouse senior had shared botanical walks with Hooker; Hooker now identified the plant as one 'not previously found in the British islands'. The Backhouses and friends had discovered the bog sandwort or Teesdale sandwort (*Minuartia stricta*), still unknown elsewhere in England. They found that the Woodsia fern was much less abundant and less luxuriant than when gathered by James Backhouse senior in 1821; they saw much bear berry, noting that it was formerly collected for medicinal purposes in the neighbourhood, and rediscovered, though in a more restricted area, the bog whortleberry 'which had been gathered there thirty years previously, by the late Dr Oliver and James Backhouse'.

This earlier collecting excursion would have been in 1813, the year in which Richard Garland published Oliver's list of rare Teesdale plants, including the bear berry and bog whortleberry, along with the apothecary's measurements of the height of High Force (56 feet) and the length of Cauldron Snout (596 yards). In 1792 Oliver had discussed his measurements of High Force with John Byng, whose tour we next consider.

# 10

## *The Hon. John Byng takes A Tour to the North in 1792*

*'I am in that sort of wild country, and unvisited village that I wish to explore'*

In 1792 the Hon. John Byng (1743-1813) took a *Tour to the North*, 'to fly from the hateful noises, hours, and stinks of London'. Three years previously Byng had explained his touring, this comment having particular relevance to Teesdale:

> for I leave London that I might see Nature in her wild, and most becoming attire …
> I come abroad to view old castles, old manors and old religious houses, before they be
> quite gone. I enjoy a grove of venerable old oaks; feel transported at the sight of a wild
> water-fall …

Having left the army (as Lieutenant Colonel of the 1st Foot Guards) in 1780, Byng, now working in the Inland Revenue, made at least one tour a year until 1794, 'Not to be worried, every morning by revenue prosecutions, and every evening, by sights, and relations of follies, and fashions' in London. Writing in 1782, he declared that 'Tour writing is the very rage of the times', but thought he would not risk publishing his own diaries: 'I shall never hazard a bookseller's window.' But by 1789 he indulges 'in a little hasty vanity, and satisfaction, in thinking how pleasant my tours will be to readers, an hundred years hence; if they, or the ink of them shall abide'.

Fortunately, the manuscript tour diaries did survive, complete with Byng's own watercolour sketches, inn bills and prints pasted in. Byng succeeded his brother George as 5th Viscount Torrington in December 1812, but held the title for only a few weeks; he died in January 1813. *The Torrington Diaries* were not published until the 1930s. Although they did not influence any other travellers at the time, Byng was right to think how pleasant his tours would be, especially over two hundred years later. Because he made notes in his pocket book and then wrote up his 'Tour Book' each evening, Byng's accounts seem immediate; he enjoyed writing up his journal during the winter following each summer tour and, as he was not writing for publication, his descriptions appear genuine. We get a good impression of the actual conditions encountered by travellers near the end of the 18th century: 'In all my descriptions, I have trusted to my own eye sight, and opinions, without borrowing from any touring books.' John Byng seems to have adhered to this premise, though he does use information from another printed source.

In the introduction to his *Tour to the North* he hints at the part played by the publication of prints and descriptions in bringing sites to the notice of potential tourists: 'I am happy (vain perhaps) in thinking that I enjoy the pleasure of Touring as much, if not more than most men; and each Tour three times over; viz., by anticipation, by the present enjoyment, and by a record of the past.' Part of the 'anticipation' was the collection of prints and maps, just as we might read a guidebook when planning a holiday. 'Before I set forward upon this new progress, let me well examine Dr C.'s collection of topographical prints; that I might not trot by a place I shall afterwards learn was an object of admiration.' Byng compares buildings with prints he is carrying, and the following year mentions the drawings of waterfalls he had taken to the North. The diarist further explains the planning behind his northern tour:

> It is from publications, and descriptions (and sometimes the puffs of natives) that places and countries are visited: had I not read the poem of Wensley-Dale ... and had I not studied 'The Tour of the Caves', and 'A Description of Malham, &c.' I had never come this way: therefore of infinite advantage to a place and country are such publications.

During his tour Byng takes every opportunity to consult maps; at one inn he studies 'an excellent map of Yorkshire by Tuke which hung in the parlour, and afforded me many hints of my near and distant progress'. Byng must have consulted some maps before setting off from London, for he mentions calling at Post Offices where he had ordered his letters, and on a previous tour he temporarily lost his portmanteau containing his map and 'intentions'. His maps, if he was following his earlier custom, may have been 'very antient, and before the baneful luxury of turnpikes was very public'.

On 26 May 1792 the 49-year-old John Byng set off on his *Tour to the North*. 'My chestnut mare, Spot, who is in fine order, I shall ride from Town; and when at Biggleswade, shall take up my bay gelding, Bumper ... for the carriage of G[arwood his servant] and our baggage.' Byng's heavy travelling baggage includes a case containing his own sheets, powder-bag and medicines; his great coat is buckled behind him, and his night cap in his pocket, and a friend's dog Ranger accompanies him. He returned home on 17 July, having ridden 931 miles. Byng summarises his tour at the beginning of his 'Tour Book'; the Teesdale section is as follows:

| Day | To What Place | Inn | County | Miles |
|-----|---------------|-----|--------|-------|
| June 11 | To Richmond | Kings Head G. | Yorkshire | 10 |
| 12 | A Morning Ride & | | | |
| | To Barnard Castle | Bull T. | Durham | 27 |
| 13 | A Ride and back | Alehouse at Middleton | – | 34 |
| 14 | A Morning Ride | – | – | 18 |
| 15 | To Askrigg | Kings Arms | Yorkshire | 22 |

Byng was perhaps the first traveller to grade the inns he used; by reading his comments on the food, stabling and accommodation, we can understand his code: G is 'good', T is 'tolerable' and B 'bad'. Inn keepers invariably either have no knowledge of the road ahead, or give Byng 'ignorant guidance'; only occasionally does he receive

**47** *South East View of Egglestone Abbey. Engraving for* An History of Richmondshire, *1823.*

'tolerable direction'. Four years earlier he had bemoaned the lack of information to be had while on tour, 'from the ignorance and want of curiosity in the natives!' The individual tourist on horseback does not seem to be well catered for, as most inn keepers were interested only in coach or chaise travellers.

When leaving the inn at Ripon, Byng has a dig at tourists travelling by carriage. 'The chaise tourists … civilly offer'd me a seat in their chaises; but I do not envy chaise tourists, who are to be hurried, and jolted along, in danger of bad roads, and without ever seeing a County to advantage.' Byng doesn't leave the care of his horses to his servant. At the beginning of his tour he attends to the shoeing of a horse, 'for a lame horse ruins us, and defeats my plan'; during his tour he usually checks the stabling himself : 'The evening stable inspection I never omit.' He also prefers to bring with him on his tour a new set of horseshoes with steel tips.

Leaving Richmond (map, plate 35) on 12 June, Byng finds a good road that brought him on to 'the high Northern Road from London to Port Patrick; when, being unused to levell or gravell, I seemed to bound along.' His first experience of Teesdale is rather mixed. Byng finds the Greta valley well wooded and Greta Bridge 'of pleasant situation'. A 'well grown plantation' tempts him to ride down to Rokeby where, unlike other visitors, he does not approve of Sir Thomas Robinson's Palladian design, and obviously does not see the prospect house above the river Greta:

> The house is a vile, ill-fashion'd tasteless building; – but what is modern art – if not lent to assist the purposes of noble Nature? for here runs the River Tees, in a wide, rattling stream, betwixt two well wooded banks, and yet no sight of it is caught from the house, nor any of its woods, and wildness introduced into the place!

Byng also dislikes Abbey Bridge, built by the owner of Rokeby in 1773, as well as the paper mill and ruins of Egglestone Abbey, though the print of *The North View of Egleston-Abbey* by Samuel Buck he later pastes into his 'Tour Book' should perhaps have prepared him for the state of the ruins, which are 'entirely neglected; and choak'd up by weeds and nettles!'

Byng rides on to Startforth where he obtains a good view of the bridge and castle of the 'black, shabby town' of Barnard Castle, before an imminent storm encourages him to find an inn. He chooses *The Bull*, where he 'procured a tolerable parlour for myself, and tolerable stabling for my horses: the best bed room was,

**48** *Barnards Castle in the Bishoprick of Durham. Engraving by S. Hooper, 1776.*

unluckily, just painted.' Naturally the inn receives a 'T' grading in Byng's system, despite the landlord being 'very ignorant about the country'. After a stroll around Barnard Castle, on which Byng consults his print of *The West View of Bernard Castle* (plate 20) and makes a sketch where the 'Castle Walls beautifully overhang the River Tees', he enjoys a supper of boiled trout, cold beef and an excellent Teesdale cheese.

The next day Garwood calls Byng early 'as I propose a long ride'. Breakfast is hurried over and a tolerable road on the Yorkshire side of the river leads to Cotherstone, 'where the excellent cheese is made', and Romaldkirk, 'a goodish village, with sash windowed houses, and a well-built Church'. Two engravings of High Force have prompted him to take this long ride, the large *High Force* after Thomas Smith and a smaller copy (see plate 30 and plate 31). Towards Middleton-in-Teesdale conditions deteriorate:

> The road now became worse; and in 3 more miles led to the bank of the Tees, in a wild, bleak country, only inhabited by miners, or visited by grouse shooters, who come in parties into this country, at this season … here we were stop'd by the Tees, who though not violent, nor stoney, afforded a wide, and no easy pleasant ford; but thro' it we must, and did go … – I am here in that sort of wild country, and unvisited village that I wish to explore; and wherein to lose the memory of all the midnight follies, and extravagant foolish conversations of the Capitol.

Byng had made preparations suited to the conditions: 'Trembling for their roads, and miles, I had brought a nt. cap in my pocket. – Having order'd dinner, hired a guide, and cramm'd his and G's pockets with bread, cheese, and ale (Brandy I idly forgot) we resumed our march.'

Byng and his servant leave their horses at a cottage and are taken by their guide through 'many hilly, boggy fields' for a mile before entering a wood where,

> being anxious to stand beneath the fall, we endured a most fatiguing descent, and a very dangerous crawl at the river's edge, over great stones, and sometimes up to our knees in

**49** *High Force, or Fall of the Tees on the West of Durham. Engraving after Kanguisseer for* The Gallery of Nature & Art; or, A Tour through Creation and Science, *1814.*

water, till we arrived at the very bottom of the fall. – The sweat running from my brow, and a flap of my coat, my only coat, nearly torn off by the bushes … – These are noble falls of water, unequall'd I suppose in this country, of about 69 feet; and must be yet more wonderful after heavy rains, or hard frost.

Here we have to remind ourselves that Byng is not writing for anyone but himself; the descriptions, though perhaps coloured by the prevailing Picturesque, are not copied from other writers. However, Byng does seem to depend on one of his prints of High Force for the height of the fall, which 'falls down a Rock of Granate about 23 Yards into a Large Circular Bason', converting the 23 yards into 69 feet. Also, as he later recalls climbing to the top of the falls for the sublime viewpoint, Byng notices the anglers depicted at the foot of the falls in both prints:

> I recrawled up the wood, and then to the summit of the cascade, as near as possible: the basin at the bottom I should suppose a fine place for fishing; and here the salmon must stop –

Ranger the dog had somehow crossed the river and the guide offered to wade through 'a rapid stream, and scrambling up and over great stones' to retrieve the animal.

> We then crept thro' the boggy wood into the field, there opening our budget … we eat and drank voraciously; I walking about, for my head was as wet, as my feet. –

Despite such misadventures, Byng reassures himself about his annual tours, before returning to the inn at Middleton-in-Teesdale: 'But I am right in this touring, for I expand my mind and limbs; enjoy, tho' alone, the present, and record it hereafter.' Once at the inn and before dinner, Byng recovers from his ordeal: 'I stripp'd off my wet shoes, and stockings, and put on a warm woolen pair of the landlords; and my head I rubbed with brandy with some of the half pint I quickly finished.' Here as usual, Byng includes his inn bill: 'I insert bills – that I may compare this – with those of ten years hence'.

SHERLOCK.
MIDDLETON. BRIDGE END.

| | | |
|---|---|---|
| Coffee and Tea | – | – |
| Dinner | 1 | 0 |
| Supper | – | – |
| Wine | – | – |
| Negus | – | – |
| Rum and Brandy | 1 | 0 |
| Punch | – | – |
| Ale, Beer and Porter | 0 | 4 |
| Fire, Pipes & Tobacco | – | – |
| Horses hay & Corn | 1 | 4 |
| Chaise and Horse Hire | – | – |
| Servants Eating and Ale(with Apothecary) | 1 | 2 |
| | 4s.10d. | |

Byng's servant Garwood 'had made an acquaintance with the apothecary of the place … with whom, in the kitchen was a long discourse held about this aforementioned water-fall; which the apothecary told me he had measured, and that from the top of the upper fall it was 63ft, – from the top of the lower fall 56ft.' The apothecary was of course William Oliver. As well as Latin, geography and drawing, Oliver had studied mensuration at Grammar School before attending medical sessions at Edinburgh University; he purchased a surgeon and apothecary business at Middleton-in-Teesdale in 1783. As well as collecting the rare plants of upper Teesdale, he had used his measuring skills at High Force. 'He, the apothecary seem'd sorry to part with such good company; and he would have relished our passing the night here.' Byng, however, decides to return to Barnard Castle by the Durham side of the river; despite the road over the moors being very stony and boggy he makes good time. After a day of 'plunging over rocks, and into bogs' and a supper of trout, he sleeps for nine hours.

The next day Byng has his suit mended from 'the wounds of yesterday' before setting off with the landlord to Raby Castle, of which he has three prints in his 'Tour Book'. Here he finds a great deal to criticise:

We now came into Lord D's farming grounds, which are fenced by clipp'd hedges, and white gates; a sad pressage of the taste in Raby Park? Wherein are very few single trees; and all the plantations are mean, of ill make, and without bold sweeps; the river, likewise, running thro' the park, which should form a Thames, is turn'd to no account! The whiten'd ill fancied Gothic buildings in the park, are of a most wretched taste, and in full exposition. Behold the grandeur of Raby Castle. How is the Castle mann'd? I was obliged to send in my name to Lady D; – and ask permission of entrance. I am told that many are refused! Why not a fix'd day, or fix'd hours?

The house-keeper shows Byng into the Castle where in 1768 John Carr had carried out improvements. Byng finds fault with the Great Hall through which the carriageway had been taken, affecting the chapel above. He is also disappointed at there not being a picture gallery, and the library is kept locked. Asked to be shown something old, Byng does approve of the Baron's Hall, still with its hammerbeam roof, and the high-roofed mediaeval kitchen. The house-keeper

**50**  *Raby Castle, Durham. Engraving by S. Hooper, 1783.*

took me into a room, above stairs, that charm'd me, of 90 by 30 feet – with old windows, and a lofty wooden roof. – There is a plan of ascending this room by a grand staircase from the back of the hall; and a noble thing this would be. – Why I should not sleep till it was executed.

Writing up his tour later, Byng muses on the improvements he would make to Raby:

Lord D, will your lordship permit me, a stranger, to lay out £20,000 for you? And I, then, think that I could make your house a wonder of beauty; – your park should be studded with trees; your hills should be cover'd with woods; a Thames should flow thro' your park; the kitchen garden should be removed; and that develish nuisance the dog kennell carried out of hearing: – the hall should be in eternal warmth; I should build a chapel; and a Gothic stair-case; and I should render that great room, fitted up with cedar, and glazed with stain'd glass, one of the grandest libraries in the universe.

The 2nd Lord Barnard had commissioned Thomas White to landscape the grounds; Byng suggests that the ponds, constructed by 1748, must be destroyed and that landscaping must be removed to restore a view of the river.

Leaving Raby, Byng doesn't stop in Staindrop, of which he has a print:

The view from Raby Castle is very rich, towards the Church of Staindrop, and over a fine country … – Adjoining to Raby Park, is the small market town of Staindrop; one of the mart towns that can be seen; and largely adapted for a place of retreat, from the cheapness of provisions, and where a good fire (the first of comforts) may be kept up for a penny a day!

After three miles Byng leaves the road temporarily to view Streatlam Castle, 'a house of the late Mr Bowes's, a place in neglect and wild disorder … with a miserable kind of park!' The diarist rides to dinner at the *Bull Inn* at Barnard Castle before taking his evening walk along the Yorkshire side of the Tees to Towler Hill, to the north-west of the town. He describes the view of the castle and hanging woods as 'remarkably fine … of wonderful beauty, worthy of undertaking any difficulty for'. Before a supper of cold fowl, Byng attends to his horses, 'at their nightly feeding, and littering up (a duty I owe to them and myself)'.

After preserving his inn bill, he makes one more entry for the Teesdale part of his Tour: on his way south to Swaledale he stops at the river Greta, where Rutherford bridge (see maps, plate 51 and plate 35), 'whose most grand and lofty arch – seemingly never trod – caused me a stay of 2 minutes attempting a sketch'. This pencil sketch would be worked up later that year and fixed in the written-up 'Tour Book'.

## 11

# A Tour in Teesdale

*'The beauties of Teesdale have powerful claims on the Painter and the Tourist'*

Ten years after the Hon. John Byng's unpublished 'Tour Book' of Teesdale, a local writer was less reticent about his knowledge of the area. On 14 August 1802 *The York Herald* printed a letter from 'S' 'very anxious' that 'the wonders of Teesdale' should be better known. As no one else had written about these 'wonders', and as the area would soon be busy with grouse shooting, 'S' in six subsequent letters to the paper detailed a 'Tour of Teesdale' aimed particularly at visitors returning from the Lakes.

A slim pocket-sized book called *A Tour in Teesdale* was anonymously published at the *Herald* office in York the following year, the 'Advertisement' stating that it was based on letters in that paper. The author does not seem to have divulged his name, the 'S' appearing on the last page of the first edition, and no name being given in *The Gentleman's Magazine* review in June 1805. Locally, however, the author's name was perhaps known; at Barnard Castle Charles Fothergill (1782-1840) in his diary entry for 21 October 1805 acknowledged that when choosing an inn at which to stay, Garland's recommendation in his *Tour in Teesdale* of the *King's Head* had decided him.[1]

So who was Garland? The 'Tour' ran into at least eight anonymous editions, four after the author's death. An obituary notice in *The Gentleman's Magazine* gives some details: 'Died at Hull February 11th 1827 aged 51 Mr Richard Garland, Solicitor. He was a man of great literary attainments and author of "A Tour in Teesdale, including Rokeby and its environs." ' However, it was not really until after 1869, when William Boyne in his *Yorkshire Library* authoritatively gave the author as Richard Garland, that other writers started to refer to 'Garland's *Tour*'. Boyne states that Garland had written his letters to *The York Herald* from Barnard Castle, and had practised as a solicitor in Hull from 1802 until his death. Before moving to Hull, he may have been a managing clerk with a Mr Weldon, a solicitor at Barnard Castle.[2]

In the first edition of *A Tour in Teesdale* Garland states that

> It is by a very slow and gradual progress, that the wild graces of Nature are won to the enjoyment of Taste … From whatever cause it is that the beauties of Teesdale have been hitherto concealed, they have powerful claims on the Painter and the Tourist, that ought to be discussed.

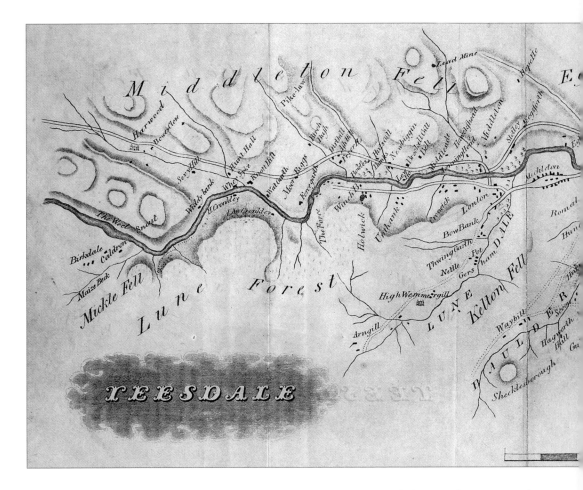

Garland is here being disingenuous; in his descriptions and choice of viewpoints he demonstrates a knowledge of Arthur Young's *Six Months Tour in the North of England* and the Barnard Castle solicitor William Hutchinson's *Excursion to the Lakes*. It may have been Hutchinson's regret for 'a neglect which has long attended the delightful scenes at home' which prompted Garland, 'intimately acquainted with the topography' of Teesdale, to act as a guide to the tourist on his way to the Lakes. *A Tour in Teesdale* does show detailed local knowledge and introduces walks and rides not mentioned by these previous writers; unusually for Tours of the time, it also includes a map.

The first walk is up the river Greta from the *Morritt Arms* (see map, plate 55), Garland's preferred inn at Greta Bridge; a number of factors make this walk 'highly romantic': 'The fine transparency of the stream, its amber colour, and rapid but silent course; the beauty of the banks, shaded with oaks; and the rocks and rich hanging-wood which terminate the Vista up the river.' The return walk provides another view:

> The bridge with its two handsome inns,[3] backed by the deep groves of Rokeby, over which you just see the old Tower of Mortham Hall rear its venerable head – the surrounding country, and the noble grounds of Raby in the distance, form altogether such an assemblage of objects in the most finished beauty, as are rarely collected in one picture.

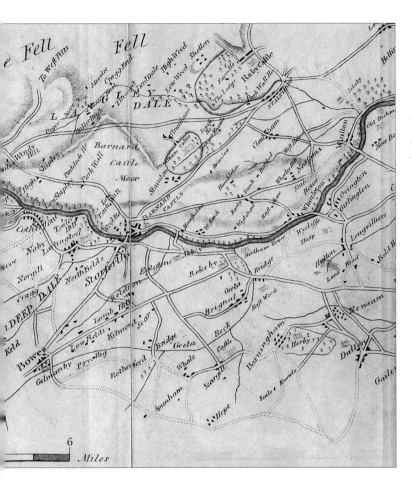

**51** *Teesdale. This map, with slight amendments, appeared in all editions of* A Tour in Teesdale *from 1803.*

A short walk from the inn is Rokeby Park, with its needle-work, antiquities and delightful walks: 'the Rock-walk, under a precipice by the bawling Greta, is particularly pleasant', with Dairy Bridge and tea room. Here Garland perhaps depends on Arthur Young for some of his information, and he may have emulated Hutchinson in quoting Mason's poem *The English Garden*, additionally suggesting (as we saw earlier) that Mason may have described Rokeby in the poem.

After dining at the *Queen's Head* at Staindrop and viewing Raby Castle, the 'Tourist's head-quarters, for two or three days, will be at Barnard Castle, where the *King's Head* is the best inn.' Garland suggests a morning walk to the partly wooded 'elevated plain' of the Flatts to the north-west of the town, borrowing William Hutchinson's description of the extensive views of the castle ruins, the bridge over the Tees, and the small valley called Deepdale. He adds the distant hills near the river's source, and a Picturesque comment: 'A scene worthy of the pencil of a Claude, to whose style the whole landscape is closely approximate!' The following description of an area in the Flatts is Garland's own:

> Keep the river, and you will gain a most truly solemn and sequestered spot, completely closed in by wood, and undisturbed by any sound, but the remotely dashing water. The rude forms of the venerable oaks that skirt the old moss-covered wall of the inclosure,

beneath which you stand; the noble height of the opposite hill, covered to the top with lofty trees; the glassy smoothness of the river at your feet; and the scattered masses of rock in its channel, impress you with delicious awe.

We then experience a sense of *déjà vu*; like John Byng 11 years previously, Richard Garland has some advice for Lord Darlington, in this case to make 'a distant pleasure-ground to Raby'. For a 'comparatively trifling' sum he advocates the development of the chalybeate spring, with the construction of walks, the opening of views, and the building of a banqueting house or inn; then Barnard Castle would rival even Rievaulx Terrace or Harrogate spa. Later we will see that in the fifth edition of his *Tour* Garland could record walks subsequently constructed in Flatts Wood.

The afternoon should be spent in examining the ruins of the castle and rambling through the town. Here again Garland relies on Hutchinson's *History and Antiquities of the County Palatine of Durham* for the history of the castle and details of the marble font in the church; he uses the same source for an evening walk to Abbey Bridge and Egglestone Abbey, complete with viewpoints. Garland adds 'a sort of vignette view' through the bridge of the Abbey, though even this is perhaps taken from an engraving in Hutchinson's *History* (see plate 41); he does, however, add 'the best view of the Abbey, and an extensive and richly diversified country' from a further viewpoint of his own. The view, over the river Tees, had been discovered by J.M.W. Turner some six years previously, and would be used again on his tour of 1816. On the way back to Barnard Castle Garland describes a 'station' or viewpoint at Startforth, where 'the town is laid before you like a map', a fine landscape especially in the evening sun.

Garland picturesquely sets the scene for an excursion 'of much fatigue, and some danger' to 'the boldest and most daring of the wild features of Nature' – in upper Teesdale. A great coat and provisions are necessities, and a hired horse used to the country a desirable option. The tourist has to rise early and ride 12 miles to breakfast at Middleton-in-Teesdale. The road 'possesses a succession of the most delightful prospects', but the best is from Foggaforth near Eggleston and is marked on the map supplied with the *Tour*; Garland relies on Arthur Young and William Hutchinson for this viewpoint, now called Whistle Crag and still used today:

> Below, the windings of the Tees through an Arcadian country, chequered in the most agreeable variety, with arable and pasture grounds, trees, villages, and farm-houses, present a very striking contrast to the bleak and barren heaths around you. To the west is a wild and confused heap of mountains: and, eastward, the eye is only arrested by the very distant hills of Hambleton. Directly opposite, the river Lune contributes its stores to the Tees, and affords a long perspective up its pastoral Dale.

A few miles past Middleton-in-Teesdale a short walk leads to Wynch Bridge; here Hutchinson's account provides Garland with the description, though he adds an account of the death of one of a group of 11 crossing the bridge in 1802:

> This extraordinary structure is composed of boards, with a slender railing on each side, and is hung on chains; the breadth of the river, the height of the rocks, and the impetuosity of the floods preventing the erection of any other kind. It is by no means pleasant to cross

**52** *Barnard Castle, Inner Courtyard and Keep Tower. Etched by J.H. Le Keux after R.W. Billings.*

> this bridge, on account of the swinging motion; nor is it at this time safe, as it has not been repaired of some time, and has got a considerable cast to one side.

At Moor Rigg a guide brings the tourist to the top of High Force,

> by far the best situation for a first sight of it, but dreadful indeed. You suddenly look down upon a cataract, rushing almost under your feet, but at some distance below, over a precipice of 69 feet, in one sheet of foam, shaking the very rocks on which you stand, and stunning the ear with its deafening noise.

A steep and difficult descent is made for a view from the bottom of the fall. A 'remarkable castle-like rock (the palace of the Genius of the river)' divides the river, 'precipitated with a graceful, though perpendicular fall' and a narrower fall which occurs when the river is in flood. Although obviously using Thomas Smith's engraving (plate 30) or *The Complete English Traveller* for the height of the fall, and Hutchinson for the foam, noise and castle-rock and other details, Garland's account seems very low-key compared with one earlier; he is at pains though to compare High Force favourably with Lodore Falls and the Falls of Clyde.

Garland makes much better use of his sources for his excursion to Cauldron Snout, one of 'mental and bodily fatigue'; his description, like the scenery, is 'in the purest style of vast and gigantic sublimity'. The guide should be directed to take the easier though longer route beside the river; even here the track is used only by lead miners and shepherds, and at Cronkley Scar 'you are entirely hemmed in by rude and barren rocks'. For a view of the whole of 'this astonishing cataract' Maize Beck is forded, horse left with the guide, and the Snout approached from its base:

> The awful and tremendous grandeur of the sight that arrests your attention, is almost more than the mind can bear. The painful, pleasing expansion of heart – that internal sensation and best criterion of the true sublime – seizes you with instantaneous and overwhelming energy. Directly before you, the river is hurled headlong from rock to rock, in a deep recess, down the declivity of a mountain, all but perpendicular, for several hundred feet.

**53** *The keep of Bowes Castle, built c.1136. Engraving for* An History of Richmondshire, *1823.*

Another sublime viewpoint is near the top of Cauldron Snout:

> Ascend the hill to the wooden bridge, which you will see at a dreadful height, and in the most romantic position, near the top of the Fall. It is a single plank, but broad and firm, with a railing on each side, so that you may safely cross it. The stand in the centre is sublime indeed! – not wholly divested of a sense of personal danger, you look downward, through a shaggy cleft, on the tumbling waters, wetting you with their spray, and shooting, in their most impetuous career, white as snow, and swifter than the arrow, beneath your feet!

Before leaving this spot, Garland exhorts the tourist to explore the 'boundless waste' of the 'deep lethargic pool' of the Weel above the Snout (covered by Cow Green Reservoir in 1971).

The return to Barnard Castle is by way of Towler Hill, from which is the 'grand view of the ruins of Barnard Castle' previously suggested by William Hutchinson, and the riverside Holmes pasture land recommended by Thomas Gray. If not exhausted by the day's excursion, Garland suggests a walk up Deepdale with 'a rock scene in every romantic diversity' and a pretty waterfall. After leaving Barnard Castle and approaching the village of Bowes, he describes a panoramic view of the road over the 'dreary' Stainmore and the whole 'sweep of the Teesdale Tour' from Rokeby to near Cauldron Snout.

Garland's *Tour in Teesdale* ends at Bowes with its Norman castle lying in a corner of the Roman fort of *Lavatrae*. He leaves the tourist in the churchyard contemplating the story of two young lovers, Roger Wrightson and Martha Railton, a story made famous in the 18th-century ballad *Edwin and Emma* by David Mallet:

EPITAPH.

Ye, dear to feeling, and the Muse,
　'O'er Stanemoor's wint'ry waste' who rove!
Scorn not the humble verse, that strews
　The grave of Virtue and of Love.[4]

There is some evidence that the owner of Rokeby would soon be using a copy of Garland's book to help his visitors make their own tour of Teesdale.

## 12

## *John Sell Cotman*

*'the most perfect examples of pure water-colour ever made in Europe'*

In 1803, in his first edition of *A Tour in Teesdale*, Richard Garland thought that 'the beauties of Teesdale [had] powerful claims on the Painter' as well as the tourist. That year the artist John Sell Cotman (1782-1842) sketched at Barnard Castle, and two years later he was painting in the area around Greta Bridge.

Dr Thomas Monro, as we have seen, regularly had a group of young artists at his home in London copying works from his art collection. In the mid-1790s both J.M.W. Turner and Thomas Girtin were to be found there, and later, J.S. Cotman. Paul Sandby Munn possibly introduced Cotman into the Drawing Society, an informal circle of artists, mostly with a Monro 'Academy' background. It was probably through such connections that Munn and Cotman met the art patron Sir Henry Englefield, who in turn recommended the two artists to his sister Teresa Cholmeley of Brandsby Hall, some 13 miles north of York.

Mrs Cholmeley found the sketches of Munn and Cotman 'superior to any I have ever seen'.[1] After a week at Brandsby in the summer of 1803, the two artists made a short sketching tour. In Teesdale they visited only Barnard Castle. Munn chose a view of the castle and bridge from downstream; Cotman made a detailed panoramic sketch from higher up the river bank opposite Thorngate Mill. After more

**54** *Ordnance Survey map of the river Greta, first edition, 1857; Brignall*

**55** *Ordnance Survey map of the river Greta, first edition, 1857; Rokeby and Greta Bridge.*

touring, Cotman would spend six weeks at Brandsby, giving further lessons to the Cholmeley girls.

On 30 July 1805 the 'Commonplace book' of Brandsby Hall records: 'Mr Cotman & Francis set off for Rokeby Park.' The 23-year-old John Sell Cotman was spending his third summer with the Cholmeley family and seems by 1805 to be regarded almost as an adopted son. He accompanied the family on sketching trips and on visits to other houses. The owner of Rokeby, J.B.S. Morritt, had readily agreed to the 22-year-old Francis Cholmeley's request that Cotman accompany him on a visit to his estate: 'We shall also be very happy to see Mr Cotman, and to shew him a little of the banks of the Tees.'

Although the neo-classical Rokeby Hall, its contents and its landscaped park had a marked influence on the young artist, few of his watercolours can definitely be placed inside the park. The best known of the Greta watercolours are two versions of *Greta Bridge* made from a pencil sketch which has survived. The sketch carefully shows the single arch, the open balustrades and roundels and niches of the Palladian bridge by John Carr (see plate 75); it had been re-built by Morritt's father after the flood damage of 1771. In the two watercolours, made in 1805 and 1810, the geometry of the bridge with its reflection and the *Morritt Arms*[2] is placed against the apparently random but carefully arranged pattern of boulders and river banks. Interestingly, although Cotman's sketch shows the curved parapet of the bridge, for both watercolours he returns to the pre-1771 triangular shape depicted in an 18th-century painting hanging in Rokeby Hall. In this classical picture the bridge is very prominent and frames the lodge to Rokeby.

Within Rokeby Park itself, Garland had described the 'delightful' Rock walk (see plate XI for a 1930s view) along the Greta from near the house towards Dairy Bridge and the junction with the River Tees. Here Cotman revelled in the same 'romantic variety of glen, torrent and copse' as Walter Scott would describe three years later. Although Cotman records bathing under Dairy Bridge, he prefers to paint a little

**56** *Greta Bridge & Old Morritt Arms. Illustration by J.A. Symington for* A Picturesque History of Yorkshire, *1901.*

foot bridge further upstream. Writing in 1937, Sydney Kitson in his biography of Cotman describes Greta Woods in Rokeby Park:

> A gully on the steep bank of the river is spanned at the top by a little stone foot-bridge, which stands up dark against a blue sky. The trees cling to the rocks, and obtain a root-hold where they may. There has been no change in all the years since Cotman drew the scene. The descendants of his trees have found the same root-holds and have grown as he drew them. The picture is there, composed by Nature: Cotman saw it and endowed it with a magic quality which was all his own.

With echoes of William Gilpin's 'Picturesque' observations 33 years earlier, Cotman comments on the Greta being 'so rapid at times as to carry down rocks of 70 or 80 tons weight,' and in particular mentions a stone at the junction of the Greta and the Tees. The Greta is prone to flooding and in *A View on the Greta or the Tees* depicts the boulders at the Meeting of the Waters.[3] After a stay of more than two weeks Francis Cholmeley left Rokeby for Northumberland. Cotman stayed on for a few more days until his hosts had to leave to visit friends in Lancashire, not before saying a 'great many good things' about his work.

The artist moved to the *Morritt Arms* for another two weeks. Along with the watercolours, Cotman's letters to Francis Cholmeley allow us to gauge something of his response to this locality, a response which art critic Miklos Rajnai suggested stimulated a sudden change from traditional artistry into unexpected brilliance and singularity. We can relate some of the scenes Cotman chose to paint to descriptions in Garland's *Tour in Teesdale*; perhaps Morritt had provided a copy to Francis Cholmeley and Cotman to aid their discovery of the area. *Barnard Castle from Towler Hill* was most probably painted before the departure of Francis Cholmeley; it echoes the view described by Garland:

> At Towler Hill, you have a grand view of the ruins of Barnard Castle, at the termination of a fine avenue of the Tees, of near a mile long; one bank of which is a magnificent hanging wood for the whole extent, and the other a verdant flat, but soon rising to a gentle swell, which bounds the eye, and directs it to an extensive prospect over the town into Richmondshire.

**57** *On the Greta at Rokeby. Illustration for* Rivers of Great Britain, *1902.*

The watercolour was exhibited at the Royal Academy the following year.

While he was sketching and painting alone it was the wooded banks of the Greta that appealed most to Cotman; he wrote to Francis Cholmeley, perhaps recalling the Drawing Society,

> I have not been far from the Inn but once … All my studies have been in the wood [Mill Wood] above the bridge … I think it grows upon me in my regard every day, it really is a delicious spot. And much should I like to have a house near it that I might have a Study of artists down to see me and to do it justice. We might then talk and draw it over in a high style.

In the same letter Cotman describes how he bathes each day 'under the tree we looked at together on our going that scrambly walk up the Greta to the rock. I have coloured a sketch of it which I call My Bath.'

This watercolour sketch must be *Hell Cauldron* (plate VI), now in Leeds City Art Gallery; the Greta leaves a narrow channel in Mill Wood to open into a deep pool, and echoes Garland's description of 'the fine transparency of the stream, … the beauty of the banks, shaded with oaks'. This outdoor study was evidently for Sir Henry Englefield, as his sister Teresa Cholmeley would write in the following March: 'I am very glad his Hell Cauldron is a good one and hope Bob [Englefield] will like it.' Kitson describes a more refined, considered and almost abstracted studio version of this watercolour, now in the National Gallery of Scotland, which was exhibited at the Royal Academy in 1806 and at the Norwich Society of Artists exhibition in 1808:[4]

> The arrangement of the trees is studied and balanced almost to the point of artificiality, and their reflections make a perfect pattern in the water below them. Yet the colour is lovely and the air is that of some dream-land where it is always afternoon.

The scene is almost perfectly preserved today, as are a whole sequence of views sketched and painted by Cotman as he re-trod the path rising above the 'hanging woods' of the Greta valley described in *A Tour in Teesdale*. Here are Cotman's 'studies of trees', as he called them; two years previously Teresa Cholmeley had praised the 'fine bold, wild trees as … show the boldness and spirit of Cotty's genius'.

These studies included many pencil sketches[5] of 'the precipices that overhang the river', as Garland put it; here the Greta makes a sharp bend called the Devil's Elbow, and Cotman reported how he was 'industriously employed upon a subject that calls forth all my powers'. Two watercolours, later painted in the studio, *On the River*

*Greta, Yorkshire* and *Devil's Elbow, Rokeby Park*, with their stylised tree masses reduced to simple flat shapes, demonstrate Cotman's response to 'all this fine scenery'.

On another walk Cotman took the path on the right bank of the river Greta through Mill Wood to a viewpoint above the Devil's Elbow. Here he made a sketch which he later worked up into the watercolour *Brignall Banks on the Greta*; three white birds emphasise the trees tumbling down an apparently bottomless valley. Further along this path was Cotman's 'favourite view, from the hill looking down on the bridge', described by Garland as a beautiful view of 'the bridge with its two handsome inns, backed by the deep groves of Rokeby'. Cotman must have shown his colour study to the Morritts before they left Rokeby on 22 August, as Morritt ordered a large copy as a present for a friend; *Distant View of Greta Bridge* was exhibited at the Royal Academy the next year.

The last of the major Greta works is *The Scotchman's Stone*, the result of 'that scrambly walk up the Greta to the rock' that Cotman made with Francis Cholmeley. The 'stone' or 'rock' is a particularly large example of the many that have fallen from the steep valley side, still making access to Cotman's viewpoint very difficult. Today the Stone has trapped more tree trunks and other debris than 200 years ago. Cotman's biographer Sydney Kitson praised the way 'the brown water of the moorland trout stream, as it flows rapidly past the rock, is rendered with an ease and mastery almost magical.' *Study of a Rock, Greta River* was exhibited at the Norwich Society of Artists in 1808.

In 1810 Cotman exhibited *The Harvest Field – A Pastoral* at the Norwich Society of Artists. In this large watercolour exhibition Cotman used the view from Towler Hill, but transformed his memories of an excursion to this viewpoint into a classical Arcadian scene – a 'Pastoral' in the tradition of Nicolas Poussin. Two figures in the picnic party may even relate to Cotman's recollection of a Poussin engraving pasted on the wall at Rokeby.[6]

Seven of Cotman's Greta watercolours were exhibited between 1806 and 1808, but the 'boldness and spirit of [his] genius' in portraying this 'delicious spot' were too modern for the general taste of the time and few pictures sold. Referring to Cotman's *Miscellaneous Etchings*, Francis Cholmeley reported from a York bookseller that subscribers did not like one particular view 'because it might have been anywhere. Two-thirds of mankind, you know, mind more what is represented than how it is done.'[7]

A proportion of the other third may have appreciated these Greta watercolours, 'totally original in vision, totally original in technique,' and through the Cholmeleys and their connections visited Rokeby to see the scenery for themselves. It would be some considerable time before Cotman's Greta works were being hailed as 'the most perfect examples of pure water-colour ever made in Europe'.[8] Meanwhile it would be the work of a writer that would make the names of Rokeby and the Greta better known.

# 13

## *Rokeby; a poem by Walter Scott, 1813*

*'O Brignal banks are wild and fair, And Greta woods are green'*

The Moon is in her summer glow,
But hoarse and high the breezes blow,
And, racking o'er her face, the cloud
Varies the tincture of her shroud;
On Barnard's towers, and Tees's stream,
She changes as a guilty dream

(Canto First, I)

So begins the romantic poem *Rokeby* by Walter Scott (1771-1832; created a baronet 1820) which, after its publication on 10 January 1813, was to put the area around Greta Bridge firmly on the tourist map.

Fortunately most of Sir Walter Scott's letters were published in the late 19th century. Combined with a careful reading of the poem and accompanying notes, and walks along the rivers Tees and Greta, they allow a reasonably accurate reconstruction of how this poem came to be written. The 'Advertisement' or introduction gives the setting:

> The Scene of this Poem is laid at Rokeby, near Greta-Bridge, in Yorkshire, and shifts to the adjacent fortress of Barnard-Castle, and to other places in that vicinity …
> The date of the supposed events is immediately subsequent to the great Battle of Marston-Moor, 3d July, 1644. This period of public confusion has been chosen, without any purpose of combining the Fable with the Military or Political Events of the Civil War, but only as affording a degree of probability to the Fictitious Narrative now presented to the Public.

Walter Scott's poem owed much to the owner of Rokeby Hall, the traveller and classical scholar J.B.S. Morritt. In June 1809 the Morritts returned Walter Scott's hospitality of the previous year. Scott wrote of having

> lingered a little while at Rokeby Park, the seat of our friend Morritt, and one of the most enviable places I have ever seen, as it unites the richness and luxuriance of English vegetation with the romantic variety of glen, torrent and copse, which dignifies our northern scenery. The Greta and Tees, two most beautiful and rapid rivers, join their currents in the demesne. The banks of the Tees resemble, from the height of the rocks, the glen of Roslin, so much and justly admired.

*Right:* **58** *Barnard Castle. Engraved by S. Fisher after Copley Fielding, for* Illustrations ... to the Poetical Works of Sir Walter Scott, *1834.*

*Below:* **59** *Tomb of Rokeby. Engraved by W.H. Simmons after J.H. Nixon, for* Illustrations ... to the Poetical Works of Sir Walter Scott, *1834.*

The scenery had made a great impression on Scott. In December 1811 he wrote to Robert Surtees, a Durham antiquary and topographer, explaining the necessity to write to finance improvements at his Abbotsford home. The letter explains some of Scott's methods, as well as suggesting that the setting of the poem was to be a key feature:

> I think of laying my scene near Barnard Castle, where there is some beautiful scenery, with which I am pretty well acquainted. If you can point out to me any romantic or picturesque incident of the period not generally known, you will greatly oblige me. You know that my stories are like a pleasure-walk, and can easily be turned aside, so as to embrace a fine point of view, or lead to a wild dell.

A few days later, Scott was writing to Morritt of his 'grand project ... Nothing less than a fourth romance in verse, the theme during the English civil wars of Charles I and the scene your own domain of Rokeby.' Scott advises Morritt, 'I have all your scenery deeply imprinted in my memory and moreover ... I intend to refresh its traces this ensuing summer.' Scott asks if his friend will accompany him on part of his tour and in the meantime requests some help:

> Is there not some book (sense or nonsense I care not) on the beauties of Teesdale – I mean a descriptive work – if you can point it out or lend it me you will do me a great favour and no less if you can tell me any traditions of the period.

He does not mind whether the information is 'truth or fiction or tradition', as long as it is 'picturesque'. Scott asks for particular information – the name of 'that wild dell where we had such a clamber on horseback up a stone staircase' and the 'traditionary tragedy of your old house at Mortham' (plate VIII).

**60** *Hall, Rokeby Castle. A fictitious scene engraved by C.G. Lewis after S.A. Hart, for* Illustrations … to the Poetical Works of Sir Walter Scott, *1834.*

Morritt replies that he will try and obtain 'a book of a few pages, describing the rides through and about Teesdale', which must be Garland's *Tour in Teesdale* (Chapter 11), and suggests that Scott obtains Hutchinson's *History of Durham* for 'some useful bits of information'. After giving details of the history of Barnard Castle, the Rokeby family and the ghost at Mortham, Morritt reminds Scott of their rides up Deepdale and along the Tees to Cotherstone. After filling his letter with such 'antiquarianism', Morritt 'will not conclude without repeating how much your intention has charmed us. The scenery of our rivers deserves to become classic ground, and I hope the scheme will induce you to visit and revisit it often.' Rokeby's owner offers his services as a guide, and hints at the tourist trade Scott's poem is likely to bring.

> Should I, in consequence of your celebrity, be obliged to leave Rokeby from the influx of cockney romancers, artists, illustrators, and sentimental tourists, I shall retreat to Ashestiel, or to your new cottage, and thus visit on you the sins of your writings. At all events, however, I shall raise the rent of my inn at Greta-Bridge on the first notice of your book, as I hear the people of Callender have made a fortune by you.

Scott soon started writing, but his publisher John Ballantyne urged that the poem be ready for Christmas 1812 and Scott was busy planting trees at home; instead of visiting Rokeby again he asked Morritt for more details of the area. Morritt gave particulars but tried to persuade Scott to return to Rokeby,

> if but for a few days, in order, on the spot, to settle accurately in your mind the localities of the new poem, and all their petty circumstances, of which there are many that would give interest and ornament to your descriptions.

Morritt hoped that Scott would not be pressured into writing in a hurry by Ballantyne's impatience. Scott did return to Rokeby and on 2 October he wrote to his publisher:

> My being here will prove of the utmost consequence to the poem. Indeed I now think I should have slurd the business without it. I have got quite a new stock of ideas and subjects … You will be surprised at the localities I have gotten.

Scott then requests that Ballantyne sends him Hutchinson's *History of Durham*, as it is 'necessary for my localities names &c.' From sources such as this and Morritt's 'antiquarianism', Scott's 'Notes' give us the history of Barnard Castle, Egglestone Abbey and Rokeby. Although the stories of the Danes and Stanemore are told,

61    *Glen of the Greta. Engraved by W. Miller after G. Balmer, for* Illustrations … to the Poetical Works of Sir Walter Scott, *1834.*

and attention is drawn to the waterfalls of upper Teesdale, it is the information Scott gives the reader concerning the locations he uses around Rokeby and the Greta that were to change the aspirations of tourists to Teesdale.

In the following extract Scott describes the gorge-like section of the Greta just above the confluence with the Tees; he may have been standing on Dairy Bridge, looking out from the 'prospect house' there, walking along the paths within Rokeby Park, or sitting in the 'cave' above the river where he worked on the poem for about a week (see plates 54-5 for locations in this chapter). The poet describes the foam caused by turbulence over the limestone layers, and he has obviously seen the Greta in spate or noticed the clues to the power of the river.

> Broad shadows o'er their passage fell,
> Deeper and narrower grew the dell;
> It seemed some mountain, rent and riven,
> A channel for the stream had given,
> So high the cliffs of limestone grey
> Hung beetling o'er the torrent's way,
> Yielding, along their rugged base,
> A flinty footpath's niggard space,
> Where he, who winds 'twixt rock and wave,
> May hear the headlong torrent rave,
> And like a stead in frantic fit,

That flings the froth from curb and bit,
May view her chafe her waves to spray,
O'er every rock that bars her way,
Till foam-globes on her eddies ride,
Thick as the schemes of human pride,
That down life's current drive amain,
As frail, as frothy, and as vain!

(Canto Second, VII)

In the note to this description, which extends for three stanzas, Scott gives the reader local detail. It is worth quoting the note at some length, as it not only demonstrates that he did copy 'truly what was before his eyes', but also illustrates how such notes helped locate the views the poet described:

> What follows is an attempt to describe the romantic glen, or rather ravine, through which the Greta finds a passage between Rokeby and Mortham … The river runs with very great rapidity over a bed of solid rock, broken by many shelving descents, down which the stream dashes with great noise and impetuosity … The banks partake of the same wild and romantic character, being chiefly lofty cliffs of limestone rock, whose grey colour contrasts admirably with the various trees and shrubs which find root among their crevices, as well as with the hue of the ivy, which clings around them in profusion, and hangs down from their projections in long sweeping tendrils … In one spot the dell, which is elsewhere very narrow, widens for a space to leave room for a dark grove of yew-trees, intermixed here and there with aged pines of uncommon size. Directly opposite to this sombre thicket, the cliffs on the other side of the Greta are tall, white, and fringed with all kinds of deciduous shrubs.

Morritt's 'Memorandum' of Scott's visit gives further insight not only into the part the poet played in locating the scenes used in the poem, but also his methods:

> I had, of course, had many previous opportunities of testing the almost conscientious fidelity of his local descriptions; but I could not help being singularly struck with the lights which this visit threw on that characteristic of his compositions. The morning after he arrived he said, 'You have often given me materials for romance – now I want a good robber's cave and an old church of the right sort.'

Scott was delighted with the sites which Morritt chose for him, the old slate quarries of Brignall and the ruined Abbey of Egglestone. Morritt observed Scott

> noting down even the peculiar little wild flowers and herbs that accidently grew round and on the side of a bold crag near his intended cave of Guy Denzil … I laughed … at his scrupulousness; but I understood him when he replied, "that in nature herself no two scenes were exactly alike, and that whoever copied truly what was before his eyes, would possess the same variety in his descriptions, and exhibit apparently an imagination as boundless as the range of nature in the scenes he recorded'.

**62**   *Eglistone. Engraved by J. Smith after H. Gastineau, for* Illustrations … to the Poetical Works of Sir Walter Scott, *1834.*

> 'Twas silence all – he laid him down,
> Where purple heath profusely strown,
> And throatwort with its azure bell,
> And moss and thyme his cushion swell.

(Canto Third, VIII)

In the note Scott gives details of one of the flowers: 'The *Campanula latifolia*, Grand Throatwort, or Canterbury bells, grows in profusion upon the beautiful banks of the river Greta, where it divides the manors of Brignal and Scargill, about three miles above Greta-Bridge.'

Other flowers are noted in Thorsgill, 'a beautiful little brook and dell' at Egglestone Abbey. Elsewhere viewpoints are described; here we have two views of the river Tees, from the castle and from Abbey Bridge:

> The view from Barnard Castle commands the rich and magnificent valley of Tees. Immediately adjacent to the river, the banks are very thickly wooded; at a little distance they are more open and cultivated; but being interspersed with hedge-rows, and with isolated trees of great size and age, they still retain the richness of woodland scenery. The river itself flows in a deep trench of solid rock, chiefly limestone and marble. The finest view of its romantic course is from a handsome modern bridge built over the Tees, by the late Mr Morritt of Rokeby.

Like John Sell Cotman some six years earlier, Morritt had obviously taken Scott to Towler Hill, 'commanding a superb view of the ruins' of Barnard Castle (see plate 96):

> Old Barnard's towers are purple still,
> To those that gaze from Toller-hill.

(Canto Fifth, I)

The poem included songs, which helped popularise both the poem and the area; in November 1812 Scott admitted to Morritt that he liked the songs, and hoped the owner of Rokeby would particularly appreciate that in praise of Brignall Banks:

> O Brignal banks are wild and fair,
>   And Greta woods are green,
> And you may gather garlands there,
>   Would grace a summer queen.

(Canto Third, XVI)

Rokeby was published on 10 January 1813 with this dedication:

TO

# JOHN B.S. MORRITT, Esq.

THIS POEM,

THE SCENE OF WHICH IS LAID IN HIS BEAUTIFUL DEMESNE

OF ROKEBY,

IS INSCRIBED,

IN TOKEN OF SINCERE FRIENDSHIP,

BY

WALTER SCOTT.

By the end of April 1813 Scott could report to his friend Lady Louisa Stuart that the poem had 'been wonderfully popular, about ten thousand copies having walked off already, in about three months, and the demand continuing faster than it can be supplied'.

Critical opinion was broadly favourable, with particularly positive reviews appearing in the *British Critic* and *Monthly Review*. The *British Critic*'s reviewer called it 'pure poetry' and predicted that 'the name of Scott will descend to the latest posterity with those of the most established poets'. There was particular praise for the vigour and variety of Scott's characterisations, though reservations were expressed regarding the coherence of the plot.

However, it was the poem's romantic scenery and Scott's meticulous description of its 'petty circumstances' which appealed to its readers; now a new type of 'discoverer' descended on Teesdale.

## 14

## *After Rokeby*

### *A Tour in Teesdale; including Rokeby, and its environs*

Four further editions of the poem *Rokeby* followed in 1813, the sixth in 1815. As Morritt had predicted, the 'cockney romancers, artists, illustrators, and sentimental tourists' soon beat a path to Barnard Castle and Greta Bridge, a copy of *Rokeby* in hand, to find the scenes described in the poem. The inclusion of a *Map of the Scenery of the Lady of the Lake* in the list of new editions of Scott's works given at the end of the first edition of *Rokeby* suggests the prevalence of this type of activity. The Lake poet Robert Southey (1774-1843) wrote to a friend in January 1813, 'Have you seen *Rokeby* yet? I enjoyed it the more from having so recently trod over the ground.'[1] Greta Bridge was an important staging post, so access to the sites was easy; in 1804 there were two inns at Greta Bridge but by 1834 a third had been built a few hundred yards to the south east.

In the way tourists today try to capture photographs of the scenes presented in a guide book, amateur artists in the early 19th century would sketch in front of the word-pictures of the tour book or, as in this case, the poem. Eight weeks after the publication of *Rokeby*, Scott had been given a present of 'two views very well done indeed by Miss Arden one of Mortham tower and one of the Tees and Greta in the park at Rokeby. They are really extremely clever very like the scenes they represent and require none of the allowance usually indulged to amateurs.'

References to *Rokeby* soon appeared in the guide books. Richard Garland was the first off the mark with a second edition of his *Tour in Teesdale*; to the title he now adds *including Rokeby, and its environs*, and makes references to the poem published earlier that year: 'to the lover of poetry, Rokeby, immortalized by the strains of Scott, will be for ever dear'. The correct spellings of Rokeby and Mortham Tower are now given on the map which accompanies the *Tour* (see plate 51), and 65 lines of *Rokeby* are quoted. As we have seen, Scott may have used the first edition of Garland's *Tour* in his research for *Rokeby*; it seems fitting that Garland in turn has attempted to give the second edition of his book more appeal by referring to the popular poem.

**63** *Cave on the Greta. Engraving by Thomas Macquoid, for his book* About Yorkshire, *1883.*

The section of the second canto of *Rokeby* describing 'the romantic ravine through which the Greta finds a passage' through Rokeby Park is quoted to illustrate Garland's observations: 'The grounds are well laid out, and afford many delightful walks: that called the Rock-walk, under a precipice by the bawling Greta, is particularly pleasant.'

When describing the situation of Barnard Castle and its fine view, Garland inserts the following extract from Rokeby into his earlier account:

> Where Tees, full many a fathom low,
> Wears with his rage no common foe;
> For pebbly bank, nor sand-bed here,
> Nor clay-mound checks his fierce career,
> Condemned to mine a channelled way,
> O'er solid sheets of marble grey.

> (Canto Second, II)

In his first edition Garland at Egglestone Abbey had described only the views of the Abbey. In 1813 he expands the mention of 'a rude bridge over a small rivulet' to include 12 lines from *Rokeby* describing Thorsgill, with Scott's 'petty circumstances' of this 'beautiful little brook and dell, running up behind the ruins of Eglistone Abbey':

> Yon tufted knoll, with daisies strown,
> Might make proud Oberon a throne,
> While, hidden in the thicket nigh,
> Puck should brood o'er his frolick sly;
> And where profuse the wood-veitch clings
> Round ash and elm in verdant rings,
> Its pale and azure-pencilled flower
> Should canopy Titania's bower.

> Here rise no cliffs the vale to shade,
> But, skirting every sunny glade,
> In fair variety of green
> The woodland lends its sylvan screen.

> (Canto Fourth, II & III)

**64**   *'Fairy Thorsgill'. Engraving by Thomas Macquoid, for his book* About Yorkshire, *1883.*

Garland's last use of lines from *Rokeby* is to embellish his walk up 'Romantic Deepdale's slender rill' to the west of Barnard Castle; here Scott refers to the Roslin glen he had made famous in his *Lay of the Last Minstrel*:

> Who in that dim-wood glen hath strayed,
> Yet longed for Roslin's magic glade?
> Who, wandering there, hath sought to change
> Even for that vale so stern and strange,
> Where Cartland's crags, fantastic rent,
> Through her green copse like spires are sent?

(Canto Second, III)

The publication of *Rokeby* revived John Sell Cotman's memories of his stay at Greta Bridge in 1805 (Chapter 12), and he seriously considered making a series of works for an illustrated edition of the poem. Having avoided making sketches of the localities such as Egglestone Abbey, Brignall church, or even Rokeby, he wrote to the Cholmeley girls asking if they had any suitable sketches. Anne had one of Dairy Bridge, but in a letter to her brother Francis in February 1813 Katherine feared Cotman's sketches 'would not be sufficiently local for the purpose of illustration'. Another artist, Thomas Stothard (1755-1854), produced illustrations for an edition of *Rokeby* published in 1813; apart from the title page, which included an untitled view of Barnard Castle, the engravings were of figures in a scene from each canto, with no local scenery depicted.

The Revd T.D. Whitaker's (1759-1821) *History of Richmondshire* was published in 12 parts from 1819 to 1823. To make the rather old-fashioned antiquarianism of the author more palatable to potential subscribers, Longmans the publishers proudly advertised in 1816 that 'superior artists will be engaged for subjects of landscape and architecture', naming J.M.W. Turner and J. Buckler as the artists. The publishers apparently appointed a committee to choose the viewpoints for Turner. Significantly, four of the 20 landscape engravings of the large area of Richmondshire were of subjects near Greta Bridge, two having 'Rokeby' in their titles.

Whitaker breaks off from his learned history to mention Walter Scott or to quote passages from the recently published *Rokeby*: 'the banks of the Greta have been made the scene of an highly spirited poem.' The parish of Rokeby,

> rich in natural scenery, adorned by modern elegance, distinguished by the site of a Roman station, and the remains of a religious house, but still more distinguished by a line of patriots and soldiers in its lords, has in later days been the retirement and the theme of great poets.

A footnote adds that these poets are Mason and Walter Scott. Whitaker's description of Rokeby Park is almost a commentary on the engraving after Turner, *Junction of the Greta and Tees at Rokeby*. In describing Dairy Bridge and its associated small building in Picturesque terms, Whitaker identifies the latter as a 'prospect-house' rather than the tea room of Arthur Young:

> A short walk from the house leads to a modern bridge over the Greta, and to an apartment placed on the brink of the rock … from which all the outrages of this dreadful torrent may be contemplated in perfect security, though it sometimes washes the foundations of the building above thirty feet perpendicular from the channel. When I saw it in tranquillity, a marble bed, over which a clear and lively mountain-stream hurried to the Teese, deep and abrupt crags to right and left, and aged overhanging woods, as various in their forms as their species, formed the character of the scene.

The church at nearby Brignall would perhaps not normally merit inclusion in a history of the area, yet Turner was commissioned to produce a watercolour of the church for engraving. In *Brignall Church* he shows that he is aware of the poem by including the 'dismal grove of sable yew' transposed from Scott's description of the 'romantic glen' of the Greta, and Whitaker quotes the song in praise of Brignall Banks. The engraving to illustrate Whitaker's discussion of Wycliffe was titled *Wycliffe, near Rokeby*, as if to borrow some publicity from the poem. In *Egglestone Abbey, near Barnard Castle* Turner includes the long line of cottages in which Whitaker presumes live the paper mill workers, the 'wide yawning east window' with, instead of tracery, perpendicular mullions, which Whitaker considers a 'singular deformity', as well as the 'beautiful little brook and dell' of Thorsgill. Thorsgill is also mentioned when Whitaker comes to discuss the Scandinavian place-names in Teesdale; here lines from *Rokeby* lighten the text:

> Where Tees in tumult leaves his source,
> Thundering o'er Caldron and High-Force;
> Beneath the shade the Northmen came,
> Fix'd on each vale a Runic name,
>
> …
>
> Remembered Thor's victorious fame,
> And gave the dell the thunderer's name.

(Canto Fourth, I)

Other engravings in the *History of Richmondshire* connected with the poem included Mortham after J. Buckler, the tomb from Egglestone Abbey (plate 16), and the Roman antiquities in the grounds of Rokeby (plate 10); even the engraving of the font in Brignall church may owe its inclusion to the interest in Brignall that the poem had generated.

*The Gentleman's Magazine* of 1826 listed Rokeby in the 'Eminences and Views' of the North Riding of Yorkshire: 'Rokeby is the scene of Sir Walter Scott's poem, the junction of the Greta and Tees here is truly picturesque.' As we have seen, the Darlington artist William Bewick recorded a group of Friends having a picnic at Rokeby in a watercolour sketch in 1825 (see plate 44).

We have seen from his sketchbook that John Glover had discovered the Greta before *Rokeby* was published; after 1813 we find Greta subjects in other sketchbooks that have survived. Henry Cave (1779-1836) was the son of a York engraver whose bound book of sketches of 1826 includes Dairy Bridge and 'Mortham Tower near Rokeby', as well as tree studies along the Greta. David Cox's Northern Sketch Book of 1837 includes the Greta, Greta Bridge and Egglestone Abbey.

Another source of information is the lists of works shown at the annual exhibitions of the painting societies. After 1813, paintings exhibited at the Old Water Colour Society started to include the names of Rokeby or the Greta. In 1814 there were *Six Views to Illustrate the Poem of Rokeby* by Copley Fielding, Henry Gastineau in 1824 showed *Rokeby*, and in 1825 George Fennel Robson exhibited *Rokeby*.

However, it was by engraved views that the scenery of this area of Teesdale was brought to the attention of a wider audience. In 1828 the fourth edition of *A Tour in Teesdale* was illustrated with eight rather crude woodcuts after Joseph Miller; Mortham Tower was the only scene connected with *Rokeby*. This volume would perhaps reach only a regional market, but six years later Charles Tilt published *Illustrations; Landscape, Historical, and Antiquarian, to the Poetical Works of Sir Walter Scott, Bart.* Six steel engravings illustrate *Rokeby*; each is accompanied by the lines from the poem that it represents. As well as a portrait of *Matilda*, the fictitious *Rokeby Castle* and the *Tomb of Rokeby*, there are three scenes from the poem: *Glen of the Greta* after George Balmer, *Eglistone* after Henry Gastineau and *Barnard Castle* after Copley Fielding (plates 58-62).

In 1813 songs, ballads and glees based on the ten songs in *Rokeby* and written by John Clarke-Whitfield appeared, some with an accompaniment for harp as well as piano, to reflect the circumstances of the poem; these songs included *Brignal*

**65**  *Mortham Tower, Rokeby. Engraved by R. Branston after J. Buckler for* An History of Richmondshire, *1823.*

*Banks, Edmund's Song* and *Matilda's Song.*[2] Another nine writers brought out in the following two years a whole flurry of songs with the same or similar titles; this wealth of music would have helped promote the poem and swell the number of 'sentimental tourists' to the area on which it was based. As well as a continuing list of published songs, illustrations of *Rokeby* scenes with accompanying quotations from the poem continued to appear in guide books throughout the 19th century; the name of Sir Walter Scott is still used today to promote Teesdale.

Turner made in 1822 a set of highly finished watercolours for his patron and friend Walter Fawkes. Designed to illustrate poems by Byron, Moore and Scott, five of the six watercolours illustrate specific lines from the chosen poems. For *Rokeby* Turner inscribes on two rocks in the bed of the Greta the lines from the second canto describing the 'romantic glen' so admired by Scott; he does not neglect to include a 'sable yew' and the narrow 'flinty footpath'.

We now consider Turner's sketching tours to Teesdale in more detail.

## 15

## *J.M.W. Turner*

*'the passage out of Teesdale leaves everything far behind for*
*difficulty–bogged most compleatly Horse and its Rider'*

Britain's greatest landscape artist, Joseph Mallord William Turner (1775-1851), made four sketching tours to Teesdale between 1797 and 1831. The area became the source of some of his most inspired and expressive watercolours; many of these reached a wide audience through being engraved, and helped to promote Teesdale as a tourist attraction.

Basing his journey north on a commission from Edward Lascelles (1764-1814, the eldest son of Lord Harewood) to produce watercolours of Harewood House near Leeds, the 22-year-old Turner spent the summer of 1797 covering over 1,000 miles on a sketching tour through the north of England. In Yorkshire he largely concentrated on antiquarian views, and within Teesdale he sketched the ruins of Egglestone Abbey and Barnard Castle.[1] Turner may well have received advice on his tour from Thomas Hearne, who had painted in Teesdale some years previously. For his two sketches in Barnard Castle, he chose almost identical viewpoints to those used by Hearne.

As we have seen, Turner was back in Teesdale in 1816, sketching for the Revd T.D. Whitaker's *History of Richmondshire* project to be published by Longman. As well as the subjects near Greta Bridge largely related to Scott's *Rokeby*, Turner sketched at Barnard Castle and then along Teesdale as far as Cauldron Snout; he stayed at inns at Greta Bridge, Barnard Castle and Middleton-in-Teesdale. 1816 was 'the year with no summer' due to the volcanic explosion the previous year at Tambora in Indonesia. In letters to a friend, Turner described the weather as 'miserably wet' and later reported that his tour earlier that summer was 'a most confounded fagg, tho on horseback'; he was 'bogged most compleatly' on the ride out of Teesdale towards Appleby and the Lakes. The art critic John Ruskin (1819-1900) proclaimed, that of all Turner's watercolours, 'those of the Yorkshire series have the most heart in them, the most unwearied, serious, finishing of truth'. Ruskin saw these Yorkshire watercolours as 'indicating one of the culminating points in Turner's career'.[2]

We know from a letter to his friend James Holworthy that in October the following year Turner was in Teesdale again; he had received a commission from the Earl of Darlington (1766-1822) for an oil painting of Raby Castle, and then for a

**66** *High Force or Fall of Tees. Engraved by J. Landseer after J.M.W. Turner, 1822.*

watercolour for an engraving in Robert Surtees' *The History and Antiquities of the County Palatine of Durham*. In the first volume of his *History*, Surtees explained that the subscription raised to provide illustrations should not cover 'the Castles or other residences of Gentlemen'. Turner's last visit to Teesdale was in 1830 while on his way to Scotland to illustrate an edition of Sir Walter Scott's poems; he revisited Barnard Castle, Egglestone Abbey and the Greta.

In discussing the watercolours and engravings which resulted from these four sketching tours, we should bear in mind the remarks of Margaret Hunt, the daughter of Dr Raine of Crook Hall, Durham, who on behalf of Longman had chosen the Teesdale views for Whitaker's *History of Richmondshire*. In *Richmondshire Illustrated by Twenty Line Engravings after Drawings by J.M.W. Turner, R.A. with Descriptions by Mrs Alfred Hunt* in 1891, she commented on the way in which landscape was viewed in the early 19th century: 'it was almost the whole duty of all hill scenery to inspire alarm, and every painter ... who wished to give a good impression of any particular place always painted it ... as if it were twice its real size'. This 'impression' was achieved by exaggerating hill slopes, by compressing the width of a scene, or diminishing the size of animals or people to dramatise nature. However, we must also remember that these watercolours were prepared for purposes of engraving to a certain size in order to fit the relevant book; compression of the width of a scene was inevitable.

There are many records of Turner's interest and involvement in the engraving process. The engravers would send proofs to the artist who would annotate them to show the changes he required so that they would faithfully render the subtleties of texture and shading in the watercolours; figures and animals added interest for the viewer, who would often be using a magnifying glass.

**67**  *Eggleston Abbey.*
*Engraved by T. Higham*
*after J.M.W. Turner,*
*1822.*

Whitaker's *History of Richmondshire* contained five engravings of Teesdale scenes. *High Force or Fall of Tees*, engraved by J. Landseer, was based on two of the seven sketches made at the site; these were done at the edge of the plunge pool at the foot of the fall, a viewpoint first described by Thomas Amory. As well as the columns of Whin Sill above the horizontal layers of limestone, Turner records the rainbow in the spray from the main fall, a feature found in the descriptions from Arthur Young onwards, and an artist sitting sketching on a slab of fallen rock. The artist does not appear in the engraving, but Turner adds two anglers; these echo figures in *The High Force* after Thomas Smith (see plate 30); however, Turner was a keen angler himself and would have noticed, as did John Byng 24 years earlier, that 'here the salmon must stop'. Byng thought that the waterfall would be 'yet more wonderful after heavy rains'; Turner sketched in the 'miserably wet' 1816 and clearly shows the double fall.

Byng disliked the noisy mill at Egglestone Abbey, but Turner was perhaps professionally interested in the paper mill. *Egglestone Abbey, near Barnard Castle*, engraved by T. Higham, is based largely on a rain-stained sketch from 1816 with details from one of 1797, both from the viewpoint on the Durham side of the river commended by Richard Garland in 1803. In the sketches Turner notes the rather dilapidated old mill with two millstones, together with the east window and south transept of the abbey. A wealth of detail is added to the watercolour for engraving: Henry Cooke, the paper mill owner, is fishing in the Tees, while his wife Hannah is drying the felts used in the paper-making process, and builders with their horse and scaffolding are also at work. The fact that the eastern range of the abbey had been converted into a mansion in the 16th century is emphasised by the girl feeding poultry while cows rest under the trees or drink in the river; another girl carries a pail on her head as she crosses the small packhorse bridge built by the Canons over Thorsgill. For this last detail Turner relies on another sketch from 1816, from the Yorkshire side of the Tees and including Abbey Bridge.

**68** *Junction of the Tees and Greta. Etched by S. Middiman and J. Pye, engraved by J. Pye after J.M.W. Turner, 1819.*

The conditions in 1816 seem to have limited Turner's usually meticulous sketching for *Junction of the Greta and Tees at Rokeby,* engraved by J. Pye. Working in the rain, he made five quick sketches of the banks of the Greta at Rokeby and of Mortham Tower. Even in the study in his large sketchbook there are only a few quick notes of the channels of the rocky Greta and the Tees, with the trees and rocks merely suggested. In the watercolour the huge boulders brought down by the flooding Greta, and first described by Thomas Pennant in 1773, as well as the prospect-house at Dairy Bridge, were added largely from memory. By 1891 Margaret Hunt noted that the three large elms in front of Rokeby Hall, conveniently concealing the lack of detail in the house, had grown considerably since 1816; now only their stumps remain. In describing the nearby inn Mrs Hunt also hints at the importance of Scott's *Rokeby* in the choice of subjects, by her father, for this commission:

> It is the inn which, as soon as Rokeby woods begin to be clad in green, and Brignall banks to be starred with primroses, is always filled with visitors who year after year find themselves drawn there, almost in spite of themselves, by the fascination exercised by the spot.

From the inn Turner followed the Greta upstream to record the secluded *Brignall Church* in six sketches (map, plate 55). As the watercolour was lost in a fire, the engraving by S. Rawle is all that remains of what Ruskin termed 'the perfect image of the painter's mind at this period'. Turner again brings his individual touch to the commissioned scene; as well as adding a yew tree from *Rokeby,* he exaggerates the depth of the valley, minimises the size of the church, and sets the whole scene at twilight. Ruskin writes:

> the Greta glances brightly in the valley … every leaf of the woods is still in the delicate air; a boy's kite, incapable of rising, has become entangled in their branches … the lonely church is seen in its secluded field between the rocks and the stream; and around it the low churchyard wall, and a few white stones which mark the resting-places of those who can climb the rocks no more, nor hear the river sing as it passes.[3]

**69** *Brignall Church. Engraved by S. Rawle after J.M.W. Turner, 1822.*

**70** *Wycliffe near Rokeby. Engraved by J. Pye after J.M.W. Turner, 1823.*

The engraving of *Wycliffe, near Rokeby*, more than any other in the Richmondshire series, shows how Turner portrayed not just the topographical details of a place, but incorporated the whole gamut of associations that place had for him. In 1823 he is said to have added rays of light above Wycliffe Hall at the engraving stage. The artist apparently explained to Pye 'that is the place where Wickliffe was born and the light of the glorious Reformation'; he also confirmed the meaning of the addition of the geese and girls to the watercolour, 'Oh, they are the old superstitions which the genius of the Reformation is driving away!' Only a few proofs of the engraving with an additional inscription referring to John Wycliffe (1324-84) were printed, but they proved Turner's intention to create an allegory of English religious and political liberty.

In 1817, for the important commissions at Raby, Turner used 27 pages in his large *Raby* sketchbook and 15 in his pocket-book. The oil painting *Raby Castle, the*

**71** *Raby Castle. Engraved 1820 by S. Rawle after J.M.W. Turner for* The History and Antiquities of … Durham.

*Seat of the Earl of Darlington* (now in The Walters Art Gallery, Baltimore) is based on a double-page panorama in the *Raby* sketchbook, with a fox hunt crossing in front of the castle. The basis of the engraving for Robert Surtees' *History* is a detailed sketch of the castle, plus another showing the main groupings of huntsmen, dogs and stags in relation to an outline of the castle. The pocket-book has studies of the individual markings of some of the hounds, along with their names, and some of these can be related directly to the engraving. On one page Turner appears to have ticked the sketch of a particular huntsman he intends to use in his watercolour.

The print-publisher Charles Heath said in 1825 he had 'just begun a most splendid work from Turner the Academician. He is making me 120 Drawings of England and Wales – I have just got four and they are the finest things I ever saw.' Each watercolour would cost Heath 30 guineas, but he already had collectors willing to give him 50 guineas after the watercolours had been engraved. Obviously Turner could have obtained more by selling directly to collectors, but was willing to accept less as he wished his images to be more widely known through the engraving project. Closely supervised by Turner, the engravers reached new heights of interpretation. The main process used was the more delicate one of etching the copper plate with acid rather than line engraving with a tool called a burin. Eventually only 96 watercolours were engraved for Heath's *Picturesque Views in England and Wales*, brought out in 24 parts. The artist worked up watercolours of three Teesdale sites for the series. The project has long been considered one of the greatest series of prints made from Turner's watercolours.

**72** *Fall of the Tees, Yorkshire. Engraved by E. Goodall after J.M.W. Turner for* Picturesque Views in England and Wales, *1827.*

For the composition of his watercolour of *Barnard Castle* (now in the Yale Center for British Art, Paul Mellon Center) made for *Picturesque Views*, Turner used three sketches made in the rain on his 1816 tour, when he had included something of the Yorkshire side of the river. However, for details such as the building on the bridge (demolished by 1823) and the various towers of the castle, the artist depended on his very careful 1797 sketches made in better conditions. Turner manufactures a high viewpoint, with the castle and bridge silhouetted against the bright sky; sun streams through the castle's 15th-century oriel window and a woodsman works in high foreground trees above two anglers.

*Fall of the Tees, Yorkshire* was engraved in 1827 by E. Goodall also for *Picturesque Views*. Turner used a sketch from his 1816 tour, showing that he had crossed over the river above High Force and found a more distant viewpoint on the Yorkshire side of the Tees which set the fall into the context of its gorge of recession in the foreground, and its catchment area of the moors of upper Teesdale beyond; the viewpoint is still very popular today. In two sketches from 1816 Turner shows another artist – at the top and bottom of the falls; he includes this artist in his watercolour of High Force. Ruskin would later admire the portrayal of the 'concentric zones and delicate curves of the falling water itself'.[4]

In 1836 Turner had the opportunity to use the hard-won sketches of Cauldron Snout, made twenty years earlier, for *Chain Bridge over the River Tees* engraved by W.R. Smith for the last part of *Picturesque Views*. As well as using more than one viewpoint to encompass the staircase of falls between the columns of Whin Sill, Turner had carefully sketched the planked bridge which local writers had proclaimed as a 'sublime' viewpoint. Turner transformed Cauldron Snout into an almost Alpine scene; the Tees descends an apparently bottomless chasm, with exaggeratedly steeper slopes than exist in reality. In the watercolour there is no evidence of the columnar rocks, nor of the pool at the foot of the falls; the planked bridge is replaced by a

**73** *Chain Bridge over the River Tees. Engraved by W.R. Smith after J.M.W. Turner for* Picturesque Views in England and Wales, *1838.*

chain suspension bridge, sketched at Wynch Bridge in 1816 and emphasised by the title *Chain Bridge Over the Tees*. John Ruskin noted how 'the wind takes the spray up off the edges, and carries it back in little torn, reverted rags and threads'.[5]

Sir Walter Scott's publisher Robert Cadell was determined to commission Turner to illustrate new editions of the author's *Poetical Works* (1833-4). Cadell told Scott, 'there is about Mr Turner's pencil ... that which renders familiar scenes more striking and lovely than before'. He could sell 8,000 copies with Turner's illustrations as against 3,000 without; and sets of the engravings would be separately printed from the steel plates for collectors. Scott was easily persuaded, as he was impressed with the 1830 illustrated edition of *Italy* that Samuel Rogers (1763-1855) had sent him, for which Turner had supplied 25 vignette illustrations. The harder steel was a more suitable material than copper for printing book illustrations as very fine lines could be engraved and large editions printed without loss of quality. As well as providing new challenges for the engravers, producing detailed watercolours for book illustrations meant a new approach for the artist. Turner must have been aware that the lack of information in his studies of Rokeby made in 1816 would not suffice for the smaller but more delicate landscape of the *Junction of the Greta and Tees* with which to illustrate the poem *Rokeby*:

> And when he issued from the wood,
> Before the gate of Mortham stood.
> 'Twas a fair scene! the sunbeam lay
> On battled tower and portal grey,
> And from the grassy slope he sees
> The Greta flow to meet the Tees

(Canto Second, XVI)

On his way to Scotland in 1831, Turner broke his journey to visit Teesdale for the last time. The site at Rokeby posed the same difficulties as 15 years earlier; Turner had to

74  *Junction of the Greta and the Tees. Engraved by J. Pye after J.M.W. Turner, for Sir Walter Scott's* Poetical Works, *1833-4.*

manufacture a panoramic sketch stretching from Mortham Tower through the Greta to the Tees. A detailed study of the buildings at Mortham was also required to match the lines from the poem; but sketches of the prospect house at Dairy Bridge and of Rokeby Hall itself do not find their way into the finished composition. For the vignette of the castle keep at Bowes, Turner relied on sketches made in 1816:

> Distant and high, the tower of Bowes
> Like steel upon the anvil glows.

> (Canto Fifth, I)

When on his sketching tours Turner did not restrict himself to the commissioned views. In 1816 he went to Towler Hill to the west for the well-known view of Barnard Castle, and sketched at Cotherstone and Middleton-in-Teesdale on the way to High Force; in 1831 he revisited Egglestone Abbey and at Barnard Castle found some different viewpoints. By now the sketches were much more economical, though at Barnard Castle details such as the oriel window in the Great Chamber and buttresses of the Great Hall are depicted, and the bridge has lost its chapel.

It was through his prints, combining his sketching and painting skills with his careful supervision of the engraving process, that Turner became so widely known during his lifetime. The Director of the Berlin Museum, visiting the Royal Academy Exhibition in 1835, sought out 'the landscapes of the favourite painter, Turner, who is known throughout Europe by his numerous, often very clever, compositions for annuals and other books, where they appear in beautiful steel engravings'. The 11 scenes in Teesdale, engraved between 1819 and 1834 from Turner's sketches and watercolours, helped to make the scenery of the dale more widely known.

## 16

## The Lake Poets and Charles Dickens

*'went by Greta Bridge, seeing Rokeby of course'*

Walter Scott was not the only writer to find source material in Teesdale; he was preceded by William Wordsworth, and followed by Charles Dickens.

William Wordsworth (1770-1850) produced a guide book to the Lake District in various forms from 1810. The fifth version was published as *A Guide through the District of the Lakes* in 1835. This was republished three times in Wordsworth's lifetime, and then another three times by 1864. It is with the 'Directions and Information for the tourist' that we are concerned, for Wordsworth starts by supplying the tourist with directions to 'certain interesting spots which may be confidently recommended to his notice, if time can be spared before entering upon the Lake District' from the south.

Wordsworth could confidently recommend certain spots in Teesdale as a result of his own journeys; we know of some of these through those family letters which have survived. The Bristol bookseller Joseph Cottle (1770-1853) had published in September 1798 *Lyrical Ballads*, a collection of poems by William Wordsworth and Samuel Taylor Coleridge (1772-1834), including *The Rime of the Ancient Mariner*, largely written during the previous year while the two poets were living in Somerset. In late October 1799 Wordsworth and Coleridge were returning with Cottle from the Hutchinson's farm at Sockburn near Darlington (see plate 19) where they had discussed the next enlarged edition of *Lyrical Ballads*. (Mary Hutchinson would marry Wordsworth in 1802.) The two poets were on foot, but Cottle was on horseback, his legs 'hugely muffled up' because of his rheumatism.

Having stayed overnight at Piercebridge, Wordsworth, Coleridge and Cottle explored the area around Greta Bridge before making for Barnard Castle. In his notebook Coleridge describes Egglestone Abbey as a grey ruin on a slope, the river Tees 'in wild turns' below it. On Abbey Bridge, built like a castle wall with battlements, Colcridge is struck by the sound of the river 'pouring itself down thro' a steep bed of rocks' with a wall of woods on each side. There are vistas of the church tower and houses of Barnard Castle, and of Rokeby, 'a handsome Gentleman's house', where Coleridge refers to J.B.S. Morritt's interest in Troy. He registers the 'shootings of water' and the white eddies of the Greta just before its junction with the Tees and also mentions the floods – especially those of 1771, which have 'flashed' over Greta

Bridge – and Brignall church. The three friends spent the night at Barnard Castle; at nearby Greta Bridge the following day Cottle took the coach to London to meet publishers, and the two poets took 'the Mail over Stainmore, the road interesting with sun and mist' on their way to a tour of the Lakes.

The following year Wordsworth records being at Greta Bridge with his brother John, and in 1802 he writes to Coleridge with a copy of *The Glow Worm*, which he had written while travelling between Raby and Staindrop. Wordsworth recalled their stay in Barnard Castle in 1799, but had mistaken the inn at which they stayed.

These, and other, journeys resulted in the following 'directions' in *A Guide through the District of the Lakes*; Rokeby, Barnard Castle and High Force are suggested as worthy of breaking one's journey:

**75**  *Inn at Greta Bridge. Engraving for* About England with Dickens, *1883. This inn, on the southern side of the bridge, was the original* Morritt Arms; *its name and licence were passed to the* George Inn *on the other side of the bridge, c.1845.*

There are three approaches to the Lakes through Yorkshire: the least adviseable is the great north road by Catterick and Greta Bridge, and onwards to Penrith. The Traveller, however, taking this route, might halt at Greta Bridge, and be well recompenced if he can afford to give an hour or two to the banks of the Greta, and of the Tees, at Rokeby. Barnard Castle, also, about two miles up the Tees, is a striking object, and the main North Road might be rejoined at Bowes. Every one has heard of the great fall of the Tees above Middleham [i.e. Middleton-in-Teesdale], interesting for its grandeur, as the avenue of rocks that leads to it, is to the geologist. But this place lies so far out of the way as scarcely to be within the compass of our notice. It might, however, be visited by a Traveller on foot, or on horseback, who could rejoin the main road upon Stanemoor.

In a letter of 1833 William Wordsworth's daughter Dora suggests that Rokeby was a popular stop on the journey to see the Hutchinsons, then living in Stockton on Tees. Dora and her aunt Dorothy (Wordsworth's sister) had driven themselves in their little open carriage to Stockton, by way of Ullswater, Appleby, Greta Bridge, 'seeing Rokeby of course', and had returned by Richmond (see map, plate 1).

The castles of Raby and Barnard Castle found a place in Wordsworth's poem *The White Doe of Rylstone*, the plot of which revolved around the Rising of the North. In

1569 the Nevills of Durham and the Percys of Northumberland plotted to overthrow Elizabeth I and reinstate Roman Catholicism. The rising was planned at meetings in Brancepeth and Raby Castle:

> Now was the North in arms: – they shine
> In warlike trim from Tweed to Tyne,
> At Percy's voice: and Neville sees
> His Followers gathering in from Tees,
> From Were, and all the little rills
> Concealed among the forked hills –
> Seven hundred Knights, Retainers all
> Of Neville, at their Master's call
> Had sate together in Raby Hall!

Published in 1815, extracts from the poem appeared in guide books such as *The Darlington Half Holiday Guide* in 1882. Its author William Cudworth quotes the last three lines of the above extract to give authority or added interest to his description of Raby castle and its 'Baron's Hall, a noble hall, truly baronial, and worthy of the head of the great Neville house'. The rebels captured Durham and marched south to Tutbury near Nottingham where Mary Queen of Scots was imprisoned. George Bowes, a steward of Elizabeth, defended his castle at Barnard Castle against the rebels but was defeated.

> 'Tis night: in silence looking down,
> The Moon, from cloudless ether, sees
> A Camp, and a beleaguered Town,
> And Castle, like a stately crown
> On the steep rocks of winding Tees.

Another Lakes poet, Robert Southey, visited Teesdale. Southey met Coleridge in 1794 and the two became close friends; the following year they married sisters Edith and Sarah Fricker. Southey became Poet Laureate in 1813 when Walter Scott declined the post in his favour. In a letter of July 1812 to his wife, Southey tells how he and his brother Tom looked at Raby and Barnard Castle before visiting Rokeby. They met Mr and Mrs Morritt walking beside the Greta, and were invited to dine and sleep at Rokeby. Southey found the grounds 'the finest things of the kind I have ever seen'. As well as describing how another poet, William Mason, had decorated the summer house at Dairy Bridge, J.B.S. Morritt had related the damage done by the river Greta in 1771. The river 'rose in the most extraordinary manner during what is still called the great flood' and piled up an immense dam of trees and rubbish against Dairy Bridge. A huge stone knocked down Greta Bridge, removed this dam of material, 'carried off' Dairy Bridge, and broke into three or four pieces when it came to rest on the river bank above the junction with the river Tees. Southey tells his wife that Playfair (1748-1819, mathematician and geologist) a few days previously had estimated the weight of the stone at about 78 tons, 'the most wonderful instance, he said, he had ever heard of the power of water'. A tree had broken the window of the room beneath the summer house, and the couple living there had to be rescued. Southey remarked on the needlework pictures of Anne Morritt, and one of the oil paintings showing Sir Thomas Robinson's proposals for the grounds of Rokeby.

He does not tell his wife of his visit to the head of Teesdale, but in November 1812 Walter Scott wrote to Southey: 'I heard at Rokeby of your pilgrimage to the head of the Tees, which seems to have been as desperate a job as my old acquaintance Bruce's to the head of the Nile.' Southey confirms this expedition in a letter to Scott in the following January, three days after the publication of *Rokeby*:

> I did not go to bed till I had read the poem through ... I enjoyed your poem the more, being for the first time able to follow you in its scenery ... The glen is, for its extent, more beautiful than anything I have seen in England. If I had known your subject, I could have helped you to some Teesiana for your description – the result of the hardest day's march I ever yet made. For we traced the stream from its spring-head, on the summit of Cross-Fell, about a mile from the source of the Tyne, all the way to Highforce.

Charles Dickens (1812-70), like Sir Walter Scott, is closely associated with the area around Greta Bridge and Barnard Castle, which he visited in 1838. *The Life & Adventures of Nicholas Nickleby* first appeared in monthly parts before being published in book form in 1839; from then until today this novel has spawned not only a wealth of comment but also a steady stream of visitors to the area. In the Preface Dickens states that he was always curious about the Yorkshire schools which were run by 'the lowest and most rotten' of schoolmasters, and that when at last he had an audience was resolved to write about them. There is little doubt that the famous advertisement for Dotheboys Hall in *Nicholas Nickleby* was a little altered version of actual advertisements which were to be found in regional newspapers in various parts of England:

> EDUCATION. – At Mr Wackford Squeers's Academy, Dotheboys Hall, at the delightful village of Dotheboys, near Greta Bridge in Yorkshire, Youth are boarded, clothed, booked, furnished with pocket-money, provided with all necessaries, instructed in all languages living and dead, mathematics, orthography, geometry, astronomy, trigonometry, the use of the globes, algebra, single stick (if required), writing, arithmetic, fortification, and every other branch of classical literature. Terms, twenty guineas per annum. No extras, no vacations, and diet unparalleled.

On the whole the 'Yorkshire schools' were utterly bad, being 'hot-beds of oppression, extortion, and neglect' as J.S. Fletcher put it in 1908 in *A Book About Yorkshire*.

What is in doubt is the identity of Dotheboys Hall and of its headmaster Mr Squeers. Despite Dickens declaring that 'Mr Squeers is the representative of a class, and not of an individual', William Shaw of Bowes Academy was almost immediately identified as Wackford Squeers, not only because they shared the same initials. In 1821 an outbreak of what may have either been trachoma or 'pink-eye' occurred in the village of Bowes and in the Bowes Academy School; despite getting medical help from London, William Shaw (1782-1850) was left with a scale covering one eye and three schoolboys went blind. Dickens in his private diary had noted under

**76**   *Dotheboys Hall. Engraving for* About England with Dickens, *1883.*

2 February 1838, that 'Shaw, the schoolmaster we saw to-day, is the man in whose school several boys went blind some time since from gross neglect. The case was tried, and the verdict went against him … Look this out in the newspapers.'[1] The case had come to court in 1823, when the practice of many boys sharing two towels was examined; this practice would later be described in *Nicholas Nickleby*. Despite the court case, the school had apparently continued to flourish.

After the publication of *Nicholas Nickleby* there were conflicting points of view which school Dotheboys Hall was based on. The *Glasgow Weekly* in 1886 serialised *Life of an Actor*, the autobiography of Horatio Lloyd; he recalled the year he had spent at Bowes Academy as a schoolboy:

> the headmaster … was a most worthy and kind-hearted, if somewhat peculiar, gentleman named William Shaw … I can see him now as plainly as I did then, and can testify to the truth of the outward presentment of the man as described by Dickens … a sharp, thin, upright little man, with a slight scale covering the pupil of one of the eyes …

Lloyd went on to say that the school itself was kept scrupulously clean, with 12 female servants; the food was excellent, and the boys were clothed as well as boarded and educated, all for £20 a year. Mr Shaw was kind and would play the flute to amuse an ill boy lying in bed.

Lloyd did recall another school, as bad as that described by Dickens:

> There, indeed, you might have found many a Smike. Boys in rags, half starved, and otherwise cruelly used, and taught scarcely anything, except haymaking, carting

manure, and kindred departments of industry. They were continually running away and almost as regularly caught, brought back, and frightfully punished. Schools like this there were in Yorkshire which deserved all the exposure they got.

William Cudworth in *The Darlington Half Holiday Guide* (1899) states that the Bowes Academy was rather a superior school; there were three other schools in Bowes, and Dickens had intended to caricature Bowes Hall, at the foot of the village. However, Dickens used William Shaw, his initials and his physical peculiarities as a model for Wackford Squeers; in this way the Bowes Academy became associated with Dotheboys Hall. So great was the effect of the novel that of the 800 boys in the four schools in Bowes when its serialisation started only 20 were left when it was completed.

In the novel, Nickleby and Squeers and the new schoolboys brought from London were put down at 'the *George and New Inn* at Greta Bridge' at 6 o'clock at night. There has been some

77　*Yard and Pump at Dotheboys. Engraving for* About England with Dickens, *1883.*

debate as to which inn at Greta Bridge Dickens and his illustrator 'Phiz' or Hablot Knight Browne stayed at and then used in the novel. From 1785 a mail coach ran on the Great North Road from London to Glasgow by way of Greta Bridge, Bowes and Carlisle, changing horses every 15 miles or so. A directory of 1822 states that there were two handsome inns at Greta Bridge (see map, plate 55), the older *George Inn* on the north side of the bridge, and the *Morritt Arms* on the south, both posting-houses. By 1838 the *George* had ceased to exist as a licensed house, and a farmstead called Thorpe Grange less than half a mile to the south east had been converted into the *New Inn*. George Martin, the tenant of the *Morritt Arms*, became landlord of this new inn in 1826, and the Glasgow mail coach was transferred from the old *George Inn*; the mail went north at 2.20 a.m. and south at 3 p.m. It was at this *New Inn* or the *George and New Inn* that Dickens and Browne stayed on 31 January 1838; this is perhaps corroborated by another characteristic of Dickens, as in the novel he refers to the landlord as Swallow, a play on Martin's name.

In a letter dated 1 February 1838 Dickens describes his journey to Greta Bridge, giving further clues as to the inn's location, well away from the bridge itself:

> As we came further north the snow grew deeper. About eight o'clock it began to fall heavily, and, as we crossed the wild heaths hereabouts, there was no vestiges of a track. The mail kept on well, however, and at eleven we reached a bare place with a house, standing alone in the midst of a dreary moor, which the guard informed us was Greta Bridge.[2]

Dickens and Browne stayed that night at the *New Inn* in a comfortable room.

The next day, after a huge breakfast, they went on to Barnard Castle and put up at the *King's Head Inn* (see plate 90), staying two days. It was probably here that Dickens met a solicitor, perhaps John Barnes, to whom he had a letter of introduction from a solicitor in practice with a school friend of his. John Barnes may have served as the original of John Browdie in the novel, Dickens again using the same initials for his character. It is at the *King's Head* that he is also likely to have met Thomas Humphrey, a clock maker in Barnard Castle whose name appeared in the title of the novel *Master Humphrey's Clock*. There is no evidence to support the belief that Dickens persuaded Humphrey to go on one of his clock repairing journeys to Bowes and to take the novelist with him, posing as the clockmaker's assistant so as to gain admittance to one of the schools.[3]

Dickens and Browne probably saw the few schools at Startforth before making for Bowes. As we have seen, the novelist and illustrator saw William Shaw, but either they did not see inside Shaw's school, or Dickens used another as the basis for Dotheboys Hall. In a letter the novelist recalled stumbling over a gravestone in the churchyard at Bowes; an eighteen year old boy had died suddenly: 'I suppose his heart broke … he died at that wretched place. I think his ghost put Smike into my head upon the spot.' On 2 February 1838 Dickens lunched at the *George* (called the *Unicorn* since about 1840) in Bowes; the next night was spent in York on the way back to London.

As a newspaper article of 1924 put it, 'to trace the footsteps and literary wanderings of the author of *Nicholas Nickleby*, whose magic pen has filled our homes with so many friends, becomes an irresistible quest.' This quest would be followed by guide book writers through the 19th century and beyond.

## 17

## *Walter White*

*'You are here shut out from the world amid scenes of savage beauty'*

By 1840 William Howitt in *Visits to Remarkable Places* could describe how improved roads and the development of the railways had enabled a wider audience to participate in a form of the Picturesque Tour. Some of the middle classes were able to take a summer tour in one of the wilder parts of the country, drawn by the widening 'love of poetry and nature, of picturesque scenery and summer-wandering.' One of the century's greatest walkers, Walter White (1811-93), an attendant or librarian at the Royal Society, had already written walking tours of the Tyrol and southern England when in 1858 he paid 6s. 6d. to travel for 26 hours in the cabin of the ship *Vivid* from London to Hull; in *A Month in Yorkshire* he describes the 375 miles of his rambles in the county. In the fifth edition of his book (1879) White explains the growing trend to get away from the city; rather like John Byng 87 years earlier, the earnest explorer escapes from the 'laborious hum and restless movement' to 'remote valleys and far-away hills'. It was in Yorkshire that White first undertook long walking holidays, and he returns to the county in 1858, again drawn by 'the remote dales where crowding hills abound with the picturesque'. Using the railways to travel between areas of interest within Yorkshire, White usually walks 14 to 18 miles a day, quoting poetry (48 lines from *Rokeby* alone) and demonstrating his love of nature.

Having viewed the mouth of the river Tees from Roseberry Topping, Walter White takes the train from Stockton to Darlington (see plate 1) on his way to trace the river to its source 'through many scenes of romantic beauty'. The next morning he catches an early train to Barnard Castle, the line having been opened in 1856. There is so much to see, 'scenes made classic by the pen of Scott', that he delays his journey further up the dale until evening and spends the day in Barnard Castle; his account of the history of the castle is mingled with a description of the view from the tower. Scott's lines from the second canto of *Rokeby* listing the tributaries of the Tees are quoted before White walks to Rokeby

> And Greta, to whose banks ere long
> We lead the lovers of the song.

**78**  *Rokeby, from Abbey Bridge. A Rock & Co. engraving for* Views & Scenery of Barnard Castle, *1857.*

White possibly leans on William Hutchinson's *History of Durham* in describing the view from Abbey Bridge towards Rokeby Hall, as he mentions the earlier writer's 'avenue' of oaks. Predictably, the river Tees here channels its way through Scott's 'sheets of marble gray'. White also uses the poet's description from the Dairy Bridge of the 'headlong torrent' of the Greta with its 'foam-globes', transposing it to the 'noisy current' of the Tees as it 'engirdles the boulders with foamy rings', as seen from the Abbey Bridge. At Egglestone Abbey White stops to talk to an artist and his wife who were using a fortnight's rail excursion ticket to visit as many abbeys and as much picturesque scenery as possible. The couple had walked across from Stainmore, seeing Dotheboys Hall at Bowes; White muses on the fact that Bowes was once a station on the Roman road from Lincoln to Carlisle and would soon (1868) be a station on the railway from Stockton to Liverpool. He continues to Greta Bridge, passing a large party of excursionists from Newcastle on their way to view the grounds of Rokeby. Here he uses Scott's Notes on the 'romantic glen' of the Greta, puts the scene in the context of the story of *Rokeby* and quotes passages from the second canto describing Mortham and the Meeting of the Waters: the glen

> will surprise you by its manifold combinations of rock, wood, and water, fascinating the eye at every step amid a solitude profound … You cannot fail to recognize how truly Scott describes the scenery; the 'beetling brow' is there, and the 'ivied banners' still hang from the crags as when the minstrel saw them.

White suggests that the reader may ramble to Wycliffe, possibly the birthplace of John Wycliffe, or along the river Greta to Brignall Banks and Scargill, though he does not quote from *Rokeby*. His comments on the inns at Greta Bridge are of interest; the noise and activity of the stage-coach era on the London to Edinburgh route has been replaced by the silence of a farm house; only one inn remains, used by walkers and anglers. As the railway to Middleton-in-Teesdale had not then been constructed, White returns to Barnard Castle in time to catch the horse-drawn omnibus at half-past five. The journey through Lartington, Cotherstone and Romaldkirk takes two hours; the driver is an important man, carrying messages and parcels between the town and the upper dale. White does not delay at Middleton-in-Teesdale but sets off to the inn at High Force; his comments on the walk demonstrates that he has read Arthur Young's description of the same journey: 'Every step makes us

**79** *Egglestone Abbey. Illustration for* Rambles in Teesdale, *1877.*

feel that we are approaching a region where Nature partakes more of the stern than the gentle'. After an excellent tea 'a solemn roar – the voice of High Force in its ceaseless plunge' – lulls him to sleep.

In the morning White sees the long white sheet of foam of High Force from his window and sets off on a two-hour exploration. In his choice of viewpoints and imagery he almost provides a catalogue of the techniques of picturesque description, gleaned from his reading of Thomas Amory, Arthur Young and William Hutchinson in particular. First is the delayed view: White takes us along the path until 'at a sudden turn the noise of the fall bursts full upon you'; the fall is not seen until a little further on, when the trees no longer screen it. Secondly there are the viewpoints or stations and the difficulty of reaching them: White has only to 'scramble down' to the viewpoint at the foot of the falls identified by Amory and followed by Young, who had to use his hands and reach 'from bough to bough'; White also follows Hutchinson to the top of the bluff where 'the river

**80** *Abbey Bridge. Illustration for* Rambles in Teesdale, *1877.*

rushes to its leap'. Thirdly, and perhaps subconsciously from his reading of these earlier writers, White adopts the restrictive vocabulary of the picturesque; nearly fifty years previously Jane Austen, in *Sense and Sensibility*, had noted that 'admiration of landscape scenery has become mere jargon'. At High Force White describes how

> you see the deep stony chasm, and the peat-stained water making three perpendicular leaps down a precipice seventy feet in height. It is a striking scene, what with the grim crags, the wild slopes, and the huge masses lying at the bottom and in the bed of the stream; and the impressive volume of sound.

However, White does show a firm 19th-century interest in geology and detailed observation: he notes 'where something like crystallization has been produced by a highly-heated intrusive rock' and he lies on the rock at the top of the fall admiring how the peat-stained water contrasts with the white foam and has worn the rocks in the river bed quite smooth.

At breakfast White quizzes the waitress about the inn. He learns that the house was built about twenty-five years before, when the road was made to connect the lead mines of Alston Moor, in Cumberland, with the highways of Durham. In winter they see few people, only farmers, cattle dealers, and miners; but in summer the place is kept alive by the numerous visitors to the waterfall. Sometimes they entertain a school party on a day's holiday.

White sets off to Cauldron Snout, commenting on the whitewashed farms of upper Teesdale where the ground-floor is used as a barn and stable, the dwelling above being reached by an outside stone staircase. After passing the 'greenstone' of Cronkley Scar, with rare and interesting plants nearby, he descends the trackless ling-covered moorland to the Weel, which he follows to a rift in the hill-side. The faint sound of rushing water grows louder, and 'presently coming to the brink of a rocky chasm we behold the cataract of Caldron Snout. The Tees here makes a plunge of 200 ft, dashing from rock to rock, twisting, whirling, eddying, and roaring in its dark and tortuous channel.' White uses William Hutchinson's words: the black crags contrast with the white foam, and 'you are here shut out from the world amid scenes of savage beauty.' The rough bridge has a rude hand-rail, enabling a view of

**81** *Mickle Fell. Illustration by J.A. Symington for* A Picturesque History of Yorkshire, *1901.*

the twisting course of the river. He muses on the therapeutic effect of sitting beside a waterfall, watching the swift play of the water and listening to its splash and roar: 'And what a joy it is to recall–especially in a London November–or rather to renew, the happy mood inspired by the waterfall among the mountains!'

On his way to climb Mickle Fell White stops at Birkdale farm – still today believed to be the most remote farmhouse in England – for a meal of bread, butter, milk and cheese. He hears of the Ordnance Surveyors once staying at the farm for months while surveying Westmorland and toiling to the top of Mickle Fell to find conditions unsuitable for their observations, and of the farmer guiding photographers and visitors to High Cup Nick. From the summit White enjoys the glorious panorama and is almost able to trace his journey along the Tees from near the Cleveland Hills towards its headwaters on Cross Fell.

White's book had gone into five editions by 1879 and, as well as having some influence on the number of visitors to Teesdale, may have prompted other writers to produce guide books to the dale.

# The Nineteenth Century and the Railways

*'A person may thus leave London at 2-30 and be at
Middleton-in-Teesdale at 9-15 the same day'*

Walter White used the growing rail network to spend a month rambling in Yorkshire; his book was the first of a plethora of guide books which reflected the expansion of the railways into Teesdale in the 1850s and '60s and the resulting increase in visitors. The 19th-century guide books, while showing the continued influence of Scott and Dickens, also describe the facilities provided for the tourist, such as the local guides and the lodgings which largely followed on from the development of the railway network. Walks to High Force, Cauldron Snout and less well-known scenes were also included.

The publication of the second edition of Richard Garland's *A Tour in Teesdale*, with the addition of material from Scott's *Rokeby*, may have prompted W.R. Robinson to add a section on the Greta Bridge area to his *Guide to Richmond* in 1833. This *Guide* comprised *historical and descriptive notices of the castle, monastic remains, walks, views, &c. embracing Aske and Rokeby*. Robinson's guide book quotes lines from Scott's poem and notes, referring to the Roman camp at Greta Bridge, Mortham Tower, the tomb of Fitzhugh brought from Egglestone Abbey, and the river Tees at Abbey Bridge; illustrations included 'View on the Greta' and 'Fitzhugh's Tomb, Rokeby'.

Hugh Railton in his *Hand-Book to Teesdale* (*c*.1857) suggests going to the *Morritt Arms* to arrange a visit with a guide to Rokeby, 'rendered immortal by the pen of Sir Walter Scott'. He quotes the song 'Brignall Banks' and recommends the 'exceedingly beautiful' walk from Rokeby, past the Roman camp at Greta Bridge, to Brignall old church (see maps, plates 54 & 55), painted by Turner. Although Richard Garland in the second edition of his *Tour in Teesdale* (1813) suggests an agreeable walk up the Greta to Rutherford Bridge and the 'curious caverns', he fails to quote from Rokeby. With his limited time in Teesdale in 1858, Walter White, as we have seen, didn't go up the Greta, only suggesting Brignall Banks as a possibility, and not quoting from the poem at this point. So, despite Scott's note about the site, no other writer before Railton seems to have recommended this walk.

*Rokeby* is quoted more extensively by M.J. Ward in *An Excursionist's Guide to Barnard Castle*, printed there about 1858. There are 140 lines from the poem, relating to Barnard Castle, Deepdale, Egglestone Abbey, along the Greta in Rokeby

*Above:* **82** *View on the Greta. Lithograph by W.R. Robinson for his* Guide to Richmond, *1833. Drawn from below Eastwood Hall, before the Greta enters the Devil's Elbow.*

*Right:* **83** *Fitzhugh's Tomb, Rokeby. Lithograph by W.R. Robinson, 1833.*

Park, and Brignall Banks. Ward quotes 14 lines on the cave in which Guy Denzil and his band of ruffians assembled, along with the song 'O Brignall banks are wild and fair'. *The Teesdale Mercury Penny Guide to Barnard Castle, Rokeby, The High Force, etc.* of 1874 quotes over 40 lines of *Rokeby* and recommends the walk from Greta Bridge along Brignall Banks, to include the cave and returning by Scargill.

**84** *Dairy Bridge. Illustration for* Rambles in Teesdale, *1877.*

Written and illustrated by two Sunday School teachers, *Rambles in Teesdale* was published in 1877 and summarises the attractions of Teesdale at the time:

> We were well aware that for grandeur, and romantic, sylvan scenery, Teesdale may vie with any part of the kingdom; it is immortalized by poet and painter; the geologist and the antiquarian find a wide field for research; whilst the botanist hails upper Teesdale as one of his richest fields of wealth.

It is soon apparent that it is the poet that has most influenced the teachers' choice of holiday. 'Rokeby! the very name inspires romantic visions; for years it had been with us a treasured dream, floating in the distance.' They feel that it would be presumptuous for them to describe the glories of Rokeby in their own words, so 218 lines are quoted from Scott's poem, first published 64 years earlier.

They go on to say that the poem cannot be fully appreciated until a visit is made to Rokeby, when the fidelity of Scott's descriptions is fully realised. Despite apparently having a copy of the poem with them, the two writers make use of a guide to the grounds of Rokeby; he shows detailed knowledge of locations used in the poem. A copy of Lockhart's *Life of Scott*, published five years earlier and thoughtfully provided for visitors at the *Morritt Arms*, enables Morritt's comments on Scott's meticulous gathering of details as they walked in Rokeby Park to be quoted at length. When rain enforces a morning in the inn, the two writers can give a full account of the writing of the poem, with Morritt's references to Garland's *Tour* and Hutchinson's *History of Durham*.

On one day's visit a short rest on a seat, admiring the 'wild, bare rocks jutting o'er the dell', gives an opportunity to quote a stanza in full:

> The cliffs, that rear their haughty head
> High o'er the river's darksome bed,
> Were now all naked, wild, and grey,
> …
> And so the ivied banners gleam,
> Waved wildly o'er the brawling stream.
>
> (Canto Second, VIII)

The Sunday School teachers then point out the cave (see map, plate 55) where Scott wrote his 'pictures painted on the spot' before entering 'the dismal grove of sable yew'. They pass Dairy Bridge, with an illustration of its 'glossy tendrils of clasping ivy', to where the Greta rushes 'with headlong speed to lose its identity in the bosom of the Tees'.

An illustration of Abbey Bridge (plate 80) and a description of the views from it allow for further quotation from *Rokeby*, along with Leland's mention of the marble quarries nearby, noted in Whitaker's *Richmondshire*. At Egglestone Abbey a hermit conducts them around and the ruinous state of the remains prompts another look at the poem:

> The reverend pile lay wild and waste,
> Profaned, dishonoured, and defaced.
> …
> And peasant hands the tombs o'erthrew
> Of Bowes, of Rokeby, and Fitz Hugh.
>
> (Canto Sixth, XXVIII)

A sketch of the abbey (plate 79) shows some of the tombs in the nave, along with the weathered and vegetation-clad east window. In nearby Thorsgill, Wilfred, Redmond and Matilda from *Rokeby* 'flash before the mind's eye'; Richard Garland quoted Scott's botanical detail in the second edition of his *Tour in Teesdale*.

A walk along Brignall Banks would not be complete without a reference to Turner's portrayal of the old church at Brignall, and without quoting from Scott's song and searching for the cave, 'A little entrance, low and square'. It was here that Morritt had remarked on Scott's meticulous noting down of the flowers along Brignall Banks, and over 60 years later the two Sunday School teachers recall 'the vivid picture drawn by the poet'. Perhaps following M.J. Ward's *An Excursionist's Guide to Barnard Castle*, or *The Penny Guide*, the two ramblers suggest going the three miles above Greta Bridge, quoting the passage where Bertram, lying on the heather and throatwort,

> listless eyed
> The course of Greta's playful tide;

on the opposite bank, one cliff

> A thousand varied lichens dyed
> Its waste and weather-beaten side …
>
> (Canto Third, VIII)

**85**  *Junction of the Greta and the Tees. Illustration for*
Rivers of Great Britain, *1902.*

In their remarks on the Roman fort at Greta Bridge and the castle at Barnard Castle, the two ramblers make reference to the histories of William Hutchinson and the Revd T.D. Whitaker, as well as quoting extensively from *Rokeby*. The names of the tributaries of the Tees are introduced, the Balder 'named from Odin's son', 'silver' Lune, Greta, Thorsgill, and 'Romantic Deepdale's slender rill'.

John Bousefield, in his *Pleasant Memories of Darlington and Neighbourhood* published in Darlington in 1881, continued the tradition of quoting extensively from Scott. On 'A Summer Day up the Tees' Bousefield joined the many visitors to Rokeby, which is 'endowed with great natural beauties: rushing streams and towering rocks; rich pastures and verdant woods; those beauties have been increased from the resources of art, and gilded by the magic of poetry.' At Rokeby, Scott's cave and the tomb of Fitzhugh (plate 83; 'Old Tomb' on map, plate 55)[1] are visited, as are Barnard Castle, Brignall Banks and Deepdale.

Copying an idea borrowed from Birmingham's *Saturday Half-Holiday Guide*, William Cudworth in *The Darlington Half Holiday Guide* of 1882 described what could be seen in a half day's excursion from Darlington. Rokeby Park might be visited on Tuesdays and Thursdays, in the company of a guide from the *Morritt Arms*. Cudworth accompanies his description of Rokeby with references to Scott's poem, and also gives an outline of the story of *Rokeby* and details of how it came to be written. He advocates seeing Barnard Castle where *Rokeby* begins, and Egglestone Abbey where it ends; also the caves of Brignall Banks, the location of Guy Denzil's band of robbers.

As we have seen, William Cudworth also considered the part played by William Wordsworth and Charles Dickens in making Teesdale more widely known. In *Rambles in Teesdale* the Sunday School teachers were careful to discover which inn at Greta Bridge Charles Dickens used in *Nicholas Nickleby,* and at Bowes asked for

**86**  *Egglestone Abbey. For* The Darlington Half Holiday Guide, *1899.*

Dotheboys Hall (plate 76) to be pointed out to them; in their imagination they 'follow the chaise and cart, as they emerge from the *New and George Inn*, along the frozen road, in the dark, drear, cold night, until the wretched freight is deposited at the door of Dotheboys Hall'.

The expansion of the railway network into Teesdale was crucial for the growth of tourism in the dale. After many delays, mostly caused by the Duke of Cleveland's objections to the railway going through his estates of Raby Castle and Selaby Hall, the Darlington and Barnard Castle Railway Act of 1854 was passed. This brought the rail connection of Barnard Castle to the main London line two years later; by 1863 Barnard Castle was connected to Bishop Auckland. By 1861 the South Durham and Lancashire Union Railway had extended the route from Barnard Castle to Lartington then westwards to Bowes, over Stainmore to Kirkby Stephen (map, plate 1). This highest railway crossing in England was built primarily to carry iron ore from Lancashire to the blast furnaces at Teesmouth, and Durham coal to the iron manufacturers of Furness. From 1865 the Tees Valley Railway Company constructed a line from Lartington through Cotherstone, Romaldkirk and Mickleton to Middleton-in-Teesdale, opening up the upper dale. By 1882 the network was all part of the North Eastern Railway Company.

Hugh Railton's *Hand-Book to Teesdale* was published shortly after the railway came to Barnard Castle; it was advertised as being available at Barnard Castle station, and every station on the Stockton and Darlington Railway. The rail link would transform tourism in Teesdale: 'Until recently, few were permitted to view the bold and romantic scenery of Teesdale, owing to expensive transit,' but now tourists are provided with cheap and ready transport to the dale. On alighting at Barnard Castle station an 'imposing and majestic scene' awaits: a 14 mile panorama. Railton names five hotels

**87** *Opening of the South Durham and Lancashire Union Railway: The Tees Viaduct.* Illustrated London News, *24 August 1861.*

in the town and three places to get transport further up the dale; there are also coaches running twice a day to Middleton-in-Teesdale. Both sides of the dale have good roads and 'the various objects of interest in Teesdale are daily becoming better known'.

M.J. Ward, in *An Excursionist's Guide to Barnard Castle and Rokeby* of about 1858, integrates views of the recently built railway viaducts into his walks. In Flatts Wood to the north-west of Barnard Castle is the Tees Railway Viaduct; the visitor may ascend a winding path to the level of this structure, which is 132 feet above the river bed and cost £25,119. Deepdale Viaduct, 161 feet in height and built at a cost of £20,687, is a feature on a walk through the 'charming glen' of Deepdale to the west of the town.

By 1891 *The Teesdale Mercury* was recording that 'the absorbing topic of the hour is railways and railway travelling'. In June of that year the newspaper was praising a new express service that was shortly to be introduced, from London to Edinburgh by the east coast route; this, with changes to the regional timetable at York and Darlington, would benefit Teesdale: 'A person may thus leave London at 2.30 and be at Middleton-in-Teesdale at 9.15 the same day, and this, moreover, after numerous changes and not a little stopping.' The North Eastern Railway Company's new summer timetable in 1891 sports a different design for the cover. Among the sketches of the principal tourist resorts on the north-eastern section, the castle at Barnard Castle occupies a prominent position: 'Barnard Castle thus receives a free advertisement which ought to still further assist in popularising the capital of Teesdale, both as a watering place and also as a health resort.' Three years later the paper reports that Barnard Castle, Cotherstone and Middleton-in-Teesdale have a very fair quota of visitors, and praises the Town Improvement Committee for providing an evening musical treat 'amid historical surroundings the like of which can hardly be excelled in the north country'.

**88** *Cotherstone. Illustration by A. Barraud for* A Picturesque History of Yorkshire, *1901.*

James Backhouse (1861-1945)[2] described in *Upper Teesdale Past and Present* (1896) how Middleton-in-Teesdale had overtaken Barnard Castle as the starting point for a trip into Upper Teesdale; because of the Tees Valley railway branch constructed in 1868 (see map, plate 26). Backhouse notes that tourist tickets, weekend and 10-day tickets are available from all North Eastern Railway stations for travel to Barnard Castle, Cotherstone and Middleton-in-Teesdale. In Teesdale there are special cycling and walking fares, allowing the return journey to be made from a different station. An N.E.R. poster of 1898 advertised the 'East Coast Route to the Lake District via Darlington and the Picturesque Valleys of the Tees, Greta and Eden' with a view of Barnard Castle. At the end of *Upper Teesdale Past and Present* is an advertisement for a list of furnished lodgings to let in farmhouses and villages in Teesdale. John Bousefield in *Pleasant Memories of Darlington and Neighbourhood* (1881) advocates taking the 7.13 train from Darlington which arrives at Middleton-in-Teesdale about 8.30. 'Commodious open conveyances' take walkers from the station to High Force for 1s. and to Langdon Beck for Cauldron Snout for 1s. 6d. Cotherstone was becoming a summer resort for those seeking health and relaxation in pure air and in the midst of the beauties of nature, a feature confirmed by the two Sunday School teachers in *Rambles in Teesdale* (1877). The guide at High Force, Charles Dawson, as well as conducting visitors to the top of the falls, has a good knowledge of the names and localities of the rare plants and ferns of the area.

James Backhouse includes a chapter on the Teesdale flora in his *Upper Teesdale Past and Present*. On a three-day excursion to the district in August 1889 the Botanical section of the Yorkshire Naturalists' Union recorded 301 different species of flowering plants, 27 ferns, and 41 mosses; one or two were to be found nowhere else in the country. Backhouse lists the varieties of plants growing on different rocks. John Bousefield describes an excursion from Langdon Beck to Cauldron Snout; the fields are 'gay with innumerable pansies' and 'in spring the rare *gentiana verna*, with its

**89** *Deepdale Viaduct on the South Durham and Lancashire Union Railway.* Illustrated London News, *8 January 1859.*

flowers of cerulean blue, abounds'. He notes that this is the only place in England where the flower is found. Marshy pastures glow with the golden globe flower; at Falcon Clints some of the rarer ferns used to grow, but *woodsia ilvensis* and the holly fern are now very rare. We may safely assume that the many botanists carrying presses for ferns, as met by the Sunday School teachers on their *Rambles in Teesdale*, have helped to reduce their numbers. *The Darlington Half Holiday Guide* describes the walk to Cauldron Snout as one of the richest botanical localities in England, with its alpine and sub-alpine plants; here are the carnivorous butterwort, the purple alpine bartsia (plate VII), the spring gentian, and the shrubby cinquefoil with bright yellow flowers nearer High Force. A letter to *The Teesdale Mercury* in 1885 notes that Widdybank Fell has been very busy with Whitsuntide visitors wishing to see the spring gentian.

The Darlington Naturalist's Field Club in 1896 added Teesdale to its name to reflect its area of interest. Club vice-president Richard Manson in the second edition of his *Zig-Zag Ramblings of a Naturalist* (1898) recalls how in August 1895 he was on Cronkley Fell with a party of students from Toynbee Hall in London.[3] Presumably travelling by train, they had camped for a fortnight near Forest-in-Teesdale and Manson gleefully reported on their botanical experience; they had found 320 species of plants, as well as consuming 24lbs of marmalade and 36 boxes of tinned fruits.

It was not only local guide books or publications that promoted rail travel to Teesdale. *The Illustrated London News* of 8 January 1859 included an engraving of the recently completed 'Deepdale Viaduct on the South Durham and Lancashire Union Railway'. The accompanying caption describes how the viaduct's 'beautiful simplicity and airy lightness is in admirable keeping with the fairylike glen over which it stretches … a highly picturesque and romantic valley rendered classic ground by Sir Walter Scott's *Rokeby*.' The same paper on 24 August 1861 announced the 'Opening of the South Durham and Lancashire Union Railway' with an illustration of 'The Tees Viaduct' (plate 87). The accompanying article noted that the object of this railway was to further trade, as it linked coal and iron works in the east to iron mining in the west; holiday makers would have easier access to both the Lake District and the seaside resorts of the east coast.

Teesdale followed the national trend in the growing popularity of cycling. As bicycles improved and their cost reduced, the number of cycling clubs grew. When the Bank Holidays Act of 1871 added an extra day to the Whit holiday, clubs were able to organise longer excursions and gatherings or 'meets'. The North East Cyclists Clubs gathered at Newcastle upon Tyne and then cycled to a neighbouring town where they met fellow cyclists from other north-eastern towns and villages. At Whitsuntide in 1885 *The Teesdale Mercury* recorded that in addition to the local cyclists, the amateur champion of the north and several 'crack riders' from Tyneside had entered the Barnard Castle Cricket Club Annual Athletic Sports. During the long weekend there were cycling and foot races on the town's cricket field and an evening ball. The visitors were obviously impressed, and three years later at the dinner it was decided that Barnard Castle should become the official venue for the Annual North Eastern Cyclists' Meet. The North East clubs set off on Whit Saturday afternoon, met Wearside clubs at Durham, Bishop Auckland and Staindrop, and at about 9 p.m. the cavalcade was met in Barnard Castle by the town band and, lit by Chinese lanterns, made their way to the market place where they were welcomed by town councillors.

In 1893 *The Teesdale Mercury* reported that 5,271 people had arrived by train for the Meet, most with their cycles. Many cyclists spoke highly of the invigorating air of Teesdale compared with their smoky towns and cities. As well as the Sunday mail train, five additional trains had filled the town with excursionists and others had arrived by trap and bicycle, so that by midday on Whit Monday the lavishly decorated streets of Barnard Castle were thronged. From the station the procession made its way down Galgate and Newgate to The Bowes Museum and then to the castle for the group photograph. As well as the annual sports, there were visits to Rokeby and the Teesdale hills, and walks along the river and in Flatts Wood.

*The Darlington Half Holiday Guide* lists various cycling routes from Darlington. William Cudworth describes the most interesting route as that to High Force; he refers to pages in his *Guide* for places of interest, and lists the distances involved. Greta Bridge comes after 16 ¾ miles; Barnard Castle, 20; Egglestone, 24; Middleton-in-Teesdale, 29; High Force 34; the road via Egglestone to Middleton-in-Teesdale, though hilly, commands splendid views (as described by Arthur Young well over a hundred years earlier).

Walks to the waterfalls of Teesdale naturally feature large in the guide books of the 19th century. John Bousefield describes a day in upper Teesdale and quotes William Mason:

> The thundering Tees
> Reigns there amid his cataracts sublime.

**90** *Market Place, Barnard Castle. A Rock & Co. engraving for* Views & Scenery of Barnard Castle, *1857.* The King's Head *is on the right.*

Here, in its upper course, the river roars and dashes as it forces its way through the narrow gorge of Caldron Snout, or throws itself with deafening noise over the rocks of High Force.

The two Sunday School teachers in *Rambles in Teesdale* (1877) note how the station outside Middleton-in-Teesdale is busy with visitors and the omnibus to the post office is packed with day excursionists, and they join an open pleasure-break bound for High Force. James Backhouse prefers to take the high road from Bowlees up the dale, crossing Ettersgill Beck and going on to the far-famed High Force. Because of the increasing number of visitors, access to the waterfall had been improved. Walks winding through the woods provide a variety of views, and stone steps lead to the foot of the fall, under the huge basaltic precipice. Backhouse also quotes Nathaniel Spencer's 'curious description' of High Force in *The Complete English Traveller* of 1773; perhaps it is Spencer's comparison of High Force with famous waterfalls which amuses Backhouse. Spencer had written:

> Those who have had an opportunity of seeing the cataracts of the Nile in upper Egypt, and the fall of Niagara, in North America, will have their memories refreshed by visiting this place, and those whose station in life hinders them from travelling into foreign countries to visit those natural curiosities, may see them all here in epitome.

Although this may remind us of Thomas Amory's comparison of High Force with Niagara Falls in 1756, it also brings to mind the difficulties that the earlier travellers had in their quest to see High Force. Arthur Young in 1768 had to reach 'from bough to bough', and John Byng in 1792 was up to his knees in the river. Like John Backhouse, John Bousefield (1881) can describe how a broad well-kept walk leads down from the inn, through a plantation of pines, to the foot of the Force; vistas are cut through the trees, and seats placed where good views of the fern-covered crags of Holwick Fell are to be had. Steps lead to the foot of the falls; igneous rocks rise 90 feet or more, and 'over a narrow chasm in one of them, 68 feet high, the river plunges into the deep pool beneath, churning the water into foam, and dashing the spray over the high banks opposite'. In time of flood the river covers the whole of the rocks, and rushes with a terrible noise in one stupendous fall of 84 feet.

A guide leads the way to the top of the fall where the visitor with a cool head may lean over to see the leap of the river (claimed to be the highest fall in England) into the deep pool far below. John Bousefield adds another viewpoint of High Force, a projecting cliff some forty yards below on the Yorkshire side. Surrounded by thick junipers and 'standing on the verge', the viewer has 'an unequalled amphitheatre … spread before him'; in the centre of the view are the bare rocks, down which the water falls with a sullen and ceaseless boom. This viewpoint was perhaps first found by J.M.W. Turner in 1816; earlier visitors seem to have been content to follow the tradition established by Thomas Amory, Arthur Young and William Hutchinson in viewing High Force from the top of the fall and from the edge of the plunge pool.

A letter in *The Teesdale Mercury* on 21 August 1912 recalled a visit in the early 1870s to upper Teesdale, which gives credence to the descriptions of High Force in flood.

> There had been very heavy rain for some days, and a tremendous storm set in. I remember crossing the Winch Bridge: the water was nearly up to the planking, and, when we got to the High Force, to which we could not approach very near, every bit of rock was covered, and it was practically a large horse-shoe waterfall.

The authors of *Rambles in Teesdale* quote a recent newspaper article concerning access to Cauldron Snout. As the London Lead Company had constructed a road from *Langdon Beck Hotel* to the waterfall, visitors could enjoy the scenery without having to scramble over rocks or wade through bogs. James Backhouse notes that the way to Cauldron Snout is clearly marked with guide-posts. From the lake or Weel

> the Tees takes a sudden turn into a gorge … and leaps furiously down a gigantic staircase of basalt, nearly 200 feet in height. From ledge to ledge the brown stream darts, becoming whiter with each bound, as the hissing foam is broken into thousands of bubbles and clouds of spray, by the sharp-edged basaltic columns underneath.

John Bousefield suggests starting the walk to Cauldron Snout at Langdon Beck and notes that the path is later strewn with great pieces of rock, torn down from Falcon Clints by winter frosts. A good view of the succession of falls is from the lower rocks; a winding footpath may be safely ascended by hanging on to bushes growing out of the rocks. This path leads to the top where the giddy and lofty footbridge affords a grand and impressive view. 'The Tees rushes for nearly 600 feet through the deep

**91** *Gibson's Cave. Photograph by Elijah Yeoman.*

gorge, thundering over and around the mighty rocks which constitute the Snout.'

Bousefield recommends visiting Wynch Bridge (often spelt Winch at the time) on the way from Middleton-in-Teesdale to High Force; the carriage from the station stops at Bowlees and waits further along the road. Bousefield's description at first is very familiar; the narrow suspension bridge shakes and vibrates with every step. However, we do get a description of the river at Low Force here: 'a succession of pools intersected by rocks, over and around which it swirls and rushes in glittering cascades'. The only writer to notice the island upstream from the bridge, Bousefield adds a cautionary note about crossing to it as the river could suddenly rise.

In *Upper Teesdale Past and Present* James Backhouse also suggests a number of additional walks. Near Bowlees is Gibson's Cave, caused by the overhanging lip of a waterfall. Between High Force and the Forest Post-office a cart track leads to Cronkley Bridge and Cronkley Scars, 'of botanical repute'. A little to the east of Cronkley Scars a deep gorge contains the White Force, in fine weather a mere trickle of water finding its way into a fissure of limestone, and emerging again half a mile away, but in flood worth all the trouble and discomfort of crossing bogs and spongy heather to visit. At Middleton-in-Teesdale the wooded banks of Hudeshope or Skears Beck are a favourite walk. Backhouse also gives directions for the ascent of Mickle Fell and describes the view from the summit.

In the fifth edition of Richard Garland's *A Tour in Teesdale*, published in 1834, the walks around Barnard Castle were described. At his own expense and with some subscriptions local physician Dr George Edwards (1750-1823) had made paths to open up walks along the banks of the Tees; during the 19th century the paths were developed farther into Flatts Woods, with the fords and stepping stones across Percy Beck being replaced with footbridges. Garland lists 21 named walks, including The Darlington Terrace, 'commanding a highly grand picturesque prospect over the whole extent of Teesdale', The Druid's Walk, 'having a prospect of the awful and beautiful that cannot be exceeded', and Garlands Views, suggesting that Garland had been one of the subscribers to Dr Edward's improvement schemes.

**92**  *Raby Castle. For* The Darlington Half Holiday Guide, *1899.*

Hugh Railton in his *Hand-Book to Teesdale* (1857) describes the Flatts:

The retired walks by the side of the river lead to charming woodland scenery ... whilst the river, in its summer beauty, ... ripples softly on its way, giving no token of those wintry floods, when, swollen by the streamlets from a thousand hills, it pursues its course with all the grandeur of an Alpine torrent.

William Cudworth noted that the popular Flatts Woods were amply provided with footpaths and seats. North westwards from Barnard Castle station a walk through woods which gradually became wilder leads to Cotherstone station and then on to Romaldkirk. Cudworth follows Richard Garland in recommending the walk into Deepdale, to the west of Barnard Castle. As well as the waterfall, and the stream rushing over sloping beds of limestone, Cudworth draws the visitor's attention to the large boulder of Shap granite, though he does not use the term 'erratic'.

From Winston station further downstream, a ride on the omnibus gives access to Staindrop and Raby Castle. *The Darlington Half Holiday Guide* gives directions on how to obtain tickets to view Raby Park and Castle. When discussing the changes made by the 2nd Earl of Darlington, including the opening of the Lower Hall to carriages, Cudworth refers to Arthur Young's account of the Earl's agricultural expertise; as we have already noted, Wordsworth's *The White Doe of Rylstone* is quoted in describing the Baron's Hall.

Illustrations have always played a part in the promotion of publications, from the maps in Camden's *Britannia* (plate 17) to Scott's *Rokeby* (plates 58-62). Thomas and Katherine Macquoid in 1883 produced *About Yorkshire*, describing and illustrating their Sunday journeys through the county. The chapter on Rokeby and Deepdale listed many of the locations used in Scott's poem *Rokeby*, quoting many lines in the process, as 'every turn in the woods calls up some thought of the poem'. Thomas

**93** *Mortham. Engraving by Thomas Macquoid, for his book* About Yorkshire, *1883.*

Macquoid provided illustrations, not only of Barnard Castle, Brignall Banks and Dairy Bridge, but also of the lesser-known spots such as Mortham Tower, the packhorse bridge over Thorsgill (plate 64), the cave where Scott wrote the poem (plate 63), and Percy Beck.

In the 19th century, with advances in engraving and photography, books consisting largely of illustrations helped promote the scenery of Teesdale. In 1832 Thomas Rose brought out *Westmorland, Cumberland, Durham & Northumberland, Illustrated,* with drawings made 'on the spot' by Thomas Allom (1804-72). In the introduction to this book Rose considered the 1830s to be the 'Augustine age of Pictorial art', with painters and publishers creating a refined taste for faithful and vivid portrayals of British landscapes; this had been helped by the introduction of steel engraving. Engraving on steel had started about 1822; as we saw with Turner's illustrations for a new edition of Sir Walter Scott's *Poetical Works*, steel plates could withstand several thousand impressions before showing signs of wear. Thomas Allom's Teesdale drawings were of *Caldron Snout Teesdale, Teesdale near Winch Bridge, Barnard Castle* (from Towler Hill), *Raby Castle* all engraved by W. Le Petit, and *High Force of the Tees* and *Barnard Castle* (the castle and bridge by moonlight, plate 107) engraved by S. Lacey.

Thomas Rose's topographical descriptions of these Teesdale scenes lean very heavily on previous writers. At High Force the web of plagiarism, or perhaps the Picturesque vocabulary of the time, is so intricate that it is impossible to name precisely Rose's immediate sources. Thus,

> the whole body of the Tees river rushes over a perpendicular rock of black marble sixty-nine feet in height, and precipitates itself into several caverns ... Clouds of mist and spray ... reflect all the dyes of the rainbow ... the noise of the fall is heard for many miles round the country.

**94** *Caldron Snout, Teesdale, Durham. Engraving after Thomas Allom, 1834.*

**95** *Teesdale, near Winch Bridge, Durham. Engraving after Thomas Allom, 1835.*

The 'perpendicular rock' may be traced back through William Hutchinson and Arthur Young to Thomas Amory, whereas the 69 feet possibly comes from Richard Garland, in turn derived from the 23 yards from Nathaniel Spencer's account and Thomas Smith's engraving. William Hutchinson was the first to record the spray and noise of this waterfall. The viewpoint chosen by Thomas Allom for this scene is in front of where the new inn will be, and the artist includes cattle on the track still used by farmers, cattle dealers, and miners as recorded by Walter White some 26 years later.

At Cauldron Snout Allom chooses a viewpoint looking down part of the staircase of falls from above the railed footbridge, though he does not depict the columnar Whin Sill at all realistically. Rose's description emphasises the horror the tourist could expect to feel at this sublime spot; again there are parallels with Richard Garland's 'powerful, pleasing expansion of heart' on the sight of this waterfall, and

**96**  *Barnard Castle, Durham. Engraving after Thomas Allom, 1835.*

with William Hutchinson's assertion that only visitors with a mind fitted to aerial flight may cross the bridge without horror. Thomas Rose writes:

> It requires some nerve and intrepidity to pass the rudely-constructed bridge which crosses the fall: the roaring of the waters beneath, and the apparently unstedfast footing of the structure whereon he stands, excites a feeling of anxiety and fear in the heart of the tourist.

How many potential tourists, leafing through this volume of engravings, could resist the lure of this sublime cataract?

Although Rose describes Wynch Bridge in similar terms to the Cauldron Snout experience, he has to reflect Allom's illustration which shows the wider context of the bridge. Here again Rose bases his description on Hutchinson's account: the latter's river flowing into a 'deep gulph with vast tumult' becomes a 'terrific [i.e. terrifying] and roaring gulf'. Despite the iron suspension chains being securely fastened into the rock to prevent the bridge from vibrating, Rose follows Hutchinson's assertion on the 'swinging motion' as the traveller 'experiences all the tremulous motion of the chains', and suggests that few strangers would trust themselves to cross. Hutchinson's observation of the Tees rushing noisily through 'broken rocks, from whose brows, willows and brambles incessantly weep' becomes waters 'boiling' over a stony channel with rich foliage on the rocky promontories.

Rose's descriptions of Raby Castle and Barnard Castle (by moonlight) are largely concerned with historical details. A general description of the sights of Teesdale accompanies the engraving of Barnard Castle as seen from Towler Hill: the Tees rises on Cross Fell and 'imparts a rich beauty to the romantic and picturesque country through which it flows'; Egglestone Abbey and the walks at Rokeby where the Greta joins the Tees are almost inevitably mentioned. Testifying to the durability of the steel plates, this book of illustrations, with the addition of quotations from poetry, was re-issued, for example as *Picturesque Rambles in Westmorland, Cumberland, Durham & Northumberland* in 1847.

Artists continued to produce paintings for exhibition and sale rather than for engraving. In 1807, the year after John Sell Cotman exhibited three Greta views at the Royal Academy of Arts, George Fennel Robson exhibited two Teesdale views, *High Force Cataract: a fall of the river Tees* and *View on Ettersgill Beck, Teesdale, Durham*. Myles Birket Foster (1825-99) painted *Rocks on the Greta* and, in *A Relic of Old Times*, Thomas Creswick (1811-69) painted Barnard Castle in 1860. William Callow (1812-1908) exhibited many works at the Old Watercolour Society. *The Meeting of the Waters* (plate IX), inscribed 'Greta July 20, 1872' by the artist, shows Walter Scott's 'romantic glen'; the river Greta comes out from Rokeby beneath Dairy Bridge, which is almost engulfed by trees, and its peat-coloured waters swirl around large rocks brought down by the river.

Changes in printing technology allowed different approaches to reproducing paintings for a more general audience. Benjamin H. Heslop (1845-1915) reproduced 36 plates from his original watercolours (by the Meisenbach half-tone process as he seems proud to declare) in *The River Tees from Source to Sea Illustrated by B.H. Heslop* in 1893. Heslop briefly describes the course of the Tees from its source on Cross Fell (plate X), past Cauldron Snout, Falcon Clints 'famous amongst fern hunters', and the other features of the dale. The poem *Rokeby* is quoted at Abbey Bridge and Brignall.

The more local *Views and Scenery of Barnard Castle*, published by Rock and Co. in a number of formats from about 1857, totalled 16 views, including some less usual subjects: *Mrs Bowes' Mansion & Museum, Barnard Castle* (plate 102), two railway viaducts near Barnard Castle (plates 111, 115), *Rokeby from Abbey Bridge* (plate 78) and *Mortham Bridge* (Dairy Bridge) complete with figures on the balcony of the prospect house.

The photographer Elijah Yeoman (1846-1930) had a business in Barnard Castle from the 1870s, having succeeded or joined J.T. Bainbridge in 1864. Judging from advertisements in *The Teesdale Mercury* in the 1880s and 1890s, Yeoman seems to have made his living from portrait work, but also sold scenic prints over the counter, probably as mementoes to visitors, as his shop was strategically located in Galgate between the railway station and town centre. Surviving prints of his location portraits, and 'largest and best selection of views in the North', include walkers in Flatts Wood, Teesdale's waterfalls (plate 7), the castles of Streatlam and Raby, railway viaducts and, of course, scenes connected with the poem *Rokeby*.

In the summer *The Teesdale Mercury* printed the names of visitors to Teesdale and the premises at which they were staying. In one week in 1888 there were 110 inns and houses in Teesdale providing accommodation, including 53 in Barnard Castle, 38 in Cotherstone and 14 in Middleton-in-Teesdale. The majority of visitors came from Sunderland, Tyneside and Hartlepool, reflecting the influence of the railways

**97** *Mortham Bridge. A Rock & Co. engraving for* Views & Scenery of Barnard Castle, *1857.*

**98** *Advertisement.* The Teesdale Mercury, *1894.*

ESTABLISHED 1864.

# THE TEESDALE STUDIO,
### GALGATE, BARNARD CASTLE.
## E. YEOMAN, PROPRIETOR.

HIGH-CLASS PORTRAITURE in all the most Modern Styles. Babies, Horses, Dogs, &c., photographed instantaneously. Wedding Parties, Groups, Residences, &c., by appointment. Family and Presentation Portraits, from miniature to life size, highly-finished in Oil, &c.

THE LARGEST AND BEST SELECTION OF VIEWS IN THE NORTH,

All Sizes, Mounted or Unmounted

**99** *Percy Beck. Photograph by Elijah Yeoman.*

**100**  *Grouse shooting, from a drawing by Harrison Weir.* Illustrated London News, *25 August 1860.*

and the North Eastern Cyclists' Meet being held at Barnard Castle. According to *The Teesdale Mercury* in June 1893, The North Eastern Railways' list of furnished lodgings to be let in farmhouses and country villages in the Northern counties was in great demand.

Every August *The Teesdale Mercury* commented on the prospects for grouse shooting. On 15 August 1894 an editorial in the paper pointed out that the shooting season was of supreme importance to Teesdale: 'It is a time of great bustling and activity, and a season when full employment is afforded to all classes of people.' The paper suggests that the rage for grouse moors came into fashion in the 1830s, with a continuing demand from southerners. The shooting rights of the vast Teesdale moorlands, from the Cotherstone and Lartington Moors to those of the higher reaches of the Tees, were now leased to private gentlemen.

One of the 40 hand-coloured aquatints by Robert Havell after George Walker (1781-1856) in *The Costume of Yorkshire* (1814) is of the Moor Guide, smoking a pipe before setting off onto Bowes Moor with the hunters and their dogs. Walker's description of the scene suggests that most of the guides were lead miners:

> Sportsmen unacquainted with the moors, and the particular haunts of the game, make a point, on their arrival, of engaging one of these Guides, who from his perfect knowledge of the country, is well qualified to direct their steps and at the same time relieve their shoulders from the irksome load of the game bag and ammunition.

In 1866 there was a grand grouse-shooting story to tell; it lasted for three editions of the weekly *Teesdale Mercury*, and hinted at the effect that one visit could have on the

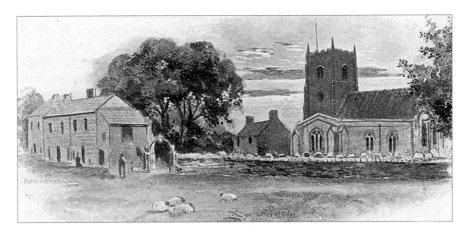

**101**  *Romaldkirk. Illustration by A. Barraud for* A Picturesque History of Yorkshire, *1901.*

popularity of the upper dale. After a morning service at the chapel at Studley Royal on Sunday 12 August, the Prince of Wales, attended by the Duke of Cambridge, General Knollys and Major Teesdale set out for the inn at High Force by way of the train to Darlington and, from there, Barnard Castle and Lartington, being greeted by crowds at each station. An 'elegant and commodious 'bus' drawn by four horses took the party on the 13 mile journey to High Force; the Prince sat on the top smoking a cigar, the servants and baggage were inside for the two-hour journey. At Cotherstone, Romaldkirk and all along the route there were large numbers of spectators, and the people of Middleton were sorry that as it was a Sunday they could not have decorations or bands. The Prince was reported as warmly approving of the bus, and being delighted with the scenery. The paper took the opportunity of doing its bit for the tourist industry of the dale:

> The road is one of the most beautiful in the County of York if not in the whole of England, and during the latter portion follows the winding of the Tees, which flows about 50 feet beneath it. High Force Inn at which the Prince is staying stands entirely by itself, by the side of the road, and within a quarter of a mile of the romantic falls from which it takes its name.

The inn was used as a shooting box every year by the Duke of Cleveland and other nobility who had shooting rights in the area; on this occasion the inn sign was removed to give the Prince some privacy.

The sport was excellent, the Prince frequently expressing his satisfaction; during the five days the number of brace of grouse shot were: Monday 1,200, Tuesday 1,007, Wednesday 565, Thursday 530 and Friday 870; apparently the count would have been higher if Colonel Hall had not been absent at the end of the week with a bilious attack. After His Royal Highness had received 12 brace, most of the rest of the 4,172 brace of grouse were as usual despatched by Messrs Arrowsmith & Sons of Barnard Castle to the metropolitan markets by the night mails. The Prince on his departure 'more than once said that he had been so delighted with the surrounding scenery and the sport that had been provided for him as well as the attention paid to his comforts, and the general arrangements, that he would on an early occasion pay another visit'.

A letter in *The Teesdale Mercury* on 22 August, referring to the old Marwood Chase and the recent visit of the Prince of Wales, hoped that Teesdale might once again become a royal sporting ground; the inhabitants of the dale would be always glad to give such distinguished visitors a cheerful and unobtrusive welcome, an observation which holds true in the dale today. The writer believed that such royal visits would help to popularise the dale and its scenery; they

> will, at the least, be the means of bringing this scenery widely and markedly under the notice of the Public; and as there is a fashion running even in such matters, it is only reasonable to conclude that a 'Tour in Teesdale' will from this time forth, become more popular.

A suggestion was made that people could subscribe towards suitable keepsakes for the royal visitors, an elegantly bound copy of the best edition of Sir Walter Scott's *Rokeby*, 'to which we owe so much', for the Prince of Wales and the Duke of Cambridge, and a portfolio of photographs of the dale for the Princess of Wales and Her Majesty The Queen.

Shooting records for Wemmergill Moor date back 134 years and one of the top drives includes the Kaiser Butt, named to commemorate a visit by Kaiser Wilhelm in 1895. Sir Frederick Millbank, a sporting tenant during Victorian times, shot 190 grouse in 25 minutes on a day when 1,035 brace were bagged. He wrote in his 1881 diary: 'In a good season, no one without seeing them, can have the remotest idea of the enormous number of birds … There are no moors in England and Scotland that can show half the number of birds on them as can Wemmergill.' A bag of 8,532 brace was recorded in 1872.

In describing the *History of Richmondshire* engravings after J.M.W. Turner, Margaret Hunt could report how a few years before the turn of the 19th century the inn at Greta Bridge was 'always filled with visitors … drawn there … by the fascination exercised by the spot.' Two well-known visitors were Charles Dickens and John Ruskin, the latter following in Turner's footsteps. Mrs Hunt quotes an entry in the visitors' book at the *George* inn which records Ruskin's stay in May 1876. The 'fascination' had of course been caused by Walter Scott's *Rokeby* and reinforced by guide books providing details of the locations in the poem and illustrations, especially those by Turner. This fascination continued into the next century; but, besides this, an additional visitor attraction was being developed.

# 19

## *The Bowes Museum*

*'It is designed in the French Renaissance style of architecture,*
*very elaborate and ornate in character'*

In 1869 the inhabitants of Barnard Castle witnessed the laying of the foundation stone of a building which as it developed appeared to be French in style. Twenty-three years later, in 1892, it was opened as the Bowes Museum. It was built by John Bowes (1811-85) and his wife Joséphine as a museum for their art collection.

As long ago as 1545 John Leland had acknowledged the long-standing position of the Bowes family in County Durham; the family's original seat was at Streatlam Castle, and in an earlier chapter we saw the part played by Sir George Bowes in the Rising of the North. His descendant John Bowes was born in 1811, the illegitimate son of the 10th Earl of Strathmore. John Bowes, with extensive land and coal interests in County Durham, made many visits to Paris, and in 1847 bought the Théâtre des Variétés, where he met Joséphine Benoîte Coffin-Chevallier. On their marriage in 1852 John Bowes gave Joséphine the Château Dubarry at Louveciennes, outside Paris. After the sale of the château ten years later and the removal of its furniture to their summer residence of Streatlam, the couple started collecting items for a future museum. From 1864, bit by bit, land to the east of Barnard Castle for the Museum and Park was 'bought for Mrs Bowes and indeed with her money', some from the sale of the Louveciennes château.

In 1867 John and Joséphine Bowes spent £560 at the Paris International Exhibition, purchasing articles from many European and Asiatic countries. Tours afforded other collecting opportunities: in 1868 porcelain and antiques were bought in Dresden. On a tour of 1845 through the Jura mountains John Bowes had noted that the landscape seemed an enlarged version of Teesdale and some 20 years later he would purchase a *View near Ornans* painted by Gustave Courbet (1818-77), to add to paintings by Eugene-Louis Boudin (1825-1908) and Jean-Baptiste-Camille Corot (1796-1875). Joséphine herself was an accomplished amateur artist, and to her paintings were added those of her fellow-exhibitors at the Paris Salons of the late 1860s; salon catalogues, inscribed for Monsieur and Madame Bowes, have survived. Paintings were also bought from picture dealers and auction houses.

In the summer of 1869 John and Joséphine came to Streatlam to supervise the building of their museum. The Parisian architect Jules Pellechet had designed the

**102**   *Mrs Bowes' Mansion & Museum, Barnard Castle. A Rock & Co. engraving, 1872.*

basic plan; but John Edward Watson of Newcastle, who had built the stables at Streatlam, was employed to make alterations to the design and to supervise the building work. The *Teesdale Mercury* recorded that the Museum 'is designed in the French Renaissance style of architecture, very elaborate and ornate in character, portions and details of which are taken from the Tuileries in Paris, the Hotel de Ville, Havre; and other public buildings in France'. The trowel used in laying the foundation stone is preserved in the museum, and commemorates the occasion with this inscription:

'On Saturday, the twentyseventh of November, Anno Domini 1869, this trowel was used by Joséphine Bénoite, Countess of Montalbo, wife of John Bowes of Streatlam Castle, Esqre., in placing the first stone of her Museum. Architect, J.E. Watson Esqr. of Newcastle on Tyne.' The plaque engraved in preparation for this event shows the intended date of 16th November; but Joséphine was unwell on that day and the ceremony was delayed.

An article in *The Builder* of 14 January 1871, on 'Mrs Bowes's Mansion and Galleries at Barnard Castle, Durham', was accompanied by a full-page engraving from J.E. Watson's drawing of the building, and a plan

**103**   *Trowel used in laying the foundation stone of The Bowes Museum, 27 November 1869.*

**104**  *The Picture Galleries at The Bowes Museum. Photograph by Elijah Yeoman.*

of the ground floor. Having described the layout and dimensions of the rooms and galleries, the article continued, 'The entrance gateway will be placed on the main road leading to Greta Bridge, and will be ornamental. The grounds are intended to be laid out with walks, terraces, lakes, gardens and an orangery, and other buildings necessary for the purpose will be erected.'

Collecting continued, with books for the Museum's library, pottery and porcelain from the International Exhibition in London in 1871, and automata such as a golden toy mouse and a silver swan which had been a great attraction at the Paris International Exhibition in 1867. The swan, bought by John Bowes in 1872, is the best known and best loved object in The Bowes Museum. It is a musical automaton in the form of a life-size model of a swan, comprising a clockwork mechanism covered in silver plumage above a music box. A simplified swan design is now used as the logo for the Museum, and the swan itself can be seen in operation daily.

In 1871 Joséphine Bowes signed her last Will and Testament, appointing her trustees, and bequeathing to them the Park and Museum for the benefit of the public. A week later, she signed a Codicil stating in the greatest detail her intentions regarding the Museum and its management. Her health deteriorated, and she died in 1874 at the age of 48.

The cost of building the Museum mounted, and the slow delivery of stone and slates delayed the construction; it was not until 1877 that it could receive the packing cases of exhibits, many of which had been stored at Streatlam. In 1879 a panelled ceiling was delivered to the Museum. John Bowes had commissioned it for the dining room at Streatlam and it consisted of panels depicting the coats of arms of the past owners of Streatlam Castle. John Bowes was heavily involved in cataloguing the paintings and other exhibits. At Barnard Castle in 1880 it became known that many pictures had arrived at the Museum, and large numbers of people were applying to view them. An editorial paragraph, fairly obviously written by John Bowes, appeared in the *Teesdale Mercury*: many paintings were still unframed, there had been no time to arrange them, and there was no catalogue for visitors; if the Curator had to spend time attending to visitors the final opening of the Museum might be deferred for years. The article ended, 'It is hoped, therefore, that the public will kindly consider that all cannot be arranged as if by magic in a short space of time, and that the labours of the Curator and his aides cannot be expedited by the presence of other parties.'

John Bowes died in 1885 at the age of 74. He left £135,000 to complete the Museum, together with £27,000 for the Chapel in the Museum Park, but his estate would not be able to pay the legacy in full until 1905. The Museum was opened on 10 June 1892. *The Teesdale Mercury* reported that the inhabitants of Barnard Castle celebrated the opening ceremony 'in the most becoming manner', displaying flags, bunting and floral decorations. Excursion trains brought extra visitors who assembled with members of official bodies, societies, clubs and schools to be led by the band of the 3rd Battalion Durham Light Infantry in a procession through the town to the Museum. About 4,000 people were on the terrace to hear Sir Joseph Pease read one item from Joséphine Bowes's will and commend it to all those present: 'And I request and adjure the inhabitants of Barnard Castle with common accord to aid the Committee as far as possible in guarding this Museum, the contents of which it has taken so much of my time and trouble to collect and bring together in this park.'

In the opening year 62,696 people visited the Museum; the average was twelve to fifteen thousand over the next ten years. *The Teesdale Mercury* in 1892 told of 'the dense crowds of people who have visited the Bowes Museum since its opening [being] proof positive that the refinement of the masses is rapidly progressing.' However, the cost of maintenance led the trustees in 1897 to impose an admission charge of 6d., with half-price for children, and 2s. 6d. season tickets for Barnard Castle families. Three years later a planned closure of the Museum was avoided when the trustees received the first payments of John Bowes's legacy. By 1905 the last of the legacy was paid and the trustees were able to abolish the charge for admission to the Museum. Soon though, the Museum had to close for two years after dry and wet rot was discovered in the roof; to compensate for the closure, improvements were made to the Park. Eight gardeners were employed in laying out the grounds with lawns, flower-beds, shrubberies and a bowling green.

The Museum was reopened in 1909, and in 1912 Lady Glamis from Streatlam Castle opened the bandstand. There were nearly five hundred pictures in the galleries, and several rooms of ceramics; as well as furniture from the Château at Louveciennes, there were fine Flemish and French tapestries. Articles commemorating the founders were in the large room above the entrance; Joséphine's pictures hung on the walls,

**105**   *The Bowes Museum. Drawing, c.1871.*

and in a case in the centre of the room were displayed items such as John Bowes' uniforms, his horse racing prizes, and the trowel used by Joséphine in laying the foundation stone of the Museum.

By 1947 financial difficulties were again felt, and the 6d. admission fee had to be re-introduced; in 1949 the Durham County Education Committee gave a grant of £1,800 to the Museum. Soon the 'Friends of the Bowes Museum' was formed. Her Majesty The Queen (descended from the 9th Earl of Strathmore, who adopted the name of Bowes-Lyon) sent a cheque for £100 and was invited to be patron of the Friends of Bowes Museum. Despite a further grant from the Durham Education Committee, and further gifts, in 1955 the Curator had to propose the closure of the Museum. After a guarantee from The Friends and some trusts, this closure was averted and the following year Durham County Council decided to take over the financial responsibility for The Bowes Museum. An illuminated scroll commemorates the event:

> 1956
> On the first day of November in the presence of
> Her Majesty Queen Elizabeth the Queen Mother
> the Durham County Council formally undertook
> responsibility for the administration of this Museum
> in order to ensure the continued realization of the ideals
> which animated its founders, John and Josephine Bowes.

In 1998 The Bowes Museum was the first museum to be awarded 'designated' status by the Museums, Libraries and Archives Council, identifying and celebrating its collections of national and international importance. However, funding from Durham County Council became more difficult, as the reorganisation of boundaries meant its population had decreased dramatically. Winter closure of the Museum in 1998/9 was averted with support from the 'Friends of Bowes Museum'. In 2000 an independent trust was formed, with Durham County Council providing core funding. With this security, and the ability to seek grants from elsewhere, improvements were made to, for example, the display of the porcelain collection, and an audio guide was introduced. *The John and Joséphine Story* Gallery opened in 2004; it tells the story of their meeting in Paris, their homes and their taste in furniture and fashion, and shows Joséphine's paintings, and the purchases from the International Exhibitions at the start of the museum project. A broader range of exhibitions also became possible, with loans from other art galleries.

Some of these exhibitions have direct relevance to the story of visitors to Teesdale. An exhibition entitled 'The Road to Impressionism: Joséphine Bowes and Painting in Nineteenth Century France' was mounted in 2003 and based on Joséphine's own paintings, and those that she and John Bowes had collected in France, with much research into the Museum's archives which included original Salon catalogues. 'Boudin, Monet and the Sea Painters of Normandy' in 2004 built on pictures in the Museum's collection, along with loans from galleries in London and New York. The bicentenary of John Sell Cotman's ground-breaking visit to the Greta (discussed in chapter 12), was celebrated by 'Sense & Sensibility: Cotman Watercolours of Durham & Yorkshire' in 2005, and the following year visitor numbers increased dramatically, drawn by 'Turner: Tours of Durham & Richmondshire'. As well as two watercolours of Gibside painted for John Bowes, the 10th Earl of Strathmore, and now owned by The Bowes Museum, a rare copper engraved plate of one of them – to illustrate Robert Surtees' *History … of Durham* – had come to light in the County Durham Archives. The exhibition looked at Turner's total involvement in his commissions, from sketching, through his watercolours to the engraving process. Local people were able to see not only the artist's sketch-book of 1831, showing a sketch of Barnard Castle, but also his watercolour *Barnard Castle* which was loaned by the Yale Center for British Art. Alongside the exhibition the Museum ran a series of watercolour workshops, 'Painting with Turner'; and number of guided walks, *Walking in the Footsteps of Turner*, were arranged.

The Bowes Museum's special connection with Queen Elizabeth The Queen Mother continued: in 2001 the exhibition 'Royal Milliners' showed 100 royal and designer hats and in 2005 the Friends of the Bowes Museum had an armillary sphere sundial installed in the Museum grounds in memory of their former patron.

In the first decade of the 20th century problems with the roof closed the Museum; in late 2005 scaffolding covered part of the building because the roof was again in urgent need of attention. This time the building has remained open, and new galleries are being formed to display more of the items gathered by John and Joséphine Bowes.

# 20

# *The Twentieth Century*

*'Scott had succumbed instantaneously to the pervasive charm of
Rokeby; my capitulation was also immediate'*

In his speech at the opening of The Bowes Museum in 1892, Sir Joseph Pease
considered that Teesdale was becoming more and more a health resort. He went on
to tell those people there of the area's attraction for visitors:

> You have that scenery, that fresh air, which the countless toiling thousands of busy
> England so much require, and which induce them at this time of year especially to
> spread themselves out away from what I may call the smoky haunts of men into the
> rural districts where fresh light, fresh air, and fresh vigour are to be found.

Quoting 18 lines from the poem *Rokeby*, Sir Joseph went on to say that they had
Rokeby and the Greta, Bowes, Streatlam and Raby: 'Many and many a summer day
can you ramble and look upon the historic places of the past and take pleasure in the
present. We stand in the middle, almost the centre, of the classic ground of Scott.'

*A Picturesque History of Yorkshire*, written from 'personal observations made during
many journeys' at the turn of the 20th century by J.S. Fletcher, provides a summary
of what visitors would find interesting in that part of Teesdale which lay south of the
Tees. The river Greta has a chapter to itself; it 'has a value altogether incommensurate
with its comparatively brief course. It is not only a stream of great beauty, most
romantically surrounded, but it possesses associations of rare interest and value.' The
Greta is not only full of memories of Sir Walter Scott, Charles Dickens and J.M.W.
Turner, but is also rich in archaeological, historical and geological interest. As well as
reciting the whole of the song 'Brignall Banks' from Scott's poem *Rokeby*, Fletcher
quotes the three stanzas where Scott describes the river within Rokeby Park, adding
his own comment: 'Here the Greta runs between mighty rocks and huge boulders,
and sometimes comes down from Stainmore with such fury that it hides even the
greatest of them beneath the overwhelming flood.' Fletcher in his chapter on 'The
Yorkshire Bank of the Tees' cites another poet, George Layton, describing Layton's
poem on Barnard Castle as 'somewhat ambitious', but choosing to quote from it 34
lines comparing the waterfalls of Cauldron Snout and High Force.

In the first half of the 20th century many of the visitors to Teesdale came by
train and surviving railway posters illustrate the attractions that could be reached by

**106**   *Scargill Castle. Illustration by A. Barraud for* A Picturesque History of Yorkshire, *1901.*

train. Images of Barnard Castle were used to advertise *Historic Monuments in North East England* (1910), *Circular Tours Through the most interesting portions of Yorkshire and the North of England* (*c.*1920), and *Old World Market-Places* (1930s). A North Eastern Railway poster of 1910, with artwork by Frank H. Mason (1876-1965), shows an impressive river Tees in flood flowing over High Force; entitled *Teesdale, Yorkshire: Magnificent waterfalls, river & moorland scenery*, lines from *Rokeby* are added:

> "Where Tees in tumult leaves his source
> Thundering o'er Caldron and High-Force" Scott.

An editorial in *The Teesdale Mercury* entitled 'With London Pressmen', in May 1905, illustrated the efforts that the North Eastern Railway company made to promote Teesdale: 'The descent upon the wilds of Teesdale of a round dozen of representatives from the leading London daily newspapers is an event utterly without parallel in the history of the dale.' Officials from the N.E.R. arranged a journey to Middleton-in-Teesdale for the journalists, who were reported as being greatly impressed with the natural beauties of Teesdale, 'as we doubtless shall presently learn'. A week later the front page of the *Mercury* led with 'Teesdale as a Holiday Resort – England's most romantic holiday ground and peaceful pastures'. One of the journalists had written in *The Weekly Dispatch* that 'Teesdale is one of the most charming holiday resorts in the whole length and breadth of England. Beautiful scenery, romantic surroundings, a pure and bracing air are its leading characteristics.' The area breathes of the past, the Roman occupation, its castles and Scottish raids; Teesdale villages can rank with the prettiest in England; the Tees boasts some of the noblest waterfalls in Britain. As well as Barnard Castle, the article mentions Dairy Bridge, Streatlam Castle, Raby Castle, Cotherstone, Romaldkirk, Lartington, Mickleton and Middleton-in-Teesdale.

**107** *Barnard Castle, County of Durham. Engraving after Thomas Allom, 1835.*

Three railway posters of the 1930s, beautifully painted by Ernest William Haslehust (1866-1948), promoted 'Teesdale by L.N.E.R.' Two of these posters depict the river Greta, at Dairy Bridge (plate XI), and at the Meeting of the Waters (the Greta and Tees). The style of poster continued to change; after the nationalisation of the railways in 1948, two 'Teesdale: See Britain by Train' posters for British Railways show people enjoying the idealised sunny river scenes at 'The Tees at Barnard Castle' (Jack Merriott 1958) and at 'High Force, Middleton-in-Teesdale' (Edward Wesson, 1962).

A Barnard Castle and District Publicity Society grew up and published an *Official Guide* to the town through the British Publishing Company; this ran into a number of editions, all with advertisements and photographs. The words 'Beauty Surrounds, Health Abounds' on the title page of the 1933 edition sum up the advertising message:

> Highly favoured with an environment of exquisite beauty, free from the excitement and turmoil of more popular rendezvous, situate on the "drier side of Britain," 600 feet above sea level, with ample shelter from cold winds, yet withal enjoying sunshine in abundance, Barnard Castle is an ideal Health Resort particularly for those who seek a rest cure and those who wish to spend a more active holiday amidst sylvan surroundings. The town possesses an excellent water supply and public health statistics stamp it as one of the healthiest towns in the North of England.

An advertisement for the *Morritt Arms* at Greta Bridge illustrates the motoring visitor which the guide is hoping to attract; the old coaching house has been re-modelled and re-furnished, 'with every convenience that the Motorist can require'. As well as references to Scott and Dickens, there are sections in the *Official Guide* on golf and fishing, and walking is promoted in Flatts Wood, Deepdale and Brignall Banks. The list of accommodation in Barnard Castle includes 13 hotels, four boarding houses and private hotels, 34 private apartments, three apartments in farmhouses, a furnished cottage and a youth hostel. In 1948 the Barnard Castle and District Publicity Society together with the Chamber of Trade brought out *Barnard Castle: A Guide to the Town & Neighbourhood*.

Grouse shooting continued to bring in visitors to the upper dale on 'the glorious twelfth' of August. According to *The Teesdale Mercury* in August 1904, the Americans 'dearly love Teesdale and its rugged grandeur. They revel in the fastnesses of the hills, and the mountain recesses.' Mr Bull, a wealthy New York banker, and Mr Smith, the champion aristocratic American boxer, were staying at Holwick Hall; 'one of the novelties of the modern sport is to see American ladies shooting grouse.' *The Teesdale Mercury* records 'Splendid Grouse Shooting in Teesdale' in 1912:

> Some remarkably good shooting has taken place, this season, on the higher Teesdale grouse moors … At the Moor House shooting by Cross Fell, it is noteworthy that one gentleman, aged 72 years, loading himself, had 116 driven grouse down to his own gun at an elevation of 2,100 feet above sea-level. This, surely, is a record performance.

The paper goes on to report the far west portion of the shoot, which included Mickle Fell, produced 724 brace on one day; 1,955 brace of birds fell in four days on the Wemmergill Moors.

The pastime of cycling continued to bring visitors to Teesdale. In 1904 *The Teesdale Mercury* could report that the Barnard Castle Meet was 'the oldest gathering of wheelmen in the world', the town being beloved of the cyclists for its picturesque surroundings and for the hospitality of the inhabitants. There must have been 25,000 onlookers at the procession: 'Lavish were the decorations at mid-day, bunting, banners, streamers, and floral adornments being everywhere profuse.' In 1905 'one of the heaviest laden trains which ever arrived at Barnard Castle' brought visitors to the Meet on Whit Monday, when 'competent observers' calculated that at least thirty thousand people were in the town.

*The Teesdale Mercury* of 29 May 1912 contained a long article on the Cyclists' Meet, the 36th annual meet of north-eastern 'wheelmen', though the cricket club sports had not survived. The cyclists, accompanied by cars and a large motor char-à-banc with thirty passengers, started on Saturday afternoon in Newcastle and continued to Durham, Bishop Auckland (where about forty took tea at the *Commercial Hotel)* and Staindrop, before proceeding to Barnard Castle where they were met by a torch-lit procession. Sunday morning was spent at Rokeby, with speeches and photographs; in the afternoon a service was held in the castle, and there were band concerts in Flatts Wood; the cyclists went to the village of Ovington for the evening. The main events took place on the Monday; the morning entertainment was held in the castle's inner bailey, with a backdrop of a magnificent river view. After the presidential address, 'remarkable for the breadth of its cordiality and pleasantries', two sketches were performed, a 'Spanish Extravaganza' by the Barnard Castle Excelsior Club, and 'The Recruiting Sergeant'. The afternoon procession, with a fancy dress competition, was watched by a surprisingly large crowd; a 'miscellaneous entertainment of song, dance and story' followed. The evening official reception took the form of a 'smoking concert' at the *Turk's Head Hotel*. The Meet finished on the Tuesday morning with the President's Reception in the castle; light refreshments accompanied 'song, speech and recitation' and were followed by the group photograph of the cyclists.

In 1946, after 50 visits to Barnard Castle, the North Eastern Cyclists Meet officially moved to Rothbury in Northumberland and Barnard Castle decided to hold its own Meet. In an open letter to the president of the North Eastern Cyclists the editor of *The Teesdale Mercury* of 12 June 1946 could applaud the success of the local Meet: over 3,000 people had paid a total of £200 to see the gymkhana, 1,000 cyclists from the northern counties were in the town, and 8,000 lined the streets for the Monday procession. By the 1950s the Meet had become more of a family weekend, with jazz bands, motor cycle races, Punch and Judy shows, a dog show and a road race. According to *The Teesdale Mercury*, the August Bank Holiday of 1950 was one of the busiest for many years; almost all the hotel accommodation was taken and there were large groups of campers in all parts of the upper dale; traffic was heavy and there were the usual numerous parties of cyclists and walkers.

In 1905 Michael Heavisides, a Stockton-on-Tees printer and publisher, produced his own *Rambles by the River Tees, from its rise to the ocean*. This was based on a number of day visits with cycle and camera and two family summer holidays, at Newbiggin and Barnard Castle, the latter holiday having the 'two-fold object of enjoying the lovely scenery … immortalized by Turner, Scott, and Dickens, and gathering material and photographs'. The family travelled by train from Stockton to Middleton-in-Teesdale via Darlington, Barnard Castle, Cotherstone, Romaldkirk, and Mickleton; father, son and eldest daughter brought their bicycles.

Michael Heavisides describes how Middleton-in-Teesdale has two main hotels, the *Blue Bell* and the *Cleveland Arms*; trains are met from both, with wagonettes running to the *High Force Hotel* and *Langdon Beck Hotel*. The return fares to these hotels are 1s. 6d. and 2s. 6d. respectively. At Middleton-in-Teesdale, Heavisides advises tourists to consult the North Eastern Railway Company's List of Furnished Apartments; 'substantial stone residences are fast springing up to meet the wants of tourists'. He notes that Cotherstone is apparently popular with the people of Sunderland; here are the *Fox and Hounds* and the *Red Lion*. Perhaps this popularity stemmed from 1888 when, at the North Eastern Cyclists Meet in Barnard Castle, the Sunderland club had led the call for the Meet to be held permanently in the town. In 1893 many cyclists had stayed in villages outside Barnard Castle, especially Cotherstone.

Heavisides illustrates his *Rambles* largely with his own photographs, proudly labelled 'taken with a No. 5 Poco Camera by M. Heavisides'; this was probably a Rochester 'Cycle Poco' folding bellows camera in a case designed to hang from a bicycle cross bar. The photographer obviously has an eye for a composition and a good viewpoint; at Cauldron Snout he leaves his bicycle and carefully steps from rock to rock to take photographs from the bridge at the top and then from the foot of the fall. Near Cotherstone he walks through fields and woods to the Fairy Cupboards to find the rocks occupied by 'a sewing party of ladies'; the rocky river bed he chooses for his view of the group is awash, 'so I heroically go into the water

**108**   *Dairy Bridge. Photograph by Michael Heavisides, c.1905.*

as I am, and take the photograph.' At Egglestone Abbey the farmer's boy is asked to drive a few cows to add interest to the foreground of the photograph. Later, visiting Dairy Bridge on the Greta with his eldest daughter, he admits having cycled the four miles earlier that morning to catch the sunlight on the scene.

After a night of heavy rain the family walk from Newbiggin to High Force, which they 'have a keen desire to see in its grandest form', after heavy rainfall in the upper dale. The waterfall obviously drew a large number of tourists; 'a goodly number of people are moving along by motor, conveyance, cycle, and foot, with the expectation of seeing a sight long to be remembered.' Entrance is by a wicket-gate, there are paths and some stone steps to help the tourist. Seven years later *The Teesdale Mercury* would report how heavy and continuous rains in the watershed area of the Tees had led to a rise in level of the river by three feet in a few hours; the waterfalls in upper Teesdale had been 'phenomenally grand' and had attracted hundreds of spectators.

Other waterfalls visited by Michael Heavisides are the Fairy Dell below High Force, Low Force at Wynch Bridge, Gibson's Cave at Bowlees, and Cauldron Snout.

A visit is made to The Bowes Museum; it is open on weekdays except Friday, and the fee is 3d. each; and at Romaldkirk the tomb to Sir Hugh Fitz-Henry is inspected. However, it seems as if, apart from the scenery, it is Scott and Dickens that have attracted Mr Heavisides to Teesdale: *Rokeby* is quoted at Abbey Bridge and Brignall Banks; at Greta Bridge, the letter from Dickens to his wife describing his

**109** *Brignall Church. Illustration for* Rambles in Teesdale, *1877.*

journey there is quoted in full, as is the preface to *Nicholas Nickleby*, in which Dickens states his early interest in the Yorkshire schools.

A special day visit is made from Stockton, where Heavisides incidentally quotes from Anne Wilson's poem *Teisa,* to Bowes, 'if only to look on Dotheboys Hall'. At the *Unicorn Hotel* Heavisides is shown the room in which Dickens stayed. Although Dickens had stated that Squeers was not based on any particular individual, Dotheboys Hall is still pointed out to visitors; the pump where the pupils used to wash is still in the yard (plate 77). Heavisides includes his own photograph of 'The old posting house, Greta Bridge': in 1905 the words 'Post Office' and 'Morritt Arms' can still be deciphered on the walls, and it was 'specially fitted for the reception of visitors during the summer months'; the rooms occupied by Dickens are pointed out, despite the fact that the novelist actually stayed at the *George and New Inn*. In Barnard Castle it is the *King's Head* (plate 90) which attracts the attention of Michael Heavisides. As well as the reference to the hotel in *Nicholas Nickleby*, it was from here that Dickens would have seen the shop of Humphrey the clock-maker, with the large grandfather's clock the printer recalls seeing in the doorway; *Master Humphrey's Clock* had been the resulting novel.

The Lake District artist Alfred Heaton Cooper (1864-1929) illustrated a number of travel guides for the publisher A. & C. Black. In 1924 *The County of Durham, Painted by A. Heaton Cooper, Described by G. E. Mitton* was published. As well as watercolours of *Barnard Castle, Banks of the Tees, The Tees at Barnard Castle, Raby Castle by Moonlight, High Force Teesdale*, there is *Cauldron Snout on the Tees* (plate XII). Here the river cascades over the blocky columnar whin sill, viewed by two diminutive figures on the footbridge; they represent the thousands of visitors which the introductory chapter tells us are drawn to the fine scenery up Teesdale, with its cascades of High Force and Cauldron Snout. The chapter on the Tees valley follows the dale upstream; Cauldron Snout forms 'a long canyon in the rocks, ending in a foaming fall with the waters broken and split by the obstacles in its way ... Cronkley Fell, celebrated for its gentians, towers overhead.'

In September 1938, to escape the atmosphere of pre-war gloom in the country, Alfred Wainwright (1907-91), later to become famous for his walking guides, spent his holiday on *A Pennine Journey, a Story of a Long Walk in 1938*. He walked alone along the eastern flank of the Pennines from Settle in Ribblesdale to Hadrian's Wall, returning down the west side; the story lay forgotten for nearly thirty years until the author remembered it when writing his guide to the Pennine Way, and his publisher persuaded him to allow it to be printed. Wainwright describes ascending and descending the progression of dales on the eastern side of the Pennine chain, Ribblesdale, Littondale, Wharfedale, Wensleydale, Swaledale, then entering the valley of the Greta and Teesdale; in addition to walking twenty miles a day he had three or four thousand feet of climbing. At Bowes he admired the picturesque cottages and charming gardens, noted the *Unicorn Inn* featured by Charles Dickens in *Nicholas Nickleby*, and visited the castle. Cotherstone had an air of quiet prosperity, but he walked on to reach Romaldkirk in the dark. At Middleton Wainwright bemoans the scars of quarries, the single-track railway from Barnard Castle and the mineral line within sound of High Force. He leaves Teesdale by Newbiggin Common, shrouded in mist, drawn by the urge to reach Hadrian's Wall.

When Una Pope-Hennessy (1876-1949) spent four years in County Durham she decided to investigate and preserve the literary associations of the county. In *Durham Company* (1941), she recalls visits to the county by Wordsworth, Coleridge and Dickens, but devotes a whole chapter to 'Rokeby and Sir Walter Scott': 'Scott had succumbed instantaneously to the pervasive charm of Rokeby; my capitulation was also immediate. No place more overpoweringly conveys the flavour and sentiment of days that can never return.' Una Pope-Hennessy traces the story of how the poem *Rokeby* came to be written, and the part played by J.B.S. Morritt in gathering historical information and sharing his local knowledge with Scott. 'To a lover of mediævalism the place was almost too perfect.' With Morritt, Scott scoured Deepdale, Cat Castle, Cotherstone with the rock still called Pendragon Castle, Wycliffe, Scargill, Brignall and the moors beyond. As Scott gazed out from Balliol's Tower, 'the countryside became re-peopled with historic ghosts – Philip of Mortham, Oswald of Wycliffe, Matilda of Rokeby. Every place was suddenly endowed with an owner and a story. Tapestry-wise a pseudo-romance of pseudo-chivalry was projected over the landscape.'

Una Pope-Hennessy says *Rokeby* was written in the cave above the Greta (map, plate 55), a spot so inspiring it must induce a flood of verse; but she admits that the poem is complicated and shows signs of having been pieced together out of separate anecdotes. With Mortham Tower behind him, Rokeby in front, and guide books, histories and maps beside him, Scott wrote the poem without which the Greta and Tees would have remained unknown outside the immediate area. It would be over forty years after Pope-Hennessy's visit before there would be a real revival in interest in Rokeby and Sir Walter Scott; in May 1986 Rokeby Park opened for two days a week in the summer months, and for the first time the house itself was opened to the public.[1]

Sir Clement Jones recalls that a short paragraph in *The Observer* in 1947 had led him, aged 66, and his wife to make a 'walking-cum-motor tour' into part of Teesdale: 'Those who know the furthest tip of Yorkshire where it meets Durham and Westmorland on the heathery wilderness of Wemmergill and soars by Mickle Fell to the tumble of the Tees in its great forces, know England at its royal best.' In *A Tour in Westmorland* published the following year Sir Clement compares the now

**110**   *Stainmoor Forest. Illustration by J.A. Symington for* A Picturesque History of Yorkshire, *1901.*

turnpiked Stainmore road with that described about the end of the 17th century by the antiquary Sir Daniel Fleming of Rydal (1633-1701), who wrote:

> From Brough the road leadeth over the ridge of fells. Here beginneth to rise that high, hilly and solitary country, exposed to wind and rains, which, because it is stony, is called in our native language Stane-moor; over which is a great (but no good) road, the post passing twice every week betwixt Brough and Bowes, and coaches going often that way, though with some difficulty and hazard of overturning and breaking. All here round about is nothing but a wild desert.

Jones can now write that Stainmore is full of interest for so many different experts: the geologist, the antiquarian, the bird-watcher, the botanist, the entomologist, the painter, the sportsman. He passes Wemmergill, famous for its grouse moor and well-known in the 1890s to readers of the illustrated weeklies for its smart shooting-parties in beards, starched collars, deer-stalker caps and spats.

However, it is the waterfalls of Teesdale that are the main draw. At High Force (plate XIII) Sir Clement Jones had 'never seen anywhere else such grandeur of setting or such a fine fall of water'; he describes the drop of more than 70 feet over the basalt lying above limestone. Caldron Snout is another magnificent waterfall where the three counties of York, Westmorland and Durham meet. Crossing the Tees by Scorberry Bridge, he notices 'a wealth of wild flowers; one field, in particular, covered with pale orchids, another with wild pansies of varying colours and sizes – purple, yellow, blue and yellow half and half, and pure white'. On a walk at Cotherstone his wife and he had seen the alpine bistort, woodruff, crosswort, wood sanicle, lady's bedstraw and milkwort.

Their tour continued by way of the train from Middleton-in-Teesdale to Kirkby Lonsdale via Barnard Castle, Bowes and Barras, over the Pennine ridge with a signboard

**111** *The Deepdale Viaduct, Barnard Castle. A Rock & Co. engraving, 1871.*

inscribed 'Stainmore summit: Height 1,370 feet', to Kirkby Stephen and Tebay. Sir Clement Jones could have added that Stainmore Summit was one of the first places to be blocked by snow-storms, snow ploughs being kept on standby at Darlington and Kirkby Stephen. After the Second World War traffic on this line declined; there was no local passenger traffic after 1952, although summer holiday trains ran to Blackpool and the Lake District until 1961. The following year the Stainmore line closed completely, the Deepdale viaduct being demolished in 1963 and the Tees viaduct in 1971. The Tees Valley line to Middleton-in-Teesdale closed in 1965.

Douglas Ramsden produced *From Stainmore to the Tees* in 1948 and a Picture Guide booklet called *Upper Teesdale* in 1961 (with map, plate 3). From these, and his manuscript notes which have survived, it is obvious that Ramsden thoroughly researched his topic. For example, he recalls the story of Edwin and Emma told in Mallet's ballad of 1760; a monument to the lovers can be found in the churchyard at Bowes, and the church register records the background: 'Rodger Wrightson, junr., and Martha Railton, both of Bowes. Buried in one grave. He died in a Fever, and upon tolling his passing Bell she cry'd out: "My heart is broke"; and in a few hours expired purely thro' Love. March 15, 1714.' Ramsden reports *The Unicorn Inn* at Bowes as remaining a perfect witness of the coaching days; one could imagine the cobbled yard bustling with activity when the Glasgow Mail arrived to change horses. Although Bowes is best known as the village of Dotheboys Hall, a large house at the western end being reputed to be the original school in Dickens's *Nicholas Nickleby*, there were at least three such schools in the village.

At Greta Bridge Ramsden was not misled, as were the other 'enthusiastic literary tramps' whom we have followed. He correctly identifies the farm house of Thorpe Grange as being the *New Inn* where Charles Dickens stayed in 1838; and the original *Morritt Arms*, with its stables and outbuildings around a cobbled courtyard, is now a private house to the east of the river Greta.

*21*

# The Pennine Way and the North Pennines

*Britain's first official long distance footpath, Britain's first UNESCO
Biosphere Reserve, and the first European Geopark*

In the last chapter we witnessed the inhabitants of Teesdale at the opening of the Bowes Museum in 1892 being reminded that 'you have that scenery, that fresh air, which the countless toiling thousands of busy England so much require'. By 1947 the *Observer* newspaper could proclaim that the area from Mickle Fell to 'the tumble of the Tees' with its great waterfalls was 'England at its royal best'. As part of the northern Pennines, Upper Teesdale's scenery and its scope for outdoor activity was soon receiving official national recognition, thus attracting more visitors.

In June 1935 the *Daily Herald* published an article by Tom Stephenson, a rambler, entitled 'Wanted – A Long Green Trail'. Inspired by the Appalachian Trail in the USA, Tom Stephenson suggested a trail along the 'backbone of England'. At the inaugural conference of the Pennine Way Association in 1938, the 'special character and attractiveness' of the Way, with its 'wide, health-giving moorlands and high places of solitude' were praised; these features should be available for all time as a natural heritage for 'all who feel the call of the hills and the lonely places'. The Pennine Way was designated as Britain's first long distance footpath in 1951, and finally opened in April 1965. More than 100,000 walkers a year now follow the 268 miles along the Pennines from the Peak District to the Scottish borders.

Usually walked from south to north, the Pennine Way approaches Teesdale by way of Stainmore, crossing the old Barnard Castle to Kirkby Stephen railway line and the A66 following the Roman road, before crossing Deepdale and Cotherstone Moor to Baldersdale. The Bowes Loop provides an alternative route over this section, allowing a visit to the village of Bowes with its castle, its associations with Dickens, its shops and accommodation. At the midway point on the Way is the Balderhead Reservoir; when finished in 1965 it had the largest earth dam in the country holding back four million gallons of water, adding to the Hury and Blackton Reservoirs (1894-6) lower down Baldersdale. The Pennine Way, now joined by the Bowes Loop, passes near Birk Hatt, the former home of Hannah Hauxwell, and through Hannah's Meadow Nature Reserve (to be considered in the next chapter). After Lunedale, with the Grassholme and Selset Reservoirs (completed in 1915 and 1960), the Pennine Way soon gives panoramic views of Teesdale before dropping down towards Middleton-in-Teesdale.

**112** *The River Tees below Wynch Bridge. Line drawing by Alfred Wainwright, c.1968.*

**113** *Falcon Clints looking east. Line drawing by Alfred Wainwright, c.1968.*

In his *Pennine Way Companion* of 1968 Alfred Wainwright enthuses over the next stretch of the walk. The five miles from Middleton-in-Teesdale to High Force are a joy to the naturalist, the botanist and the geologist. One of Wainwright's delightful pen-and-ink drawings is of the river Tees below Wynch Bridge, the most beautiful stretch of all. The fell walker also writes of the 'lovely reaches of Upper Teesdale', and High Force and Cauldron Snout feature in his 11 highlights of the whole Pennine Way. To Wainwright, High Force is the finest moment of the river Tees, especially seen from the Yorkshire side; it is a spectacle all should see, no other waterfall in England creates such an impression. The route leaves the river Tees for a while, passing near the Langdon Beck Youth Hostel before skirting Widdybank Fell of botanic fame. After Cronkley Scar and Falcon Clints are passed, Cauldron Snout dramatically comes into view. Wainwright finds Cauldron Snout a fine mountain cataract; after continuous heavy rain it is 'a tremendous spectacle, a torrent of angry, cascading waves, white with rage'; but he bemoans the fact that, despite much protest, a new reservoir above the Snout at Cow Green is to drown an area of unique botanical interest.

From Cauldron Snout the Pennine Way follows the route taken by the artist J.M.W. Turner in 1816 when he was 'bogged most compleatly', riding along Maize Beck to High Cup Nick and down to the village of Dufton on the western side of the Pennines. The Way then climbs again, passing the source of the Tees, to the highest point on the walk, the summit of Cross Fell. Here Wainwright devotes a page to comment on lead mining. His drawings include relics from the lead-mining era, all located on the route maps drawn in his own famous style; here are levels, an air shaft, a mineshop, and the iron water trough used by the ponies bringing supplies for the miners and taking the lead ore to the smelter.[1]

Alfred Wainwright walked the Pennine Way in 1966 and 1967. In November 1966 an article with the title 'Industry versus botany – in Upper Teesdale' appeared in the *Illustrated London News*. Parliament was to decide whether the Tees Valley Water Board would be allowed to build a reservoir which would flood 650 acres of moorland in the headwaters of the Tees, an area of almost unique botanical value. The growing industries and population of Teesside urgently needed more water, and of the 17 sites investigated for a reservoir, Cow Green would be the cheapest and the most productive, would require the least obtrusive engineering, with a minimal effect on agriculture, and would not interfere with any habitation. However, the Teesdale Defence Committee had argued at a mass protest meeting that the Cow Green area was part of a unique botanical community, a site perhaps unchanged since the last Ice Age which had been the delight and study of botanists for many years. Despite this, Parliament approved the Tees Valley and Cleveland Water Bill, and the building of Cow Green reservoir was completed in June 1970. The Imperial Chemical Industries, the chief beneficiary of the new reservoir, set up and financed the Teesdale Trust to research the origins of the plants and animals of the area, and the effects that the reservoir had on them. While a portion of the special habitats were lost, the effect of the reservoir has not had any adverse ecological repercussions, and access to Cauldron Snout by way of the road to the dam was much improved.

Many people seem to have a desire to trace a river's course from its source to the sea, and the river Tees is no exception. Benjamin Heslop painted 36 watercolours for his book *The River Tees from Source to Sea* in 1893 (see plate X). Twelve years later Michael Heavisides spent his holidays taking photographs to illustrate his *Rambles by the River Tees, from its rise to the ocean*. However, it is only from the 1980s that it has been possible to follow the river Tees almost from its source to its mouth, using negotiated rights of way. The 'Teesdale Way' is an extension of the Pennine Way, and was opened when both Durham County Council and the former Cleveland County Council developed the riverside footpath. Downstream from Middleton-in-Teesdale and its junction with the Pennine Way, the Durham County section of the Teesdale Way is waymarked with the logo of a dipper bird, a common sight on the river banks, and wherever feasible paths on both banks of the river are used, allowing the growing number of walkers to plan circular routes.

More recently the Teesdale environment was celebrated in 'Visual Arts UK: North of England 1996', part of the Arts Council of England's millennium project, 'Arts

2000'. 'Marking Parish Boundaries along the Teesdale Way' was Teesdale District Council's contribution to this project. Where the Teesdale Way crossed 11 parish boundaries, often at either end of a bridge or stile, or in one case across a fence, pairs of markers were set up. Designed by Richard Wentworth, the markers had the names of the parishes incised into 'split' cast-iron posts, and formed the first public art project in Britain to be supported by the National Lottery.[2] For the same 'Arts 2000' project The Bowes Museum put on an exhibition *Walking the Landscape: With Cotman and Turner in Teesdale*, and three walk leaflets entitled *Artists in Teesdale* were produced. After viewing the paintings, watercolours and engravings by Turner, Girtin, Cotman and others, visitors to the exhibition were encouraged to follow in the footsteps of the 18th- and 19th-century tourists drawn to the splendours of the natural environment of Teesdale. As well as walks to High Force, Wynch Bridge and Cauldron Snout on the river Tees, there were two routes along the river Greta.

Around the headwaters of the river Tees and stretching towards the upper end of Cow Green Reservoir, an area called Moor House was designated in 1952 as the first National Nature Reserve (NNR) in England. Upper Teesdale NNR, designated in 1963 and extended in 1969, stretches from Cow Green Reservoir and Cauldron Snout southwards to Mickle Fell and eastwards to High Force waterfall, encompassing Widdybank Fell and Cronkley Fell. The two NNRs of Moor House and Upper Teesdale were designated by the United Nations Educational, Scientific and Cultural Organisation (UNESCO) as a single Biosphere Reserve in 1976. Nowhere else in Britain is there such a range of rare upland habitats, from sub-alpine heaths and blanket bogs to juniper wood and hay meadows. Research ranges from meteorological studies in the 1930s to the present-day investigation into the effects of climate change on such upland areas. Today the local farming community works with the owners of the land – Natural England (the former English Nature) and the Raby and Strathmore estates – to manage the reserve. Special conservation programmes encourage the survival of the black grouse, of juniper woodland, and of rare alpine plants such as the yellow marsh saxifrage.

The increase in interest in conservation brings more visitors to such Reserves, with associated problems such as increased trampling on fragile habitats and the disturbance of wildlife. Within the Upper Teesdale National Nature Reserve the Widdybank Fell Nature Trail was devised by Nature Conservancy in the 1960s. The first trail booklet included a map showing numbered stops along the route to Cauldron Snout, and detailed line drawings of plants and birds. This booklet was designed to help walkers appreciate the scientific importance of the reserve and why it must be carefully managed. The geology of the carboniferous sedimentary rocks, the injection of the Whin Sill, and the production of the sugar limestone was explained, along with the signs of lead mining and the relationship between rocks and plants. Today English Nature's leaflet is in full colour, with maps of the combined Moor House-Upper Teesdale NNR and the trail alongside photographs illustrating the rare alpine plants and some aspects of conservation.

After the Second World War the establishment of National Parks was suggested as part of the post-war reconstruction of the UK. A government committee chaired

**114**   *The High Force on the Tees. Engraved by William Miller after Edward Swinburne for* The History and Antiquities of the County Palatine of Durham, *1794.*

by Sir Arthur Hobhouse in 1947 prepared legislation for National Parks and Areas of Outstanding Natural Beauty, or AONBs; each Park 'should have great natural beauty, a high value for open-air recreation and substantial continuous extent'. The significance and value of the North Pennine landscape was first officially recognised by the Hobhouse Committee who declared it a 'conservation area'. The North Pennines was also considered for designation as a National Park in the 1970s but the proposal was thought to be too difficult administratively because the area was run by five different county councils.

No action was taken until 1973, when the Countryside Commission announced their intention to seek the designation of the North Pennines as an AONB; these 'are selected for designation because they possess fine landscapes which should be protected and, where possible, enhanced.' The designation order for the North Pennines AONB was made in 1978; after a public enquiry the confirmation order, with revised boundaries, was finally made in 1988. Including Teesdale above Middleton-in-Teesdale, the AONB has 'tumbling waterfalls, sweeping moorland views, dramatic dales, stone-built villages, snaking stone walls'.[3]

The statistics are impressive: as well as rare arctic-alpine plants, the North Pennines AONB has 30 per cent of England's upland heathland, 20 per cent of its blanket bog, 80 per cent of its black grouse, 22,000 pairs of breeding wading birds, and 40 per cent of the UK's upland hay meadows.

It is estimated that the UK has lost 95 per cent of its colourful flower-rich meadows since 1945. The AONB Partnership's 'Hay Time' project, designed to save and improve hay meadows in the North Pennines, was launched in May 2006. Hay meadows survive in the North Pennines thanks to traditional farming practices, in particular the late cutting of the crop. This allows the plants time to flower and seed, compared with the modern practice of taking two or three cuts when making silage. Hay meadows provide an important nesting habitat for birds such as the skylark, lapwing and yellow wagtail. Working together with farmers, the Hay Time project harvests wildflower seeds from species-rich meadows and uses these to enhance meadows that have lost some of their characteristic plants, such as melancholy thistle, wood cranesbill and globe flower.

The black grouse is one of the most rapidly declining bird species in the UK, and the Black Grouse Recovery Project has been running since 1996 in the North Pennines. Black grouse live on the fringes of moorland, where blanket bog and shrubby woodland are also found. This project encourages farmers and landowners to improve these conditions by reducing sheep grazing on the moor edges, by small-scale planting of shrubby woodlands, and by controlling the birds' predators.

As well as its fine landscapes and rare upland habitats, the North Pennines AONB also has an important geological heritage (as discussed in Chapter 1). This geological heritage was recognised in June 2003 when the North Pennines AONB became the first area in Britain to be awarded the status of 'European Geopark' which is a place with an outstanding geological heritage which is used actively to support sustainable development. The Geopark status for the AONB is managed by the North Pennines AONB Partnership.

# Tourists to Teesdale Today

*European and Global Geopark*

We have traced the way in which the perception of Teesdale's landscape has changed over the centuries. Early travellers found the area wild and threatening, with Thomas Amory describing 'mountains tremendous to behold' as he made 'numberless windings round impassable hills'; John Byng, though determined to see High Force, thought Teesdale 'a wild, bleak country, only inhabited by miners, or visited by grouse shooters'. By the early 19th century there was a more romantic view of the dale, as shown in Walter Scott's poem *Rokeby* and the watercolours of J.M.W. Turner and J.S. Cotman. Later in the 19th century, walkers such as Walter White were drawn by 'the remote dales where crowding hills abound with the picturesque', the portrayal of the scenery by earlier artists and writers being part of the appeal. During the 20th century Teesdale's rare flora and fauna were protected in nature reserves, and its special landscapes recognised in the designation of an Area of Outstanding Natural Beauty. It is now accepted that these special landscapes, from meadows to grouse moors, based on the underlying geology, should not just be conserved, but interpreted and promoted for the benefit of both tourists and the local people. Tourism now has an essential part to play in the economy of Teesdale.

Today's visitors come to see the country house of Rokeby Park, the castles at Barnard Castle (20,000 each year) and Raby, the ruins of Egglestone Abbey, but more especially the spectacular waterfalls of High Force and Cauldron Snout, along with The Bowes Museum in Barnard Castle (120,000 visitors per year, with over two thousand Friends). An average of 26,000 people visit the Tourist Information Centre in Barnard Castle each year, while over 70,000 use each of the car parks at Cow Green and Bowlees. About 40,000 walk the High Force section of the Pennine Way, and nearly four times as many are estimated to visit the Moor House-Upper Teesdale National Nature Reserve.

Although the grounds at Rokeby Park were visited in the 19th century, the house was opened to the public for the first time in 1986. The antiquities, oil paintings, Anne Morritt's needlework pictures, and the print room described in Chapter 2 are all on view. The Meeting of the Waters, Dairy Bridge, Greta Bridge, Brignall Banks and Brignall old church are nearby. *Picturesque Paths in Teesdale* walk leaflets enable the visitor to follow in the footsteps of J.S. Cotman, J.M.W. Turner and Walter Scott. Two of the former inns at Greta Bridge, discussed in Chapters 11 and 12, continue to supply the needs of visitors: the first *Morritt Arms* is now The Coach House, a guest house in The Square, and *The George*, now the present-day *Morritt Arms*, is still a hotel.

Some consolidation of the old church at Brignall has taken place. Here is a gravestone, dated 1695 and 1728, to Christopher and Henry Thwaites respectively, post masters at Greta Bridge; those interested in the early botanists will find a modern plaque marking the Revd Johnson's grave: 'Rev. Ralph / Johnson / Vicar of Brignall / 1656-1695 / Naturalist & Friend of / John Ray'. At Middleton-in-Teesdale another botanist's gravestone is still readable: 'SACRED to the MEMORY of / William Oliver Surgeon in Middleton / who departed this life October 11th / 1816 Aged 56 Years'. In the same churchyard is the gravestone to Richard Watson, 'The Bard of Teesdale', who died in 1891: 'Enough the record of his name, his songs perpetuate his fame'.

At Middleton-in-Teesdale, the influence of the London Lead Company is still to be seen.[1] Two circular walk leaflets were published in 2002 as *Lead Mining Landscapes*, linking remains of the lead-mining industry in the Hudeshope valley above Middleton-in-Teesdale and around Eggleston; here are hushes and mine entrances, miners' cottages and mineshops, bouseteams and wasteheaps. In the 18th century the London Lead Company funded some of Teesdale's turnpike roads. From Bowlees part of the pre-turnpike road can be followed to beyond Dirt Pit; the modern road follows the turnpike road nearer the river Tees. Beyond Langdon Beck at Ashgill Head there is a level entrance, the remains of a mine shop, reservoir and washing floor, as well as signs of the turnpike road and bridge where the modern road avoids the earlier road's tight bend around Ashgill Beck (see map, plate 27).

*In the footsteps of Charles Dickens* is a leaflet which links the places where the novelist stayed, Barnard Castle, Greta Bridge and Bowes, with the former 'Yorkshire schools' whose buildings survive – at Bowes and near Eggleston. A plaque on the former *King's Head* in Barnard Castle states that Charles Dickens stayed there in February 1838 while collecting material for his novel *Nicholas Nickleby*. In the churchyard at Bowes is the gravestone to George Taylor, 'who died suddenly at Mr William Shaw's Academy'; Dickens claimed that 'his ghost put Smike into my head upon the spot.' There are also memorials to William Shaw, the headmaster of Bowes Academy, to the two young lovers Rodger Wrightson and Martha Railton, and to three workmen who were killed during the building of the South Durham and Lancashire Union Railway over Stainmore Summit.

At Whistle Crag on the road between Eggleston and Middleton-in-Teesdale is a lay-by with an information board explaining the panoramic view of the valley of the Tees and its tributary the Lune. This is the view first described by Arthur Young in 1770 and referred to by many subsequent tour writers. There is a plaque on the house in Galgate, Barnard Castle where the local solicitor and tour writer William Hutchinson lived.

A little below the Whistle Crag viewpoint and near Mickleton, the Beckstone Wath footbridge over the Tees opened in 2002, enabling another circular walking

**115**   *The Tees Viaduct, Barnard Castle. A Rock & Co. engraving, 1871.*

route around Middleton-in-Teesdale, Eggleston and Romaldkirk along the Teesdale Way. Two new footbridges have been built by Durham County Council on the Bowes Loop of the Pennine Way, across the river Greta at Swinholme and Deepdale Beck at Levy Pool, enabling walkers to use the route in all weathers. Alfred Wainwright in his *Pennine Way Companion* had previously warned of the difficulty or impossibility of making these crossings in times of heavy rain. The bridges were funded by the Countryside Agency from their National Trails budget. Sections of the Pennine Way have been paved with stones or have duckboards laid; the section downstream from High Force has both these methods of erosion control.

It is important for Teesdale's economy that tourist numbers are retained and if possible increased, although some tourist facilities have inevitably closed. *Meet the Middletons*, a tourist attraction which explored Middleton-in-Teesdale's 19th-century history through the lives of one family, closed in January 2006, within two years of its opening; only a sixth of the projected number had visited the centre. Baldersdale Youth Hostel closed at the end of the 2006 season due to falling visitor numbers and the need for substantial work to upgrade facilities. Despite being on the Pennine Way, the 37-bed hostel had been running at less than a quarter of its capacity, and improvements costing £40,000 were required. Langdon Beck Youth Hostel however, with its 'green tourism' approach, continues to be busy.

A new tourist attraction for Teesdale was proposed in 2002: the longest rope suspension bridge in the world, capable of attracting 150,000 extra visitors a year to Teesdale. Longer than the Capilano bridge near Vancouver, the suggested bridge would be suspended from the abutments of the Tees Viaduct at Barnard Castle, left when the rest of the viaduct was demolished in 1972, but there is controversy over Teesdale Marketing's proposal, with some being opposed to the extra roads, the car park, café, and other facilities which would be needed. The remains of the Tees Viaduct are in Flatts Woods; here walks originally laid out in the 19th century have been renovated, and a leaflet with the walks has been produced. Higher up the dale Wynch Bridge, the country's first suspension bridge, continues to attract visitors; an information board quotes from Anne Wilson's poem *Teisa* (1778) and from William Hutchinson's description in 1794.

To retain interest in the castle at Barnard Castle, English Heritage in the summer of 2006 put up a new information board, showing a reconstruction of how the castle and its immediate area would have looked in the 15th century, with troops marching into the castle as well as parading inside the grounds. The Bowes Museum continues to organise activities and put on exhibitions that will attract more visitors. Reflecting the Queen Mother's strong links with the Museum since the 1950s, The Bowes Museum was chosen as one of only four venues to show, in 2007, an exhibition of *Watercolours and Drawings from the Collection of Queen Elizabeth The Queen Mother.*

In 1972 a Yorkshire Television documentary *Too Long a Winter* brought a stream of journalists and then visitors to a remote part of Teesdale. The film told the story of Hannah Hauxwell's lone struggle to farm at the remote Low Birk Hatt in Baldersdale, a farm with no electricity and no running water. The sight of Hannah leading her cow into the byre from a howling blizzard had an enormous effect on the viewing public; ITV's switchboards were jammed with telephone calls and special arrangements had to be made to cope with the huge amount of mail for her. *Too Long a Winter* won many awards around the world and made Hannah Hauxwell a celebrity. Further documentaries and a book, *Seasons of My Life* written with the film director Barry Cockcroft, ensured a continuing interest in the story. Fundraising paid for electricity to be brought to Low Birk Hatt, and Hannah's farmhouse was filled with gifts; she was able to buy more cattle. Eventually, in 1988, she was persuaded to leave her hard life on the farm, which her great great-grandfather William Bayles was the first to occupy in 1826, and retire to a cottage in nearby Cotherstone. As well as telling the story of Hannah's and her parents' life in Baldersdale, a second book, *Daughter of the Dales*, followed the celebrity Hannah in her travels around the country.

A chapter in *Daughter of the Dales* is called 'Adder's Tongue, Moonwort and Frog Orchid: the Legacy of the Hauxwells'; botanist Mike Prosser found that the meadows at Low Birk Hatt were the least improved meadows and most species-rich in upland Durham. Hannah had continued to farm in the traditional way, not using fertiliser to produce silage but taking the cattle out of the meadow in early April, allowing the plants time to bloom and seed before cutting the grass in late August for fodder. As

**116** *High Force & From York Side. Illustration for* Rivers of Great Britain, *1902.*

well as grasses there were flower species such as lady's mantle, yellow rattle, frog orchid, eyebright and globe flower, and ferns such as adder's tongue and the moonwort.

Durham Wildlife Trust now manages Hannah's Meadow as a Nature Reserve with an unmanned visitor centre; the pastureland also supports breeding birds such as skylark and curlew. Visitors from across the world come to see Hannah's Meadow and her cottage in Cotherstone; through the films and books many more know of a former way of life in a remote part of Teesdale, and its botanical legacy.

A television advertisement has raised the profile of another Teesdale site. Two hundred and sixty years after the first record of a visit there by a tourist, High Force was used in 2006 by the development agency One NorthEast in its award-winning campaign 'Passionate people, Passionate places'. Requests for information on access to the waterfall poured into the Barnard Castle Tourist Information Centre.

During 2006 there was a great deal of attention given to the special landscapes of Teesdale. English Nature (now Natural England) arranged a number of events in 2006 connected with the Moor House-Upper Teesdale NNR. Walkers could investigate the geology and plants of Widdybank Fell and Cronkley Fell, assist with the Juniper Regeneration Project by picking juniper berries, or learn about farming and conservation. For children there was an art day looking at meadow flowers, and for adults a talk on climate change in the North Pennines. The Upper Teesdale Botany Group produced three walk leaflets called 'Tees Bank Flowers'. These walks, which detail the flowers and ferns to be seen on the Pennine Way between Scoberry Bridge and High Force, are accessible from car parks at the Bowlees Visitor Centre and High Force.

The Geopark concept was originally part of a European programme but it has now been elevated by UNESCO to global status. In 2004 the North Pennines AONB European Geopark became a founding member of the UNESCO Global Geoparks Network, with access to more funding programmes and shared expertise in 'geotourism'. Central to the aims of the Geopark is the interpretation of the geological heritage. The Teesdale Time Trail project was led by the North Pennines AONB Partnership and supported by the British Geological Survey, English Nature and the Durham Wildlife Trust, with money from the Heritage Lottery Fund. The Trail consists of a number of information panels and a series of leaflets to help visitors understand the geological basis of the area. At Cauldron Snout, High Force, Low Force, Bowlees Visitor Centre, Holwick and Hanging Shaw, the formation of the sedimentary rocks with their fossils, the intrusion of the Whin Sill, the formation of the sugar limestone, and the legacy of the Ice Age are all interpreted. 'Rockwalks' and 'Geotours' (minibus tours with short walks) based on the Teesdale Time Trail, are organised by the AONB team for those who prefer a guided visit. Although the Rock Detectives geology clubs for children are based in other parts of the AONB, events in 2006 included visits to some of the Teesdale Time Trail sites.

There is no way of knowing how many extra visitors have come to the North Pennines as a result of the Geopark initiatives, but, in 2006 the North Pennines AONB Partnership brought in 1,400 people to 'Northern Rocks, The North Pennines Festival of Geology and Landscape' which included themed walks to Cauldron Snout, High Force, Low Force and Widdybank Fell. The AONB Partnership is also developing many more geological trails, guided tours, art activities and other ways of bringing geology to the public. This is in addition to its wider activities on all other aspects of natural beauty.

After a three-day assessment in October 2006 the North Pennines AONB's status as a UNESCO European and Global Geopark was successfully revalidated for a further three years. The work of the AONB Partnership in using geology as a tool for sustainable development was found to be exemplary within the European Geoparks Network. Alongside the work in neighbouring Weardale, the Teesdale geotourism, education and conservation projects played a crucial part in the assessment.

For centuries visitors, writers, artists, geologists, botanists, walkers and tourists have come to explore, to enjoy and interpret the unique landscape of Teesdale. This landscape, both physical and human, has been shaped by its underlying geology. It seems fitting that the story of the discovery of Teesdale should end with 'geotourism', with visitors being encouraged to come and experience and understand the rocks and their legacy, the Whin Sill crags and waterfalls, the remains of lead mining, and the rare arctic-alpine plants.

# Notes

## Introduction

1. From the North Pennines AONB website.
2. *Ibid.*

## Chapter 1: Geological Foundations

1. Manson, R.T., *Zig-Zag Ramblings of a Naturalist* (1898).
2. With minor amendments, Forster's names are still used on official geological maps.
3. Lebour, G.A., *Outlines of the Geology of Northumberland and Durham* (1886).
4. Topley, W. & Lebour, G.A., 'On the intrusive character of the Whin Sill of Northumberland', *Quarterly Journal of the Geological Society*, vol.33 (1877).
5. In the collection at Killhope, the North of England Lead Mining Museum, Weardale; information from Ian Forbes.

## Chapter 2: Classical Foundations

1. These, and other, paintings can still be seen at Rokeby. An 18th-century copy of a bas-relief from the Villa Borghese, Roman busts and Tuscan vases from Robinson's collection can still be identified; some of the Roman altars and inscriptions are in the garden.
2. Now in the National Gallery; a copy painted about 1906 is at Rokeby.
3. The 1781 edition quoted here has 'distinction'; Mason's substitution of 'destruction' in the 1783 edition makes much more sense.
4. 'rustling' in the 1781 edition.

## Chapter 3: The Early 'Explorers'

1. Leland's *Itinerary*, Hearne's edn vol.1 (1768); vol.5(1769).
2. Some details have been added to Camden's account here; the Nevill tombs are still to be seen in Staindrop church. See Chapter 16 for Wordsworth and the Rising of the North.
3. The *Gentleman's Magazine*, August 1747. Manley, G., 'George Smith the Geographer and his ascent of Crossfell', *Cumberland and Westmorland Antiquarian and Archaeological Society's Transactions* (1948); reprinted in *North Pennines Heritage*, nos. 53, 54 (2004).

## Chapter 5: Thomas Amory's *Life of John Buncle, Esq.*

1. Brown's 'Description of the Lake at Keswick' is quoted in Hutchinson, *An Excursion to the Lakes* (1776), pp.127-30. Hutchinson used the subsequent pamphlet, *Description of the Lake and Vale of Keswick*, printed at Newcastle in 1767 and apparently sold to tourists from the *Queen's Head* in Keswick.

2. Amory makes a reference to what is likely to be Thomas Cox, *Magna Britannia et Hibernia, antiqua & nova. Or, a New Survey of Great Britain, wherein the topographical account given by Mr Cambden, and the late editors of his Britannia, is added a more large history ...* (1720-31).

### Chapter 6: The Picturesque in Paintings and Engravings

1. For Mason at Rokeby see Chapter 2.
2. George Vertue (1683-1716).
3. Einberg, E., 'Catalogue Raisonné of the Works of George Lambert', *Walpole Society*, vol.63 (2001), p.144.

### Chapter 8: Local Artists and Poets

1. Not to be confused with his son, also George, who spelt his surname Cuitt.
2. Clarkson, C., *The History & Antiquities of Richmond* (1821).
3. John Byng's *A Tour to the North* is discussed in Chapter 10.
4. Fletcher, J. S., *A Picturesque History of Yorkshire*, vol.3 (1901).
5. Scott's poem is discussed in Chapter 13.

### Chapter 11: *A Tour in Teesdale*

1. Romney, P. (ed.), *The Diary of Charles Fothergill 1805: An Itinerary to York, Flamborough and the North-Western Dales of Yorkshire* (1984).
2. A letter, Who wrote 'A Tour in Teesdale'?; University of Durham Library, Palace Green, Add MS 1415/1-2.
3. The two inns were the *Morritt Arms* (now a guest house in The Square) and *The George* (now the *Morritt Arms*).
4. Garland gives the inscription on the gravestone, though it had not yet been erected (a different inscription, on the memorial stone erected in 1848, is to be seen today), and the whole epitaph, though unused at the time through lack of money. The two lovers died in 1714.

### Chapter 12: John Sell Cotman

1. The Cholmeley Archive contains the letters sent to Francis Cholmeley and the Brandsby 'Commonplace Books'.
2. No longer an inn; the present *Morritt Arms* was not so called until the 1840s, previously having been called *The George*.
3. David Hill identified the subject of this painting in *Cotman in the North* (2005), p.123.
4. Over the years these two Cotman watercolours have had different titles. The Leeds sketch was originally bought in 1936 as *Lake Scene with Trees*, then wrongly identified as being of the Meeting of the Waters; it was later identified as being at Hell Cauldron. The National Gallery of Scotland watercolour was exhibited in 1806 as *On the river Greta, Yorkshire*, in 1808 as *Hell Cauldron, Rokeby Park*, and bought in 1913 as *The Silent Pool, where the Greta Meets the Tees*. Both works are as Hell Cauldron, a site named on some 20th-century editions of the Ordnance Survey maps of the area.
5. Three sketches survive in the Norwich Castle Museum and Art Gallery; also *Rokeby on the Greta* in the British Museum and *On the River Greta* in Leeds City Art Gallery.
6. Nicholas Poussin's *Landscape with a Roman Road*, 1648; Cotman made a rough sketch *c*.1809-10 of this engraving (Norwich Castle Museum). One figure in *The Harvest Field* is reversed, as if from a tracing; Cotman's sketch of a picnic party is in the British Museum (British Roy PV); personal communication from Timothy Wilcox, British Museum. David Hill suggests that J.B.S. Morritt and Francis Cholmeley may be recalled in *The Harvest Field*; *Cotman in the North* (2005), p.131.
7. Letter in British Museum; *The Life of John Sell Cotman* (1937), p.143.
8. Binyon, L., *Landscape in English Art and Poetry* (1931), p.132.

### Chapter 13: *Rokeby; a poem* by Walter Scott, 1813

Quotations are from the first edition of *Rokeby*, 1813.

**Chapter 14: After *Rokeby***

Quotations from and references to *Rokeby* are to the first edition of 1813.
1. See Chapter 16.
2. The ten songs, with Canto and stanza references: *A Weary lot is thine fair Maid* (Third XXVIII); *The Cypress Wreath* (Fifth XIII); *Summer Eve is gone and past, the Harper's song in Rokeby* (Fifth VII & IX); *Song to the Moon* (First XXXIII); *'And whither would you leave me then?'* quoth the Friar of orders gray (Fifth XXVII); *Allen a Dale* (Third XXX); *Brignal Banks* (Third XVI); *Edmund's Song or The Harp* (Fifth XVIII); *Matilda's Song, or the Farewell from Rokeby* (Fifth XXIII & XXIV); *The Cavalier* (Fifth XX).

**Chapter 15: J.M.W. Turner**

1. The sketchbooks are in the Turner Bequest at the Tate Gallery, London; Finberg's cataloguing system of 1909 is still used. In 1797 Turner used a large *North of England* sketchbook, TB XXXIV; in 1816 *Yorkshire 2* (TB CXLV), *Yorkshire 4* (TB CXLVII) and *Yorkshire 5* (TB CXLVIII) sketchbooks. *Raby* (TB CLVI) and *Itinerary Rhine Tour* (TB CLIX) sketchbooks were used in 1817. The *Rokeby and Appleby* (TB CCLXIV) and *Minstrelsy of the Scottish Border* (TB CCLXVI) sketchbooks date from 1830-1.
2. *The Works of John Ruskin* (1912), vol.3, p.233.
3. *Ibid.*, vol.12, p.371.
4. *Ibid.*, vol.3, p.553.
5. *Ibid.*, vol.3, p.554.

**Chapter 16: The Lake Poets and Charles Dickens**

1. Kitton, F.G., *The Yorkshire Weekly Post* (19 March 1898); quoted in Fletcher, J.S., *A Book About Yorkshire* (1908), p.249.
2. Quoted in the *Yorkshire Herald* (31 January 1924).
3. Fletcher, J.S. *A Book About Yorkshire* (1908), p.251.

**Chapter 18: The Nineteenth Century and the Railways**

1. The tomb, of Sir Ralph Bowes of Streatlam, was returned to Egglestone Abbey in 1925.
2. Son of James Backhouse (1825-90); see Chapter 9.
3. Toynbee Hall was set up in 1884 in London's East End; it was the first university settlement house, where during their holidays students from Oxford and Cambridge universities could work among and improve the lives of the poor.

**Chapter 20: The Twentieth Century**

1. Rokeby Park is still open to the public; as opening days are liable to change, check the website www.rokebypark.com

**Chapter 21: The Pennine Way and the North Pennines**

1. See Chapter 4 for Francis Cockshott's description of a mineshop and pony track in this same area.
2. The author produced a walks leaflet *Explore Public Art in Teesdale* in 2001 for Teesdale District Council.
3. From the North Pennines AONB website.

**Chapter 22: Tourists to Teesdale Today**

1. Durham County Council *Walkabout* leaflet.

# Bibliographical and other Sources

## PRIMARY SOURCES: MANUSCRIPTS, DRAWINGS, PRINTS, PAINTINGS

Ashmolean Museum, Oxford: *Junction of the Greta and Tees at Rokeby* watercolour by J.M.W. Turner.

Bodleian Library, Oxford: John Byng's manuscript *Tour to the North* Ms Eng Misc d215-7; W. Gilpin's manuscript *Tour through Cumberland & Westmorland* MS Eng Misc. e488/ 7 ; monochrome watercolour 'The ruins of Greta-bridge' fol. 666v.

The Bowes Museum: *The Abbey Bridge* watercolour by Edward Dayes; *Egglestone Abbey, Abbey Bridge* watercolour by John Bailey; *Barnard Castle* watercolour attributed to Thomas Girtin; *Barnard Castle* watercolour by Thomas Hearne; *The Meeting of the Waters* watercolour by William Callow; watercolours by Benjamin Heslop, used in *The River Tees from Source to Sea* (1893); *Mortham Tower, Rokeby* 19th century-oil; photographs by Elijah Yeoman; engravings.

British Museum: *Egglestone Abbey* watercolour by Thomas Girtin; watercolours and sketches by John Sell Cotman: *Greta Bridge, The Scotchman's Stone, Rokeby on the Greta*.

The Cecil Higgins Art Gallery, Bedford: *Rokeby* watercolour by J.M.W. Turner.

Darlington Art Gallery Collection, oil paintings: *Cauldron Snout* by William Bewick; *High Force* by Joseph Miller; *Raby Castle* by Joseph Miller.

Darlington Library, Centre for Local Studies: engravings.

Durham County Record Office: *Plan of the Silver-Band Lead Mine at Cronkley in the Manor of Lune*, by Thomas Sopwith (1828): NCB/1/P 102-103; *A Map of the Road proposed to make Turnpike from Alston in the County of Cumberland, by Middleton in the County of Durham, to the South End of Abbey Bridge, in the North Riding of the County of York. As projected by John Louden McAdam Esqr. Surveyed Septr. 1823 by Machell & Watson*: Q/D/P 11; Cockshott, Francis P., manuscript account of *A Journey through Teesdale* (1848): D/X 36/5; Ordnance Survey maps, 1st and 2nd editions.

Laing Art Gallery: *Durham* sketchbook of John Glover; *Rokeby Picnic* watercolour by William Bewick; *Barnard Castle* watercolour by Henry Gastineau.

Leeds City Art Gallery, watercolours and pencil sketches by J.S. Cotman: *Brignall Banks on the Greta, Hell Cauldron, Barnard Castle from Towler Hill, On the River Greta, The Harvest Field*.

Manchester City Art Gallery: *The River Tees, Durham* oil by John Laporte.

National Gallery of Scotland, Edinburgh, watercolours by J.S. Cotman: *Greta Bridge, Hell Cauldron*.

North Yorkshire County Council Record Office: Cholmeley Archive ZQG; maps of Yorkshire; Ordnance Survey maps, 1st edition; engravings.

Norwich Castle Museum and Art Gallery, watercolours and sketches by J.S. Cotman: *Devil's Elbow; Greta Bridge; On the River Greta, Yorkshire*.

Rokeby Park, 18th-century oil paintings: *North Front of Rookby House; South Front of Rookby House*; east aspect of the house; Greta Bridge.

Sunderland Museum: Edward Robson's herbarium; engravings.

Tate Gallery, London, Sketchbooks of J.M.W. Turner:

| | |
|---|---|
| XXXIV | *North of England* sketchbook |
| CXLV | *Yorkshire 2* sketchbook |
| CXLVII | *Yorkshire 4* sketchbook |
| CXLVIII | *Yorkshire 5* sketchbook |
| CLVI | *Raby* sketchbook |

CLIX     *Itinerary Rhine Tour* sketchbook
CCLXIV    *Rokeby & Appleby* sketchbook
CCLXVI    *Minstrelsy of the Scottish Border* sketchbook
Watercolours by J.S. Cotman: *On the Greta near Rokeby*; *Distant View of Greta Bridge*; *A View on the Greta or the Tees*; *Greta Woods in Rokeby Park*.
University of Durham Library (Palace Green): 'Who wrote "A Tour in Teesdale"?', Add Ms 1415/1-2.
Victoria & Albert Museum: David Cox's *Northern Sketch Book*; *Middleton High Force* watercolour by Paul Sandby; *View on the Tees, Barnard Castle* watercolour by Paul Sandby Munn.
The Whitworth Art Gallery, University of Manchester: *Chain Bridge over the River Tees* watercolour by J.M.W. Turner.
Yale Center for British Art: *Barnard Castle* watercolour by J.M.W. Turner.
York Art Gallery: Fawkes, E.M., *The Farnley Collection*; book of sketches by Henry Cave.

## PRIMARY SOURCES IN PRINT

Amory, T., *The Life of John Buncle, Esq; Containing Various Observations and Reflections, Made in Several Parts of the World; and Many extraordinary Relations* (1756-66)

Anon., *Rambles in Teesdale. By the authors of Holiday Rambles on the Yorkshire Moors, Illustrated by one of them* (1877)

– , *Guide to Barnard Castle, Rokeby, Middleton-in-Teesdale, Raby Castle, &c.* (after 1879)

Backhouse, J. (Jnr.), 'An Account of a Visit to Teesdale in the Summer of 1843', *The Phytologist*, vol.1 (1844)

– , 'Notes of a Botanical Ramble in Yorkshire, &c. in the Summer of 1844', *The Phytologist*, vol.1 (1844)

– , 'Teesdale Botany: historical and personal recollections', *The Naturalist*, vol.10 (1884)

Backhouse, J., *Upper Teesdale, Past And Present* (1896 & 1898)

Barnard Castle and District Publicity Society, *Barnard Castle, County Durham, Official Guide* (1933)

Bell, J., 'New locality for Saxifraga Hirculus', *The Phytologist*, vol.1 (1844)

Bousefield, J., *Pleasant Memories of Darlington and Neighbourhood* (1881)

Buckrose, J.E., *Rambles in the North Yorkshire Dales* (1913)

Burlington, C., *The Modern Universal British Traveller* (1779)

Byng, J., *The Torrington Diaries*; Andrews, C.B. (ed.) (1934-8)

Calvert, R., *Notes on the Geology & Natural History of the County of Durham* (1884)

Camden, W., *Britain, or a chorographical description of the most flourishing Kingdomes of England, Scotland, and Ireland … Beautified with Mappes of the several Shires of England: Written first in Latine by William Camden … translated newly into English by Philémon Holland … Revised, amended and enlarged* (1637)

Coburn, K. (ed.), *The Notebooks of Samuel Taylor Coleridge*, vol.1 (1957)

Cook, E.T. & Wedderburn, A. (eds.), *The Works of John Ruskin (Library Edition)* (1903-12)

Cudworth, W. (ed.), *The Darlington Half Holiday Guide* (1899)

Defoe, D., *A Tour through England and Wales* (1724-6)

Dickens, C., *Nicholas Nickleby* (1839)

Fletcher, J.S., *A Book about Yorkshire* (1908)

– , *A Picturesque History of Yorkshire*, vol.3 (1901)

Forster, W., *A Treatise on a Section of the Strata, from Newcastle-upon-Tyne, to the mountain of Cross Fell, in Cumberland* (1809 & 1821)

Garland, R., *A Tour in Teesdale* (1803-4)

– , *A Tour in Teesdale; including Rokeby, and its environs* (1813-52)

*The Gentleman's Magazine* 1739, 1747, 1761, 1771, 1803, 1805, 1826, 1827

Gilpin, W., *Observations, Relative Chiefly to Picturesque Beauty, Made in the Year 1772, on several parts of England; particularly the Mountains, and Lakes of Cumberland, and Westmorland* (1786)

Goodrich, L., *By Greta Bridge* (1936)

Gough, R., *Anecdotes of British Topography. Or, an Historical Account of what has been done for illustrating the Topographical Antiquities of Great Britain and Ireland* (1768)

Gray, T., *A Catalogue of the Antiquities, Houses, Parks, Plantations, Scenes, and Situations in England and Wales, arranged according to the alphabetical order of the several Counties* (1773)

Grose, F., *The Antiquities of England & Wales* (1773-87)

Haslam, S.H., 'Remarks on the threatened extermination of rare Plants by the rapacity of Collectors', *The Phytologist*, vol.1 (1844)

Hauxwell, H. & Cockcroft, B., *Hannah: The Complete Story* (1991)

Heavisides, M., *Rambles by the River Tees* (1905)

Heslop, B.H., *The River Tees from Source to Sea* (1893)

Holcomb, A.M. & Ashcroft, M.Y., *John Sell Cotman in the Cholmeley Archive* (1980)

Hooker, J. D., 'Moraines of the Tees Valley', *The Reader*, 15 July 1865, p.71

House, M. & Storey, G. (eds.), *Letters of Charles Dickens*, vol.1 (1965)

Hunt, M., *Richmondshire Illustrated by Twenty Line Engravings after Drawings by J.M.W.Turner, R.A. with Descriptions by Mrs Alfred Hunt* (1891)

Hurtley, T., *A Concise Account of some Natural Curiosities, in the environs of Malham, in Craven, Yorkshire* (1786)

Hutchinson, W., *An Excursion to the Lakes, in Westmorland and Cumberland, August 1773* (1774)

– , *An Excursion to the Lakes, in Westmorland and Cumberland; with a Tour Through Part of the Northern Counties, in the Year 1773 and 1774* (1776)

– , *The History and Antiquities of the County Palatine of Durham* (1785-94)

Jones, Sir C., *A Tour in Westmorland by Sir Clement Jones* (1948)

King, S., 'A Botanical Excursion in Teesdale', *The Phytologist*, vol.1 (1844)

Layton, G., *Castle-Barnard, a poem* (1823)

Lebour, G.A., *Outlines of the Geology of Northumberland and Durham* (1886)

Leland, J., *Itinerary* (ed. Hearne, T.) vols.1, 4, 5 (1768-9)

Mackenzie, E. & Ross, M., *An Historical, Topographical and Descriptive view of the County Palatine of Durham* (1834)

Macquoid, T. & K., *About Yorkshire* (1883)

Manson, R.T., *Zig-Zag Ramblings of a Naturalist* (1898)

– , *Outlines of the Geology of South Durham* (1899)

Mason, W., *The English Garden: A Poem. In Four Books* (1783)

Mavor, W., *The British Tourist's; or Traveller's Pocket Companion, through England, Wales, Scotland, and Ireland. Comprehending the most Celebrated Tours in the British Island* (1798)

Morritt, J.B.S., *A Grand Tour: Letters and Journeys* (1985)

Moule, T., *Great Britain Illustrated: A Series of Original Views from Drawings by William Westall, A.R.A. Engraved by, and under the Direction of, Edward Finden, with descriptions by Thomas Moule* (1830)

*The Newcastle General Magazine or Monthly Repository of Useful and Curious Intelligence, and Literary Performances* (January 1748, April 1755)

Pennant, T., *A Tour from Alston-Moor to Harrowgate, and Brimham Crags* (1804)

Phillips, J., *Illustrations of the Geology of Yorkshire Part 2: The Mountain Limestone District* (1836)

– , *The Rivers, Mountains and Sea-coast of Yorkshire*, 2nd edn. (1855)

Pope-Hennessy, U., *Durham Company* (1941)

Railton, H., *The Hand-Book to Teesdale* (*c.*1857)

Ramsden, D.M., *From Stainmore to the Tees* (1948)

– , *Upper Teesdale* (1947)

Rimmer, A., *About England with Dickens* (1883)

Robinson, W.R., *Robinson's Guide to Richmond* (1833)

Rock & Co., *Views & Scenery of Barnard Castle* (1857)

Rose, T., *Westmorland, Cumberland, Durham & Northumberland, Illustrated. From Drawings by Thomas Allom, &c. with Historical & Topographical Descriptions, by Thomas Rose* (1832)

Scott, W., *Rokeby; A Poem* (1813)

Sedgwick, A., 'On the Association of Trap Rocks with the Mountain Limestone Formation in High Teesdale, &c.', *Transactions of the Cambridge Philosophical Society*, vol.2 (1827)

Simpson, S., 'Botanical Excursion to Teesdale', *The Phytologist*, vol.1 (1844)

Smith, J. E. & Sowerby, J., *English Botany; or, Coloured Figures of British Plants, with their Essential Characters, Synonyms, and Places of Growth* (1790-1814)

Sopwith, T., *Geological sections of Holyfield: Hudgill Cross Vein, and Silverband Lead Mines in Alston Moor and Teesdale* (1829)

– , *An Account of the Mining Districts of Alston Moor, Weardale, and Teesdale, in Cumberland and Durham* (1833)

Southey, R., *Letters from England: by Don Manuel Alvarez Espriella. Translated from the Spanish* (1807)

Spencer, N., *The Complete English Traveller; or, A New Survey and Description of England and Wales* (1773)

Surtees, R., *The History and Antiquities of the County Palatine of Durham* (1816-40)

The Teesdale Mercury, *The Teesdale Mercury Penny Guide to Barnard Castle, Rokeby, The High Force, etc.* (after 1880)

Tilt, C., *Illustrations; Landscapes, Historical, and Antiquarian, to the Poetical Works of Sir Walter Scott, Bart.* (1830)

Wainwright, A., *A Pennine Journey. A Story of a Long Walk in 1938* (1986)
– , *Pennine Way Companion: A Pictorial Guide* (2004 edn)
Ward, M.J., *An Excursionist's Guide to Barnard Castle and Rokeby* (c.1890)
Watson, R., *Poetical Works of Richard Watson* (1884)
– , *Poems and Songs of Teesdale by Richard Watson, 'The Teesdale Poet'* (1930)
West, T., *A Guide to the Lakes, in Cumberland, Westmorland, and Lancashire*, 7th edn (1779)
Whitaker, T.D., *An History of Richmondshire* (1823)
White, W., *A Month in Yorkshire* (1858)
Wilson, A., *Teisa: a descriptive poem of the River Teese, its towns and antiquities* (1778)
Winch, N.J., Thornhill, J. & Waugh, R., *The Botanist's Guide through the Counties of Northumberland and Durham*, vols.1 & 2 (1805-7)
Wordsworth, W., *A Guide through the District of the Lakes in the North of England*, 5th edn. (1835)
Wordsworth, W. & D., *The Letters of William and Dorothy Wordsworth*; Shaver, C.L. (ed.) *The Early Years 1787-1805*, 2nd. edn (1967)
– , *The Letters of William and Dorothy Wordsworth*, Hill; A.G. (ed.) *The Later Years Part II 1829-34*, 2nd. edn (1979)
*The York Herald* 1802: 14 & 28 August; 4, 11 & 18 September; 9 & 23 October
Young, A., *A six months tour through the north of England. Containing, An Account of the present State of Agriculture, Manufactures and Population ... interspersed with ... views of some picturesque Scenes, which occurred in the Course of the Journey* (1770)

## SECONDARY SOURCES

### A: ARTICLES

*Archives of Natural History*
Horsman, F., 'Ralph Johnson's Notebook', vol.22 (2) (1995)

*The Burlington Magazine*
Binyon, L., 'The Art of John Sell Cotman', No.472, vol.81 (1942)

*Country Life*
Worsley, G., 'Rokeby Park, Yorkshire', 19 & 26 March, 2 April 1987

*Durham County Local History Society Bulletin*
Barnby, R.A., 'The influence of the London Lead Company on the development of Middleton-in-Teesdale', 15 (1972)
Kirby, M.H., 'Some recent developments at the Bowes Museum', 16 (1973)

*Past Times in Teesdale*. Teesdale Record Society Seminar Papers
Wilkinson, A., 'Tourism in Teesdale' (2001)
Conran, E., 'Teesdale's Grand Tourists' (2001)
Shaw, E., 'Charles Dickens' Teesdale Legacy' (2001)

*The Teesdale Mercury*
15, 22 & 29 August 1866; 4 July 1877; 5 November 1884; 20 May, 3 & 24 June 1885; 15 August 1888; 27 May, 17 & 24 June 1891; 3 & 15 June, 3 August 1892; 24 May, 7 June 1893; 25 July, 8, 15 & 22 August 1894; 25 May 1904; 3 & 31 May, 7 & 14 June 1905; 29 May, 7 & 21 August, 4 September 1912; 12 June 1946; 2 & 9 August 1950

*The Teesdale Record Society Journal*
FIRST SERIES
Oliver, Rev. W., 'Rev. James Farrer, Vicar of Brignall, 1739-1780', vol.8 (1942)
– , 'A Local Vicar of the 17th century: The Rev. William Parish, Vicar of
Rokeby, 1661-1688', vol.10 (1943)
– , 'A Local Postmaster of the 17th century: Christopher Thwaites of Greta Bridge, 1626?-1693', vol.10 (1943)

THIRD SERIES

Coggins, D., 'The First Winch Bridge', vol.6 (1998)

Heyes, W.F., 'Road Improvements in Teesdale, circa 1820', vol.4 (1996)

Heyes, W.F. et al, 'Who Was Who in Teesdale', vol.8 (2000)

Horsman, F., 'Ralph Johnson (1629-1695) of Brignall', vol.11 (2003)

– , 'William Oliver (ca.1761-1816) Surgeon Apothecary and Botanist of Middleton in Teesdale', vol.13 (2005)

Moore, D., 'Teesdale Botany and Botanists', vol.8 (2000)

Tallentire, W.L., 'Building the Castle of Barnard', vol.11 (2003)


*Women's Studies*

Keegan, B., 'Writing Against the Current: Anne Wilson's Teisa and the Tradition of British River Poetry', vol.31 (2002)


## B: BOOKS

Boyne, W., *Yorkshire Library, a bibliographical account of* (1869)

Bradshaw, Dr. M. (ed.), *The Natural History of Upper Teesdale*, 4th edn (2003)

Brown, D.B., Hemingway, A. & Lyles, A., *Romantic Landscape: The Norwich School of Painters* (2000)

Clapham, A.R. (ed.), *Upper Teesdale: the Area and its Natural History* (1978)

Clark, J.W. & Hughes, T.M., *The Life and Letters of the Reverend Adam Sedgwick* (1890)

Cox, E.G., *A Reference Guide to the Literature of Travel, Vol.3 Great Britain* (1949)

Cross, R., Rigby, G. & Lewery, T., *Marking Parish Boundaries Along the Teesdale Way* (1997)

Einberg, E., *Catalogue Raisonné of the Works of George Lambert*, Walpole Society, vol.63 (2001)

Fairbairn, R., *The Mines of Upper Teesdale* (2005)

Fletcher, J.S., *Picturesque History of Yorkshire* (1901)

Gage, J., *Collected Correspondence of J M W Turner* (1980)

Gill, J., *Streatlam and Gibside: The Bowes and Strathmore Families in County Durham* (1980)

Graham, G.G., *The Flora and Vegetation of County Durham* (1988)

Grierson, H.J.C., *The Letters of Sir Walter Scott*, vols.1-3 (1932)

Hardie, M., *Water Colour Painting in Britain* vols.1 & 2 (1967)

Hardy, C.E., *John Bowes and the Bowes Museum* (1970)

Hermann, L., *Turner Prints: The Engraved Work of J.M.W. Turner* (1990)

Hill, D., *In Turner's Footsteps through the hills and dales of Northern England* (1984)

– , *Turner in the North* (1996)

– , *Cotman in the North* (2005)

Holcomb, A. M., *John Sell Cotman in the Cholmeley Archive*, North Yorkshire County Record Office, Publications No.22, Northallerton, 1980

House, E., Rudd, M.D.C. & Clark, P., *Joseph Mallord William Turner: Tours of Durham and Richmondshire* (2006)

Hussey, C., *The Picturesque* (1927)

Kirkland, J. & Wood, M.R., *William Bewick of Darlington* (1990)

Kitson, S.D., *The Life of John Sell Cotman* (1937)

Landseer, T., *Life and Letters of William Bewick (Artist)* (1871)

Lockhart, J.G., *Memoirs of Sir Walter Scott* (1882)

Manwaring, E., *Italian Landscape in Eighteenth Century England* (1925)

Rajnai, M. (ed.), *John Sell Cotman 1782-1842* (1982)

Rajnai, M. & Allthorpe-Guyton, M., *John Sell Cotman 1782-1842: Early Drawings (1798-1812) in Norwich Castle Museum* (1979)

Rawlinson, W.G., *The Engraved Work of J. M. W. Turner R.A.* (1908-13)

Rudd, M.D.C., *The Picturesque and Landscape Appreciation: The development of tourism in the Yorkshire Dales & County Durham 1750-1860*, unpublished MA thesis, University of Durham (1990)

Shaver, C.L., *The Letters of William and Dorothy Wordsworth*, vol.1 (1967)

Southey, Rev. C. C., *The Life and Correspondence of Robert Southey*, vols.3 & 4 (1850)

Tyler, R., *Francis Place 1647-1728: An exhibition representing all aspects of his work* (1971)

Vyner, B., *Stainmore: The Archaeology of a north Pennine Pass* (2001)

Watson, J.R., *Picturesque Landscape & English Romantic Poetry* (1970)

# Index

Numbers in **bold** refer to illustration page numbers
Roman numerals refer to colour plates

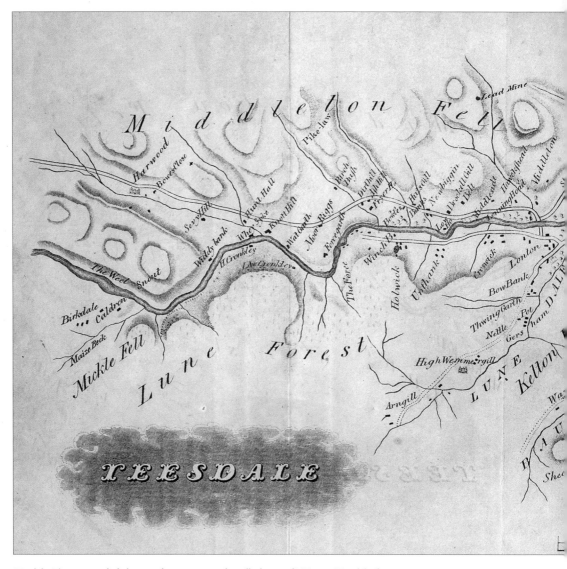

*Teesdale. This map, with slight amendments, appeared in all editions of* A Tour in Teesdale *from 1803.*